Latin American Television
a Global View

Latin American Television
a Global View

John Sinclair

Oxford University Press
1999

Oxford University Press, Great Clarendon Street, Oxford OX2 6DP

Oxford New York

Athens Auckland Bangkok Bogotá Buenos Aires Calcutta
Cape Town Chennai Dar es Salaam Delhi Florence Hong Kong Istanbul
Karachi Kuala Lumpur Madrid Melbourne Mexico City Mumbai
Nairobi Paris São Paulo Singapore Taipei Tokyo Toronto Warsaw
and associated companies in
Berlin Ibadan

Oxford is a registered trade mark of Oxford University Press

Published in the United States
by Oxford University Press Inc., New York

British Library Cataloguing in Publication Data
Data available

Library of Congress Cataloging in Publication Data
Sinclair, John, 1944–
Latin American television: a global view / John Sinclair.
Includes bibliographical references and index.
1. Television broadcasting–Latin America.   I. Title.
PN1992.3.L3S56   1998   384.55′098–dc21   98-28580
ISBN 0–19–815930–7
ISBN 0–19–815929–3 (pbk.)

1 3 5 7 9 10 8 6 4 2

Typeset by Pure Tech India Ltd, Pondicherry,
http://www.puretech.com
Printed in Great Britain
on acid-free paper by
Bookcraft Ltd
Midsomer Norton, Somerset

Preface

This book is the culmination of two decades of research interest in the television industries of the Spanish- and Portuguese-speaking worlds. More immediately, it is also the outcome of a period of sabbatical leave in the latter half of 1997, which made possible visits to Mexico, the United States, Spain, and Portugal. These have enabled me to update the state of accumulated research knowledge at a time of great transition, but such a substantial task could not have been achieved without the goodwill and cooperation of several individuals, not to mention organizational support.

So, first I would like to acknowledge my gratitude to the various colleagues who have discussed the project with me, looked over drafts, or made available their own work and research resources, both in the past as well as in the preparation of this book: in particular, Ingrid Schleicher, Enrique Sánchez Ruiz, and Francisco Hernández Lomeli in Mexico; América Rodriguez, Joe Straubhaar, Federico Subervi Vélez, Silvio Waisbord, and Kent Wilkinson in the US; Enrique Bustamante in Spain; Helena Sousa in Portugal; and José Marques de Melo in Brazil. For their inspiration and advice over the longer term, I would like to thank Emile McAnany and Fátima Fernández. Taken together, these people form a critical mass of researchers who are building the study of the Spanish- and Portuguese-language television industries into a distinct field within the broad realm of international communication and cultural industries research.

Others again have contributed more with the provision of institutional support and their sheer collegiality, again both during the recent leave, and in some cases over a much longer period: Jorge González at the Universidad de Colima in Mexico; John Downing at the University of Texas in the US; Manuel Parés i Maicas at the Universidad Autónoma de Barcelona in Spain; and, home in Melbourne, Kee Pookong at Victoria University of Technology, and Steve Niblo, Barry Carr, and Rowan Ireland at La Trobe University.

Thanks are also due to Andrew Lockett, who in his time at Oxford University Press encouraged this line of investigation and provided the opportunity for me to write such a book. Victoria University granted me the leave and the financial support which made possible the trip to Mexico and the US; while I was able to visit Spain by virtue of a scholarship granted by its government under their programme for *hispanistas extranjeros*, and Portugal with the assistance of the Universidade do Minho.

As well as the collaboration and support of colleagues and institutions, to write a book needs a great degree of cooperation in one's personal life. In this regard, my sincere appreciation goes to my partner Maggie Gundert, especially for sustaining some long periods of being left to look after our daughters Catalina and Isabel; and also to them for taking these absences and my frequent reclusion with such good grace.

J.S.

Barcelona
December 1997

Contents

1 | Introduction

Like the English-speaking world, the world in which Spanish is spoken is both diverse and vast. Also, through the imposition of a common tongue on a host of peoples in the course of colonial expansion, the extent of the use of Spanish reaches across oceans and continents. This is true of the Portuguese-speaking world as well, the history of which in its major aspects is quite similar to that of the Spanish. And just as the United States has long overtaken England as the largest nation in the English-speaking world in terms of both population and the productive output of cultural goods and services, including television programmes and their means of distribution, so it is in the Spanish-speaking world, where Mexico has eclipsed Spain, and in the Portuguese-speaking world, where Brazil has outstripped Portugal.

In order to understand how the globalization of television production and distribution has developed and assumed the ever more intensive and complex forms it has today, it is necessary, though not sufficient, to take language and culture into account as primary 'market forces' which enable the major producers and distributors of television programmes and services to gain access to markets outside their nations of origin. In this context, it becomes helpful to discard the metaphor of the 'worlds' which share a common language in favour of the concept of 'geo-linguistic region'. Such regions have been the initial basis for the global-ization of the media, precisely in television programmes and services. It should be emphasized that a geolinguistic region is defined not just by its geographical contours, but also in a virtual sense, by commonalities of language and culture. Most characteristically, these have been estab-lished by historical relationships of colonization, as is the case with English, Spanish, and Portuguese. However, in the age of international satellites, not only do former colonies counterinvade their erstwhile masters with television entertainment, but geolinguistic regions also come to include perhaps quite small, remote, and dispersed pockets of users of particular languages, most often where there have been great diasporic population flows out of their original countries, such as

1

Indians now living in the Gulf States, Britain, and North America, or the unique case of the Spanish-speaking minorities of diverse origin who inhabit the US.

In the geolinguistic regions of Spanish and Portuguese, particular media corporations have arisen which have been able to exploit the massive size of the domestic markets for which they produce as the key to the opening up of foreign markets in other nations that speak the same language. These other countries have provided them with a 'natural' constituency for their output, and, in spite of the fact that all of them also import English-language television programming and other media products such as films, the crucial fact is that the most popular programmes, indeed entire television genres such as the Latin American soap opera or *telenovela* in particular, are in the language and cultural ambit of the countries which so avidly consume them as imports.

The paradigm case of a geolinguistic region is Spanish, which is the 'mother tongue' of some twenty countries in Latin America which, together with Spain, form a geolinguistic whole. No other language is spoken in as many countries as the national native language, as distinct from an official one (Crystal 1997: 3), nor with the same degree of world-regional consolidation. The Portuguese situation is quite different, in that all the speakers of Portuguese in Latin America are in the one country, Brazil. This is the largest country in Latin America, and also in the Portuguese-speaking, or lusophone, world, with over sixteen times as many speakers as in Portugal (*El estado del mundo* 1996: 614–19). Furthermore, although there are several other former Portuguese colonies in the world, they are in Africa and Asia, where there is no common Latin heritage, the language is not the mother tongue of the majority, and the television markets are small and restricted (Rønning 1997).

Table 1 shows the scale and composition of television markets in the major countries of Latin America in 1997, but size is not everything, as the cliché goes. Although the argument will be sustained that absolute size of the Mexican and Brazilian domestic markets is a key factor in the dominance which the major networks based in each of those countries have attained over their respective geolinguistic regions, there are other countries which also have substantial populations and large numbers of television homes, but do not much figure as television producers and distributors. This is because there are also structural factors in the development of television as an institution which have a strong bearing on whether or not a nation becomes an active exporter. For example, these factors are present in Venezuela, which is a regional exporter in

Table 1. Size and composition of selected Latin American television markets

Country	Population (millions)	Households (millions)	TV homes (millions)	Pay TV homes[a]	Satellite dishes[b]
Argentina	35.0	10.6	9.5	5.2 million	3,500
Bolivia	7.5	1.9	1.0	55,000	500
Brazil	161.0	36.0	34.5	2.5 million	4 million
Chile	15.0	4.1	3.5	770,000	2,500
Colombia	37.0	7.2	6.5	250,000	75,000[c]
Dominican Republic	8.0	2.3	1.5	80,000	500
Ecuador	11.0	2.1	0.6	85,000	1,000
Mexico	96.0	19.0	16.0	2.2 million	1.6 million
Paraguay	4.7	1.2	0.7	150,000	500
Peru	24.0	4.9	3.1	180,000	2,000
Uruguay	3.2	0.9	0.8	260,000	5,000
Venezuela	21.0	4.9	3.9	190,000	75,000

[a] Pay TV homes include cable, wireless (MMDS), and DTH.

[b] Satellite dishes not providing a subscription service. In Mexico, Central America, Venezuela, Colombia, dishes are used to pirate signals from US satellites, while in Brazil they are used to enhance reception of broadcast channels.

[c] An estimated 2.5 million–3 million additional Colombian homes are connected to systems run from pirate dishes.

Source: *Variety*, 21–7 July 1997: 28. Adapted with permission of Variety Inc., © 1997.

spite of having a smaller population than Colombia, with its quite different institutional development and structure.

The table also needs to be interpreted in relation to the other major Spanish-speaking countries outside Latin America. Just as the US contains about four times as many native speakers of English as does the UK (Crystal 1997: 30 and 60), and Brazil sixteen times as many as Portugal, as noted just before, Mexico's population of 96 million is more than twice that of Spain, with its 39.7 million (*El estado del mundo* 1996: 614–19). Furthermore, as well as Spain, there is one other major Spanish-speaking nation in that geolinguistic region to be taken into account, but it is one in which Spanish is not the dominant language: the US. On the basis of the figures given in the table, and the 39.7 million figure just cited for Spain, the US would be the fifth-largest Spanish-speaking country in the world, if we take the current estimate documented in Chapter 4 of over 26 million people of Hispanic origin living in the US, or almost 10 per cent of its total population of 265.8 million (*El estado del mundo* 1996: 614–19).

Latin America as Postcolonial Space

Mil cuatrocientos noventa y dos: 1492 was the year which marks the beginning of 'a major extended and ruptural world-historical event...the whole process of exploration, conquest, colonisation and imperial hegemonisation' (Hall 1996: 249). With the fraught quincentennial commemorations not long behind us, 1492 is readily recalled as the year in which Christopher Columbus (Cristobal Colón as he is called in Spanish) landed on the islands of Cuba and Hispaniola, and claimed them for the Spanish Crown (Bakewell 1991: 57). Perhaps it is less well known that this same year saw the final expulsion of the Moors from the Iberian peninsula, after almost 800 years of occupation, followed by the banishment of the Sephardic Jews, and the subsequent creation of the 'proto-modern' nation-state of Spain. This was brought about with the marriage of Isabel of Castile and Ferdinand of Aragon, thus uniting the two main kingdoms of the peninsula in a dual regime of 'Catholic Monarchs' who laid the basis for the government of both the new nation and its nascent empire (Galeano 1973: 22; Williamson 1992: 61–3).

Having sponsored the initial voyage of discovery, Isabel and Ferdinand obtained the sanction of the Pope, Alexander VI, a Spaniard, for Columbus' subsequent settlements in the Spanish 'Indies' ('Las Indias'), and an agreement to regulate territorial rivalries with their neighbouring kingdom of Portugal, which for some time had been establishing trading colonies in West Africa and the islands of the Atlantic. This was the Treaty of Tordesillas of 1494, which prescribed an imaginary north–south line or meridian dividing the Atlantic 370 leagues west of Cabo Verde. Spain was to have rights over all the territories west of that line, and Portugal to the east. As it turned out, the line was drawn so far to the west that when the Portuguese explorer Pedro Alvares Cabral landed on the east coast of South America in 1500, he was able to claim it for Portugal under the Treaty. Although the Tordesillas line was progressively pushed much further to the west in the course of subsequent events before the borders of modern Brazil came to be defined, it reserved sufficient territory for Portugal to begin its relatively torpid colonization of the region in the first decade of the sixteenth century, at the same time as the Spanish *conquistadores* were subduing the Caribbean islands and mainland coast (Schwaller 1987: 69; Bakewell 1991: 57–80).

While it is not the intention here to provide a potted history of the Iberian nations and their American colonies, it is important to establish the main features of their colonial relationships. In this regard, it is significant to note that, although Latin America is the oldest postcolonial region outside the Mediterranean and its nations have had their independence for the longest period of time, relative to Asia and Africa, it also had the longest period under colonization, for independence did not begin to happen until some 300 years after settlement. Spain was establishing a new viceroyalty in the Southern Cone of South America, and missions in North America, while Britain's American colonies were signing the Declaration of Independence (McWilliams 1968: 25–6), or around the same time as the east coast of Australia was claimed and being settled as a British possession. Also worth noting is the extremely large scale of colonization, bearing in mind that the Spanish colonial viceroyalties covered much of the continent of North as well as almost all that of South America, with the notable exception of Brazil. Most of what is now California, Arizona, New Mexico, Texas, and Florida formed about half of 'New Spain', the colonial name for Mexico (Bakewell 1991: 58–9).

The motivation of the Spanish conquest was, in the words of one of its chroniclers, Bernal Díaz del Castillo, 'to serve God and His Majesty and also to get riches' (quoted in Galeano 1973: 23). Thus, the Christianization of the native peoples proceeded in tandem with the extraction of wealth, all administered through the viceroyalties by Spain. Colonial modes of production were established under which the native peoples (the 'Indians'), and later also slaves from Africa, worked on the estates and plantations, and down the mines. However, Isabel and Ferdinand's descendant Charles V (King of Spain 1516–56), in his role as Holy Roman Emperor, drew Spain into conflicts within Europe. His son and successor Philip II (King of Spain 1556–98) also engaged in costly wars, notably against the Protestant English and Dutch (Williamson 1992: 66–7). The cost of the Catholic monarchy's exploits was the enormous wealth of silver and gold which Spain had been deriving from the colonial economies. In this sense, 'the Spaniards owned the cow, but others drank the milk' (Galeano 1973: 34). Unable to retain the material benefits of empire, Spain had to stand back and watch Britain and France and other nations which had accumulated capital from colonial expansion become the leaders of the new industrial age.

The independence period was not precipitated until 1808, when Napoleon invaded the Iberian peninsula. This led to the Portuguese royal family and entire court exiling itself under British escort to Brazil, there to make Rio de Janeiro the capital of its considerable empire, which extended through Africa and Asia as well as half of South America. This move delayed the overthrow of the monarchy in Brazil until 1889, in spite of it becoming independent from Portugal in 1822 (de Camargo and Noya Pinto 1975: 13–14; Williamson 1992: 74). However, in Spain, the

French deposed the monarch, creating a power vacuum and a crisis of legitimacy at the very pinnacle of the empire. Although the vacuum was soon filled by a liberal 'Regency Council', and a monarch was subsequently restored, there were independence struggles initiated throughout all of Spanish America, resulting in independence for most of the colonial territories by 1825 (Williamson 1992: 210–32).

However, the banishment of Spain from Latin America ushered in an era in which other European powers and then the US could set up neocolonial relationships with the new nations through trade and investment. This initial trade with Europe laid the basis for the indebtedness and dependency which have continued to characterize the region. René Chateaubriand, French Foreign Minister at the time, observed, 'In the hour of emancipation the Spanish colonies turned into some sort of British colonies' (quoted in Galeano 1973: 216), referring to the considerable investments which Britain was able to make throughout the region, once the main barrier to its unconcealed ambitions there had been removed. Yet, within a few decades, France also was involved.

Fernand Braudel records that the name 'Latin America' was in fact first used by France in 1865, expressly to further its own interests (1993: 427). The term was 'promulgated by French intellectuals' in order to counteract British and US concerns about French ambitions in Mexico (Mignolo 1995: 180). This was at a time when the French emperor Napoleon III had taken advantage of a period of debt-prone instability and political division in Mexico in an attempt to establish what he called 'our beneficent influence in the centre of America'. His troops invaded Mexico in 1861, a Mexican throne was created, and a Habsburg monarch was put on it. With the US preoccupied with its own civil war, the French intervention lasted until 1867 (Cockcroft 1983: 76–80). Thus, although 'Latin America' since has been adopted universally as a neutral cultural-linguistic descriptor referring to all those nations which share a 'Latin' language, either Spanish or Portuguese, a geolinguistic region stretching from the US border with Mexico in North America to the tip of continental South America, as a concept it has highly politicized and tendentious origins in European colonial rivalries.

Well before the French intervention in Mexico, the US had also declared an interested stance towards all the lands to its south. In fact, by that time, the US had already fought a war with Mexico. This had begun in Texas in 1846, and, under the Treaty of Guadalupe Hidalgo in 1848, the US had annexed almost all of Mexico's former territories from Texas to California, the area it now calls its Southwest (Riding 1986: 49–51). An estimated 100,000 Mexicans already inhabited the territories so gained (Cockcroft 1983: 72). With some justification, Mexican-

Americans living in the US today can say, 'We did not, in fact, come to the United States at all. The United States came to us' (Valdez 1972).

The annexation was explained by the same notion of 'manifest destiny' as had legitimized US expansion elsewhere across the North American continent, although, in the early days of independence, the US had seemed to show solidarity with its Latin neighbours. In 1823 President Monroe had warned off European powers which might have had colonial ambitions in the region, and pledged US support for any country so threatened. As the century wore on, this 'Monroe Doctrine' came to rationalize US intervention in Latin America when it saw its interests were either at risk or could be advanced, actually culminating in 1898 in a war against Spain, out of which it acquired protectorate rights over Puerto Rico and Cuba, Spain's first and last colony in the Americas (Cockcroft 1983: 70–3; Williamson 1992: 322–3). Cuba, while nominally independent, was to remain under US influence until the revolution led by Fidel Castro in 1959, while Puerto Rico was eventually given a unique status as a 'commonwealth' of the US, with its people recognized as US citizens (Davis, Haub, and Willette 1983).

As to the rest of Latin America in this century, the US Government has a long history of direct and indirect interventions; support for client states led by repressive dictatorships and juntas; and 'covert operations' and 'low intensity conflicts'. These tactics have been motivated by its desire to protect the massive private investment by US corporations in Latin America, often denounced as 'US imperialism', and a determination to maintain the 'security' of the region against whatever forces the US Government has perceived to be inimical to those interests. Proceeding with both force and diplomacy (as in the Good Neighbour Policy between the World Wars, or the Alliance for Progress in the 1960s), the US has clearly and consistently asserted its political as well as economic hegemony over the entire region in the postcolonial era (McClintock 1992: 89–90; Williamson 1992: 322–7). In the course of this book we shall explore how this power has been manifested also in terms of communication and culture through television.

'The perfect instrument of empire'

The story is told that when, in 1492, Antonio de Nebrija presented Queen Isabel with his grammar of Castilian, the first of any modern European language, she asked him what such a work was good for. 'Language', replied the scholar, 'is the perfect instrument of empire' (Williamson 1992: 62). Castilian is the language that we now recognize as 'Spanish', which became a world language in the process of colonization, but the name serves as a reminder that although Spain was the first nation to have a national language (Klee 1991: 1), even in Spain itself today there are several other languages still widely spoken in distinct regions, now actually undergoing a revival in fact, notably Catalan, Basque (Euskara), and Galician. This is not to mention the surviving range of native languages and imported linguistic influences in the Americas over which Spanish was imposed, along with Christianity, and with a similar degree of incompleteness. As Hall observes, 'hybridisation begins with 1492, just as globalisation begins with 1492' (1997: 54).

Relative to the other languages of the Iberian peninsula, Castilian was a 'language-of-power' (Klee 1991: 1), not just as the language of administration for a vast empire, but as the language upon which a 'national print-language' could become standardized, and so create the 'imagined community', the cultural dimension of nationhood, in Benedict Anderson's influential formulation. In fact, Anderson sees the nation-states of the Americas as the first independent nations of their kind (1991: 45–6), models for the postcolonial world. He makes the point that all the new American nations established in the independence era, whether Spanish-, Portuguese-, or English-speaking, were 'creole states', that is, the colonial-born shared the same language and cultural heritage as the metropolis from which they had to free themselves. At least for these creole elites, there was no issue of an alien language, as there would be later with the new nations of the twentieth century in Asia and Africa. The dominance of the colonial languages ensured that there was a standardized 'language-of-state' common to the colonial administrative units upon which the new nations would come to be based, but also that anticolonial, progressive ideas from Europe, and news of the example of the American War of Independence, were readily communicated.

In his concern to explain how so many nations emerged in Latin America, as compared to English-speaking North America, Anderson seems to discount the fact that the Spanish-speaking nations also inherited a language in common, but over a much greater expanse. With the major exception of Brazil, and the very minor ones of Belize and the Guianas, Spanish is the language not just of all the other continental nations south of the US, from Tijuana to Tierra del Fuego, but of the region. However, as has been noted, here too Spanish was a language of power. Anderson does emphasize that the creole elite, progressively shored up in numbers by immigration, were both colonized, and colonizers, their language identifying them more with their colonial masters than with the natives and slaves over whom they in turn ruled (1991: 47–65). In this respect, they were complicit in the spreading and maintaining of the language of a colonial power throughout the region, suppressing the native languages (Nahuatl, Quechua, and Guaraní, to name some major ones) and those of the slaves brought to the plantations from Africa. A corresponding process took place with regard to Portuguese in Brazil.

The outcome is that, compared to the other postcolonial continents of Asia or Africa, Latin America exhibits a unique linguistic homogeneity, for the most part at the level of a first language, and at the very least at the level of a lingua franca, a common tongue, amongst native peoples. Even the differences between Spanish and Portuguese are not so great as those which exist between the different languages of most neighbouring countries in Asia or Africa. However, this homogeneity is tempered by some heterogeneity which must not be ignored.

First, we are familiar with sometimes considerable national variations in English, such as between British, American, Australian, and Indian English, and, furthermore, with regional variations within a nation, such as English as it is spoken in New York compared to Atlanta or Los Angeles. These variations can be differences in grammar and vocabulary as well as of pronunciation and accent, some of which might be particularly difficult to understand, or carry a negative status. Just so are there the same kinds of variations in the Spanish-speaking world: the characteristic lisp of Iberian Spanish is not used in the Americas, for example. Similarly, national groups such as Argentinians and Mexicans can be sensitive about each other's accents, in the same way as an American accent might still grate when heard on British or Australian television. Yet, although not all English-speakers are exposed to a wide range of variations, by and large English-speakers the world over can understand each other. This is one of the factors which makes English the world's principal geolinguistic region, and, as will be argued later in this book, the basis for its development as a global television market. The point here, however, is more to show how this also has been true for the Spanish- and Portuguese-speaking geolinguistic regions, and to assess how they are faring in the age of international satellite transmission and globalization.

Secondly, historical differences in language and culture are given an official recognition in Latin America, and Iberia also for that matter. These differences include the cultural combinations and adaptations which have taken place in the course of creating nations. As Shohat puts it, 'nationhood was officially articulated in hybrid terms' (1992: 110). In Mexico, for example, this has taken the form of the ideological celebration of *mestizaje*, the biological and cultural mixture of the pre-Hispanic native peoples with the Spanish conquerors, immigrants, and creoles (Mignolo 1995: 180). This includes linguistic mixing: many words in Mexican Spanish come from the native language, Nahuatl. As well, Indian heritage is given recognition by the state, for its own purposes, in its ideology of *indigenismo* (Cockcroft 1983: 147–8). Thus, while there continues to be a real racial hierarchy, Mexican national culture is officially *mestizo*, or mixed, and this is not just the ideology of the national government. Progressive figures such as Frida Kahlo and Diego Rivera were instrumental in incorporating indigenous culture into the Mexican national culture (Williamson 1992: 526), while radical groups such as the Chicano movement of the 1960s and 1970s in the US affirmed *mestizaje* with their concept of *la raza*, 'a race of half-breeds, misfits, and mongrels' (Valdez 1972: pp. xiv–xv).

Similarly in Brazil, in order to build both the fact and the sense of nationhood out of its diverse states, quite vast territories, and varied peoples with their different histories—the natives of the Amazon, the slaves of Bahía, the immigrants from Europe and, later, Japan—an ideology of ethnic integration was needed, carried by a common language. The Portuguese language today 'gives the nation a visible unity' (Hugh-Jones 1995: 3–4), while the national mythology provides white elites with a black heritage. Again, the ideology of ethnic integration cannot be explained as an imposition by the elites in control of the construction of national culture. Intellectual modernist movements have theorized Latin American hybridity and syncretism for most of this century (Shohat 1992: 108–9), while ethnic mixing is celebrated by such popular novelists as Jorge Amado, several of whose works have been made into films and *telenovelas* (Hinchberger 1997). Indeed, given Brazil's ethnic diversity and immense geographical expanse, both through entertainment and news, television became particularly important in the process of nation-building. This did not begin until the 1960s, when Brazil still could be described as 'a cultural archipelago made up of semi-autonomous geo-economic regions' (Marques de Melo 1992: 1).

In the words of Colombian theorist Jesús Martín-Barbero, what television did at this stage in Brazil, in its nation-binding role, was to transform 'the mass into the people and the people into the nation'. The next stage was the commercialization of culture, he argues, in which the media took on the 'economic function' of creating a 'consumer society' (1993: 164). Such questions of cultural fusion and national identities have become a major preoccupation with contemporary Latin American theorists. The Argentinian Nestor García Canclini prefers the term 'hybridity' over *mestizaje* to express the greater multiplicity of cultural elements, not just language and ethnicity, which the age of globalization is bringing together. Hybridity occurs at every level, he says, including the local, the national, and the transnational (García Canclini 1997: 22–3). Martín-Barbero says that in Latin America, the common Iberian languages and cultural traditions provide also a regional level of identity, but the commercialization of this fact by television is cheapening the Latin American imaginary: 'privately-sponsored initiatives to penetrate the global market with regional audiovisual collaborations are diminishing the recognition of that which is Latin American' (Martín-Barbero 1997: 18).

Setting aside for the moment some of the complexities that these theorists are raising about the degree of fragmentation of hybrid identities, but retaining the notion of distinct levels, we can think of how viewers might relate in different ways to television programming from different sources. For example, at the local level, viewers get the local news and sport in their city or district, and at the national level, networked news and entertainment programming produced in and for the national market. There are two transnational levels: the world-regional level, at which *telenovelas* and other entertainment from the major producers in Latin America circulate; and the global, which usually means subscriber services like CNN—all in Spanish or Portuguese, of course. So, viewers in Lima, for example, can enjoy watching a local league sporting match and then the national news, affirming their identities as Limans and Peruvians respectively. However, watching an Argentinian or Mexican *telenovela* reminds them of the similarities they share with neighbouring countries in their region (and perhaps also the differences), while flipping over to CBS Telenoticias or a Hollywood film dubbed into Spanish might make them feel more like privileged citizens of the globe.

This is not the place to speculate on whether any of these levels is becoming dominant over the others, as theorists of cultural imperialism and globalization have tended to fear. Rather, the point is that even though viewers in other regions of the world have access to all these levels, including the world-regional, only in Latin America are audiences in a whole host of nations able to be addressed by virtue of their more or less common linguistic and cultural heritage as a kind of 'imagined community' on a world-regional scale, a feature of the region which the larger television producers have been well placed to exploit. Furthermore, we are talking here not just of the geographic region of Central and South America and the Spanish-speaking Caribbean, but of the whole geolinguistic entities created by Iberian colonization: that is, the nations of Spain and Portugal themselves have to be included as part of the region in which their respective languages are spoken.

11

In the absence of comparative audience studies, it is not possible to say how far viewers, and which kinds of viewers, might be drawn in by the idea of a common Hispanic (Spanish) or Lusitanian (Portuguese) identity, or alternatively, how far the submerged differences between and within the Latin nations might provide a counterweight of resistance against being addressed as a member of such an international imagined community (Waisbord 1996: 24–5). What is clear is that there is a demand for local, national, and regional programming, that Latin America has developed its own television programming and genres which are popular at all these levels, and that a small number of producers have been able to seize a strategic advantage out of emphasizing similarity at the expense of difference, and so build themselves hegemonic positions over the commercialization of cultural similarities within their respective geolinguistic regions. These particular media companies will be examined in some detail over the next few chapters. A more immediate task is to sketch in the broad features of the development of television as a medium in Latin America as a whole.

The Development of Television as an Institution

To understand the development of television in Latin America, three sets of factors need to be taken into account, although the relative weight to be given to them has been much contested for both theoretical and ideological reasons over recent decades. First, most emphasis in the past has been on the influence of the US, both its government and the private interests with a stake in television development, namely the networks, the equipment manufacturers, and the transnational advertisers and their agencies. The second set of factors has to do with Latin American governments, and the highly variable relationships which they have assumed with regard to television, ranging from quite *laissez-faire* disregard to zealous hands-on control. The role of the Latin American broadcasting entrepreneurs constitutes the third set of factors. This aspect has been fairly neglected relative to the others, but this section will seek to demonstrate the influence of the collective action of the entrepreneurs, while subsequent chapters will examine the role of particular individuals in selected national contexts.

One other dimension which deserves more attention than it has received is the degree to which the establishment of radio in Latin America in the period between the World Wars cast the mould in which the subsequent development of television was formed. Radio involved the same three sets of factors as television—US interests,

Latin American governments, and entrepreneurs—and without suggesting for a moment that television is just, in the notorious epithet, 'radio with pictures', some attention to the continuities found from one medium to the next is essential to understanding the institutionalization of broadcasting in Latin America.

Responding to the active presence of US radio equipment manufacturers in the region and the discreet urgings of US officials in favour of establishing radio as a commercial medium (Schwoch 1990: 96–123), as well as to the availability by this time of US rather than European capital for investment, Latin American entrepreneurs formed partnerships with the nascent radio networks of the US. This began in the 1920s, although it was not until the 1930s that commercial radio became a popular medium in Latin America. For its part, the US Government, in the course of its efforts in the ideological defence of the hemisphere during the Second World War, set up the office of Coordinator of Inter-American Affairs under Nelson Rockefeller, which from 1940 until 1946 encouraged the expansion of the US networks into Latin America, and supplied programming in Spanish and Portuguese (Fox 1997: 19–22).

By 1945, the links between the Latin American entrepreneurs and the US networks NBC and CBS were formalized with the formation of AIR (Asociación Interamericana de Radiodifusión—Interamerican Broadcasting Association). At its first congress the following year, AIR resolved to concentrate on the establishment of television, and from then on lobbied the various national governments to ensure that television was introduced on a commercial 'American' model, rather than a 'European' state-operated basis. For this reason, the commercial model in Latin America should be seen as having been adopted by Latin interests, rather than imposed by US ones (Fernández Christlieb 1987: 35–7). Latin American entrepreneurs positioned themselves to take advantage of US official and corporate interest in their region, and supported each other in resisting regulation by national governments. AIR became particularly interventionist during the 1950s with the promulgation of its 'Panama Doctrine' which bound its members into a mutual defence of their private interests (Mejía Barquera 1989: 121–9, 181–6). For their part, NBC and CBS found common cause with the Latin American entrepreneurs, rather than with the US Government, in so far as they were concerned to prevent the US Government from setting up its own service to Latin America (Fox 1997: 17).

The first President of AIR was Goar Mestre, a radio and television entrepreneur from CMQ in Cuba, where he and his brother Abel were backed with investment from the United States network NBC, at that time the broadcast division of the US equipment manufacturer RCA.

Mestre had been one of the first exporters of radio programmes to the region, including the innovative Latin commercial genre of the *radionovela*, ancestor to the *telenovela*. Subsequently exiled from Cuba after the revolution of 1959, Mestre became active in television broadcasting and production in Argentina. This was in association with CBS and Time-Life, with whom he also invested in a Venezuelan television network. He had a further association with CBS in a Peruvian channel in conjunction with a local partner, Genaro Delgado Parker. Second President and group organizer was Emilio Azcárraga Vidaurreta, a major Mexican radio entrepreneur who had built up two chains: one affiliated with NBC and the other with CBS. Through Azcárraga's programme distribution connections, NBC was able to form affiliates in several other Latin American countries as well (Fernández Christlieb 1987: 36–43; Muraro 1985: 80).

This calls for some consideration of the various US interests and their strategies over time. Silvio Waisbord discerns three stages in the development of Latin American television, and its relation to US interests is a feature of each stage. The first is characterized by the US networks' support for Latin entrepreneurs such as Mestre and Azcárraga, and the sale of US-manufactured equipment, for both transmission and reception. The investment in Latin American networks occurred more after 1960, since the US networks were still building up their domestic television systems during the 1950s. Latin markets were too small to be profitable for them at that stage, when television was still new in the US itself, and the first Latin American television stations were established early, not far behind the US. The major television national markets of today, Mexico and Brazil, set up their first stations in 1950, as did Cuba, which soon became an avid market for US programming, and the first nation in the world to extend television to its entire, if rather compact, national territory (Bunce 1976: 81). The second-order television production nations of today, Argentina and Venezuela, commenced television in 1951 and 1952 respectively (Waisbord 1997: 1–3).

While US corporations supplied equipment, technical assistance, and in some countries up to 80 per cent of programming in this first decade, only after 1959 was there much active interest shown by the US networks in Latin American television. That was when the newest US network, ABC, established an international division, Worldvision, and actively began to set up affiliates in Latin America and other world regions. NBC, the largest US network, concentrated more on the sale of management services and equipment, and also, taking advantage of the advent of reliable videotape recording around this time, on investment in programme production (Frappier 1968: 1–7). As noted, CBS backed Mestre, and had an association with Time-Life, which in its own right made a most significant investment in Brazil. This will be discussed in some detail in Chapter 3.

While ABC made an important investment in programme production in Mexico, also to be considered in more detail further on, its most characteristic strategy involved the setting up of international networks of affiliates, based on the same model as all the US networks had built themselves upon in their domestic market, writ large over a sub-region. Thus, when the US Government and some transnationalized manufacturers persuaded the Central American countries to form the Central American Free Trade Zone in 1960, ABC signed up affiliates in the five countries involved into the Central American Television Network (CATVN) (Bunce 1976: 81–9). ABC investments in stations from Mexico to the Southern Cone countries of Chile and Argentina later formed its LATINO network (Janus and Roncagliolo 1978: 30–2). However, there is some doubt as to whether these ever attracted the advertisers necessary for them to exist as anything more than paper networks (Fox 1997: 27).

After all, the real prime movers in all of this internationalization of commercial television were the advertisers, for the most part US-based corporations that were in the process of transforming themselves into the 'multinational' or 'transnational' corporations of the 1960s and 1970s. ABC's strategy can be understood as an early attempt to provide a transnational medium for transnational advertisers, anticipating the debate about global media for global markets which would begin in the 1980s (Mattelart 1991: 48–67). The US trade journal *Television* contrasted ABC's transnational networks approach with the country-by-country *modus operandi* of the US advertising agencies abroad at the time:

ABC can sell *Batman* to an advertiser and then place *Batman* along with designated commercials in any Worldvision country where the advertiser wants it to appear.... ABC's approach is the reverse of what the agencies are doing. ABC is attempting to create a single world-wide medium that an international advertiser can buy in a centralized way, while the advertising agencies are attempting to spread their services abroad to bring them closer to the variety of media around the world. Both, however, are banking on the existence of a sizeable group of international companies with marketing plans that cover large portions of the globe. (Quoted in Frappier 1968: 4)

The second period of Latin American television as defined by its relation to US interests took place when the US networks withdrew their direct investments, and although they continued to supply programmes to the region, there occurred a significant maturing of Latin

American production companies and the growth of exportation within the region, corresponding to much growth in the size of the various national markets. Due to their strategic failures and an excess of competition, including that just referred to with the advertising agencies, the networks' direct investments were not as profitable as they had expected. Furthermore, in 1971, the FCC (Federal Communications Commission), the US regulatory body, ordered the networks to separate their distribution from their syndication activities. In these circumstances, CBS and NBC sold off their foreign investments (Read 1976: 80), while ABC also drastically scaled back its activities and retained only very minor overseas holdings (Varis 1978: 16–17).

The significance of the period of initial US intervention in the development of television in Latin America needs to be assessed carefully. Much of the critical analysis of US influence at the time which denounced it as 'cultural imperialism' (Schiller 1969; Wells 1972) jumped to the conclusion that Latin American television's apparent high levels of dependence upon direct investments and programming imported from the US were going to be permanent structural features, rather than an initial stage of adoption which would be followed by transition (Tunstall 1977: 38–40). On the other hand, it is clear that the US Government gave active encouragement to Latin American media entrepreneurs to emulate the US commercial model in the institutionalization of television, just as surely as the US networks sold them the equipment and the management services, and even invested directly, towards the same end. Furthermore, this had been the case also with radio. The reasonable conclusion is that US influence was significant not because of the incidence of foreign ownership, nor the high levels of programme imports, neither of which endured, but because of the implantation of the commercial model itself, which became the almost universal norm throughout the region, even where television was state-owned (McAnany 1984: 194–5).

Televisora Nacional, Cuba's state-owned monopoly formed in 1960 by Castro's revolutionary government out of the Mestres' CMQ and the other pre-1959 networks, is the notable exception, of course (Lent 1990: 128–9). Dating from radio days, Colombia developed its own model, even in the absence of foreign investment, whereby the state owned the television channels, but leased broadcasting time to private companies which in turn commercialized it by supplying programmes and selling advertising spots and sponsorship (Fox 1997: 89–100). In Peru, a system of majority state ownership of television prevailed from 1969 until 1981 under its left-wing military regime of the time, but without ever abandoning the commercial model, while Bolivia and Chile both have had systems in which universities owned the stations, but still were funded from commercial advertising (Roncagliolo 1995: 339–40). As will be taken up further in the next chapter, Mexico for some time had a commercial state-owned network which competed, however weakly, with the dominant private conglomerate.

The decades of the second period of Latin American television, the 1970s and 1980s, were a time in which much attention was given to the 'traffic' or 'flows' of television programming, so much so that it became one of the issues around which the movement for a New World Information and Communication Order (NWICO) was mobilized in UNESCO during those decades, and individual nations in the 'Third World', as the postcolonial world was then known (Shohat 1992: 100–1), sought to develop national communication policies to defend themselves from cultural imperialism via television, and the news and advertising it carried. In this context, two studies of television flows from the 1980s were significant with regard to Latin America in particular.

In following up a study from the early 1970s which had documented the 'one-way street' pattern of television flows from the US to the rest of the world, Tapio Varis found that while the general balance had changed very little over the intervening decade, there was 'a trend toward greater regional exchanges', particularly in the Latin American region (1984: 143–52). Amongst the other studies around that time confirming the same tendency, one in particular traced the very considerable extent to which the *telenovela* had emerged as the preferred commercial genre within the Latin American programme trade (Rogers and Antola 1985). This was a fulfilment of Tunstall's prediction from a phenomenon already apparent in 1977, that between what we now would call the global and the local levels of programme circulation, there would emerge an intermediate level of what, interestingly, he called 'hybrid media forms', such as the *telenovela* (1977: 274). Another prophetic analysis of that same year came from Ithiel de Sola Pool, although it was regarded sceptically at the time because of Pool's close association with the defence of the US 'free flow' doctrine against the NWICO advocates. He argued that linguistic and cultural barriers, and the influence of the social context in which media were received, inclined audiences to appreciate programming which was made in their own language, and had cultural familiarity for them (1977: 143).

Now that many countries have had almost fifty years of television, it appears that passing through an initial stage of dependence to a maturity of the national market is, if not universal, then certainly a common pattern, of which the Latin American experience is emblematic. Crucial in the transition is the growth not just of the audience size, but of domestic programme production, the emergent consensus amongst observers being that audiences come to prefer television programming from their own country, and in their own vernacular, or, if that is not available, from other countries which are culturally and linguistically similar. Joseph Straubhaar calls this 'cultural proximity': 'audiences will tend to prefer that programming which is closest or most proximate to their own culture: national programming if it can be supported by the local economy, regional programming in genres that small countries cannot afford' (1992: 14).

The development of Latin American national markets for television programming bears out this hypothesis, including the pre-eminence of Mexico and Brazil as 'net exporters' within the region, to follow Rafael Roncagliolo's classification. Venezuela and Argentina are 'new exporters', with Colombia, Chile, and Peru seeking to join them, but coming from far behind, while the rest of the nations in the region, most of which are the smaller nations of Central America and the Caribbean, are 'net importers' (1995: 337). This is not the place to go any further into the debate about programme flows: that will be taken up again in Chapter 6, while the special cases of the Mexican and Brazilian television industries are examined in Chapters 2 and 3, where outlines are also provided for Venezuela and Argentina.

Waisbord's third stage in which the relation to US interests must be assessed in the development of Latin American television is the recent past. This is characterized by rapid growth in channels available, due to the expansion of cable and satellite modes of distribution, which has brought in new service and content providers, including US corporations. However, the age of CBS Telenoticias and HBO Olé, and other such special Latin services provided by the major US cable channels, is already moving into a fourth stage defined by the advent of digital direct-to-home (DTH) satellite delivery. This new 'post-broadcast' technology has encouraged the major Latin American producers and distributors to enter strategic alliances with US satellite and cable services. These alliances, with their plans extending to Europe as well as Latin America, mark the beginning of a phase which brings Latin American television into the mainstream of globalization.

The fraught theoretical meaning of this rather overworked concept will be considered in a later section of this chapter, while the various trends for which we use it as a shorthand will be traced throughout the book, and discussed in the conclusion. For the present, to hark back to the three sets of factors specified at the outset of this section, it would be apparent by this stage that US influence can only be understood in relation to the Latin American entrepreneurship factor. It remains to consider the political dimension of Latin American television development. Whereas state ownership of television has been somewhat limited, as outlined above, state control is rather a different matter. That is, state policies with respect to television, or their absence, have been consequential for the development of the medium as an institution, regardless of whether the state has also been involved in the ownership of stations. Because there are complex histories of broadcast regulation different in each nation, integral to their political histories as a whole, it is difficult to draw generalizations. Nevertheless, the two main phases in which Latin American governments have taken an active role in controlling television are the 1950s, when populist dictators in Argentina, Brazil, and Colombia implemented severe nationalistic policies to direct broadcasting and other media; and the 1970s, when, in the context of the NWICO debate alluded to above, several governments took up the rhetoric of 'national communication policies'. There were moves towards reform and the strengthening of public broadcasting in Mexico, Venezuela, and Chile in the first half of the decade, and then a more prevalent discourse about the protection of television and other media industries from foreign influence and competition. This included the affirmation of their public service and civic functions, such as the construction and defence of national cultures, but no national communication policies were ever implemented as such (Fox 1988).

Consolidating itself over the 1980s and 1990s, the broad trend in the Latin American television industries has been towards ever more private control (deregulation), as well as ownership (privatization). The triumph of the commercial model is of course also the triumph of the private interests which benefit from its institutionalization, and while in the past there has been strong public criticism of private control in those countries where television is the most monopolized, there is also little faith in the state's capacity to act in the public's interest, rather than its own, and disillusion with the concept of national culture. Because of the general fragility of democratic traditions in the region, and because state regulation is associated historically with authoritarian control in the service of the state, the private media have been able to secure much greater legitimacy as an alternative base for providing political and cultural leadership than is conceivable in most English-speaking nations (Waisbord 1995: 203; 1997: 19).

As well as this degree of hegemony, Latin American television companies benefit from the heritage of discredited state control in that they enjoy a much less regulated environment in which to operate, sometimes referred to as that of *capitalismo salvaje*, 'savage' or primitive capitalism.

Whereas even the US maintains regulatory restraints against monopolization, in Latin America demonstrably monopolistic practices such as the integration of production and distribution in the television industry, while not universal, are the norm. Similarly, there is a tolerance towards the quite intensive commercialization of the medium, for example in the proportion of airtime given over to advertising, or the insertion of commercial messages in editorial or entertainment content via product placement (Straubhaar 1991: 48–9). In Mexico and Brazil in particular, where, in each case, a dominant private network emerged, the consensus of observers is that the mutual accommodation which developed between government and network was a formative factor in establishing this dominance (Rogers and Antola 1985: 27; Fox 1997: 4–5; Waisbord 1997: 11). While broadly true, this is a point easily oversimplified at the expense of real contradictions and shifts of interest between the two parties, and so is better left to the analysis in the chapters dedicated to these specific countries.

The era of national communication policies has been left far behind by the spread of deregulation and privatization, the whole overarching ideological disposition that Latin Americans call *neoliberalismo*, and the embrace of globalization. One of the mechanisms facilitating that process in turn is the formation of free trade blocs, in particular the 1993 North American Free Trade Agreement (NAFTA) between the US, Mexico, and Canada, and Mercosur, a later agreement between the Southern Cone countries of Argentina, Brazil, Paraguay, and Uruguay. In the case of NAFTA, Mexico did not seek any 'cultural exemption', as Canada did, to protect its media industries from the effects of free trade in audiovisual products, seeing itself as having the 'natural' protection of linguistic and cultural difference from the rest of North America (Sinclair 1996: 46). Since then, the sheer inequalities between the partners have begun to worry some Latin American critics (Sánchez Ruiz 1994), research is under way to monitor the impact which NAFTA might be having on the sector (Crovi Druetta 1995), and at least one prominent Latin American theorist is calling for forms of collective protection for Latin American cultural production (García Canclini 1995: 160–3).

So far, the actual effect of such treaties as NAFTA is to allow the US to insist that its intellectual property rights be upheld, specifically, the policing of copyright laws against the piracy which has been a problem for the US audiovisual industries in Latin America and elsewhere in the erstwhile Third World; and the opening up of foreign investment opportunities, not in the media, but in the telecommunications field (Waisbord 1997: 18). However, in the age of convergence, that is, the blurring of the boundaries between telecommunications and media exemplified most clearly by developments in cable and satellite television, foreign investment in telecommunications can have considerable implications for media structures. This is an effect already being felt in Argentina, as will be outlined in Chapter 3. Without going further at this stage into the particularities of how foreign and national private interests in conjunction with the state have shaped television as an institution in any given country, it is time to give some consideration to theoretical perspectives on Latin American television.

Theoretical Views from Latin America

Latin Americans have made some significant contributions to the evolution of theoretical and research paradigms in international communication studies, from the days of 'cultural dependency' in the 1970s, up to the present era of globalization, hybridized postmodern identities, and the discovery of postcolonialism. When the 'Development Decade' of the 1960s did not produce the social and economic changes foretold by the US and European theorists of 'modernization', Latin American theorists, in particular the economists involved with the UN Economic Commission for Latin America, looked for their own explanation. They found this in 'dependency' theory, essentially the idea that the continued economic and social problems of the region were attributable to the way in which Latin American national economies were unable to develop independently of foreign investment and technology. There were more and less sophisticated versions of this broad theoretical stance, amongst the former being that of Fernando Henrique Cardoso, today, quite coincidentally, the President of Brazil. Cardoso acknowledged that development did take place under conditions of dependency, but only to the benefit of the transnational investors, and the dominant classes and government of the dependent nation who collaborated with them: this was the 'tripod' of 'associated-dependent development' (Cardoso 1973; 1977).

Dependency theory was given a cultural emphasis by a number of Latin Americans interested in the neo-Marxist theory of ideology. Now sometimes referred to as 'the dominant ideology thesis', this was the most influential theoretical paradigm throughout the 1970s and well into the 1980s. Its basis was Marx's perception that the class that owned the means of the production and distribution of ideas in a society, which includes the media, could thereby control the society in its own interests (Collins 1990: 1–24). In the Latin American 'cultural dependency' perspective, the social inequalities of dependency were legitimized and

21

perpetuated by the ideas and images which circulated in the media of dependent societies, much of which was imported, particularly from the US. In fact, the US was 'the generating hub of the capitalist ideology and culture that is being diffused' (Dagnino 1973: 137). Different social classes related to this culture of dependency in different ways, with the 'local bourgeoisie' benefiting from it, while it distorted the reality of the rest of society (Salinas and Paldán 1979: 89–90).

Apart from the few Latin American theorists publishing internationally in English, there were certain national contexts within the region where the neo-Marxist theoretical critique of ideology was being applied to research on imported media content, including television. In Venezuela, for example, theorists such as Ludovico Silva (1971) denounced ideological domination, while researchers like Antonio Pasquali analysed its manifestations on television (1967). Several Venezuelan and other studies such as this at the time are reviewed in English by Luis Ramiro Beltrán, himself a pioneering researcher as well as a bibliographer of communication studies in the region (1978a; 1978b). Well before semiology became fashionable in English-speaking communication studies, Eliseo Veron was tracing its influence in Argentina (Schwarz and Jaramillo 1986). As a reference point within the English-speaking world at the time, this era corresponds to the foundation of the Centre for Contemporary Cultural Studies at the University of Birmingham.

In Chile, the era of Salvador Allende (President 1970–3) was a productive time for theory, research, and practical experimentation on the media, as supporters of Latin America's first elected Marxist president sought to find ways of combating the ideological influence of Chile's conservative media owners, and the abundant imported content in the media. Amongst them was Armand Mattelart, a Belgian, who in his own right and in conjunction with various collaborators, notably Michèle Mattelart, Ariel Dorfman, and others associated with the journal *Cuadernos de la realidad nacional*, was involved in prolific theoretical, research, and media production activities (Assmann 1974). One of the works from this period, although about comics rather than television, became widely available in English, and stands as a classic of the mode of ideological analysis being carried out at the time: *How to Read Donald Duck* (Dorfman and Mattelart 1975).

Over the next decade, Armand Mattelart was to become Europe's most articulate and active theorist working within the paradigm of 'cultural imperialism', although with an acknowledged debt to dependency theory (Mattelart 1980). Appropriately, 'cultural imperialism', or the more specific variant of 'media imperialism', is how the phenomenon of international cultural influence has been theorized by critics in the northern hemisphere, in preference to 'cultural dependency'. In the US, Herbert Schiller also took up the metaphor of imperialism, first of all with his *Mass Communications and American Empire* (1969), which traced out the connections he saw between US Government foreign policies, the overseas activities of US corporations, and the cultural role he attributed to the media in legitimizing them. As Tomlinson argues, the 'discourse of cultural imperialism', in the particular sense of it being a critique of capitalism as a homogenizing ideological force, is grounded in a Western Marxism which is only interested in the cultural meaning and social impact of the media to the extent that the media can be seen to serve political and economic functions for capitalism (1991: 34–56).

While Schiller continues to find the concept of cultural imperialism meaningful in the 1990s, in spite of various lines of criticism which have gathered weight (1990), the whole debate about cultural imperialism has been collapsed into that concerning 'globalization'. Buzzword of the 1990s, the concept of globalization is applied by different theorists in quite different senses, though quite often still it turns out to be little more than a synonym for cultural imperialism. That is, the notion that a common global culture is homogenizing the world remains intact in many formulations, even if there is now some recognition that the source of this hypothetical monolithic and pervasive culture is no longer, as if it ever was, just the US. Indeed, as Malcolm Waters asserts, 'the model of globalisation that is being globalised is itself a European model' (1995: 4) even if Europe now sees itself more as a victim than a perpetrator of cultural globalization (Schlesinger and Morris 1997: 14–16).

What is there about television in Latin America which might provide a new theoretical dimension to this debate? This book will put the case that the 'trend toward greater regional exchanges' in television programme flows observed by Varis, and alluded to earlier, confirms the need for a conception of globalization which sees it as more than the increasingly intensive penetration of national economies and societies by US- or European-based corporations, the usual suspects. That was how it was in the decades of the transnational or multinational corporation. By contrast, the global corporation is characterized by global capital: that is, interpenetration, to the point of fusion, of the former kind of transnational capital with 'national' capital from several nations. This is the kind of corporation which is globalizing not only the programme trade but also the trade in television services made possible by convergent technologies. The clearest cases in point are the new DTH satellite service ventures, mentioned earlier and examined in more detail in later chapters. In these, US-based satellite and cable companies have combined with the largest Latin American broadcast and satellite-to-cable networks to create a corporate structure able to deliver the new services to Europe as well as the whole Latin American region. This new kind of global corporation has been formed in recognition of the strength which the Latin American companies have, not just in their national, nor even in their world-regional markets, but also in the whole geolinguistic regions which they have created.

Apart from the dominance of the major networks in their own region and their substantial and active participation in the process of globalization, Latin American television has relevance to the globalization debate because of the 'text–audience' relationship which has developed between its characteristic genres and the audiences for them. In particular, a great deal of theory and research, some of it available in English, has been generated within Latin America on *telenovelas* as cultural products, and also about the audiences for them (Fadul 1993). This body of work includes quantitative (Lozano 1996), qualitative (Orozco 1995), and ethnographic (González 1997) audience research.

The consumption of television is related in the globalization literature to questions of cultural identity. In counterpoint to the trend towards cultural homogenization, a trend towards heterogenization is recognized: 'Culture is a multi-layered phenomenon; the product of local, tribal, regional or national dimensions, which is anything but a single national culture' (Richards and French 1996: 30). Rather too often, however, the 'local' becomes a catch-all category set up in contrast to the global, and tends to become equated with the 'national' (Sreberny-Mohammadi 1991). It was argued earlier in this chapter that we can usefully think of different kinds of television addressing audiences at local, national, world-regional, and global levels. In the debate about globalization, and cultural imperialism before it, there tends to be a static, zero-sum conception of culture, or, at least, the assumption that global or other foreign cultural influence carried by the media somehow necessarily drives out the local, national, and regional identities, rather than just adding another level of identification which coexists with them in any given individual. As Morley and Robins have observed,

every culture has, in fact, ingested foreign elements from exogenous sources, with the various elements gradually becoming 'naturalised' within it.... cultural hybridity is, increasingly, the normal state of affairs in the world, and in this context, any attempt to defend the integrity of indigenous or authentic cultures easily slips into the conservative defence of a nostalgic vision of the past. (1995: 130)

It is in this context that the Latin American theorization of *mestizaje* and hybridity touched on earlier has much to contribute, a perspective in which cultural identity 'is not simply an object that is acted upon by external forces, but rather has been rethought as a complex field of action' (Schlesinger and Morris 1997: 8–9). Rejecting the concept of postcolonialism as not applicable to Latin America, García Canclini is also explicit in his rejection of the dichotomies of dominator and dominated, centre and periphery, and sender and receiver. This leads to a postmodernist view of identity as deterritorialized and decentred (1997: 23–4). Martín-Barbero also draws attention to the deterritorialization of identities, in particular, as attributable to international television. He argues that Latin American television production and distribution on a regional basis is deterritorializing to the extent that the local is lost, and, as already noted, that it subsumes the cultural differences between Latin American nations, at the same time as it shapes a commercialized Latin American imaginary (Schlesinger and Morris 1997: 10–11).

Waisbord is more agnostic. While accepting Ien Ang's view that subjective identities are 'dynamic, conflictive, unstable, and impure' (quoted in Waisbord 1996: 27), he also argues that 'Perhaps the death notices written for national identities were premature' (1997: 8). Apart from this reminder that nation-states are still legitimate and effective units of political, economic, and sociocultural organization in a globalizing world, Waisbord poses the question of identities as an empirical one, a matter of audience research to ascertain 'how citizens actively build a sense of national identity beyond the interpellation of authorities and the shared consumption of mass culture'. Even if we accept that Latin America is one of the world's eight great 'civilizations' (Huntington 1997), just because Latin American nations share a similar linguistic and cultural heritage does not ensure that pan-Latin American television programming is going to be uniformly accepted and interpreted—it might have the right language and commercial properties, but the wrong cultural resonance (1997: 24–5). Evidence from regional programming executives suggests that this is indeed the case: programming 'must be flexible enough to accommodate quite distinct national market contexts' (Wilkinson 1995: 207). It follows that the sensitivity of such differences would be heightened in programme exchanges between Latin American and Iberian nations.

Rationale and Orientation

What can a book on the globalization of television in Latin America and its geolinguistic regions contribute to international communication scholarship? For one thing, it can act as a corrective to the Anglocentric assumptions of the mainstream, and show how different the world looks when viewed from Mexico City or Rio de Janeiro. For another, the massive size and growth of the Spanish-speaking markets make them too large a part of the global scene to ignore. Certainly, the global media moguls such as Rupert Murdoch and Ted Turner have not ignored them, but drawn them into their global conglomerates, and that in itself should demand the attention of concerned scholars. Thirdly, there is some comparative breadth to be gained from understanding the development, structure, and behaviour of the major Latin American producers and distributors in their respective markets, not just relative to the English-speaking world, but also to the recently privatized television markets of Europe and Asia. Worth noting in this respect is the perhaps un-expected level of technological sophistication being applied to the for-mation of new markets, such as DTH. Fourthly, there is a theoretical dimension, given that Latin American societies were the first postcolon-ial nation-states, and not only have the historical experience of cultural hybridization so much at the heart of contemporary theorizing about globalization, but as well have generated in that process some estimable theorists who deserve to be better known outside their region. Finally, there are intrinsic reasons, such as the emergence of the genre of the *telenovela*. This style of programming has grown out of the successful commercialization of Latin American popular culture, yet holds a fasci-nation for audiences in some culturally and geographically remote territories as well as in its own geolinguistic regions. Analysis of this phenomenon might provide valuable insights on processes of cultural identification and adaptation, and on their limits.

In the absence of the implicit authoritative support of the grand narratives of the past, in these times theoretical naïvety and a lack of reflexiveness about sources, methods, and logics of presentation are less excusable than ever. Thus, a word is in order about this book's strategies, empirical material, and the theoretical orientation in terms of which it is all presented. For reasons which have already been well canvassed, the television markets of Mexico, Brazil, and the Spanish-speaking US are given an intensive examination, with a more cursory look given to Venezuela and Argentina. A further chapter provides a similarly struc-tured analysis of the former 'mother countries' of Spain and Portugal, and their relations to Latin America. These chapters are all framed theoretically by the hypothesis that cultural and linguistic similarities can be and are exploited as a means to cultivate foreign markets for television programmes and services: the geolinguistic region hypothesis. In the paradigmatic case of the Spanish-speaking world, these markets have been extended from the world-regional, that is, Latin American level, to embrace the US and Spain, effectively a global level.

In each national instance, a narrative of genesis is presented in order to explain how television as an institution, and as a market, has taken the form it has, and a description and assessment is given of current developments. Particular attention is given to the relationship between entrepreneurial individuals or groups on one hand, and the state on the other, as such relationships are viewed theoretically as one kind of fundamental determinant of television as an institution in each nation. The historical accounts are based almost exclusively on academic secondary sources, but the contemporary analysis draws very much on data from trade journals and other such timely yet less proven sources. Every effort has been made to check the items cited from such sources against whatever others appeared at the same time, with the less plausible reports thus eliminated so as to form a comprehensible narrative out of the most recent data available at the time of writing, late 1997.

The emphasis in this book on ownership, entrepreneurial/corporate activities, the structural integration of the media corporations, and the relation of television to the state in each national context is consistent with the political economy tradition in communication studies. However, because that tradition, even in its most recent reformulation, refuses to engage itself with questions of the cultural meaning which media content carries for its audiences (Mosco 1996), a more supple perspective is needed, one which can reconcile both the political-economic and cultural dimensions of television as an institution. Such an approach is to be found in the 'cultural industries' school historically associated with the journal *Media, Culture and Society* in Britain, and as formulated by McAnany in the US (1984). This mode of analysis begins with the economic properties of cultural goods, and proceeds to the empirical observation of how systems of production and distribution of such goods have developed within particular countries. This is seen as a contingent, historically variable process, not the simple zero-sum domination of one nation by another, but the continuous outcome of complex relations of interest groups between nations, and the behaviour of globally interpenetrated capital in its attempts to form markets for cultural goods and services. A particular value of this approach is that it enables the global commercialization of culture to be understood in historical and structural terms, without having to invoke the conspiratorial assumptions unavoidable in the conventional cultural imperialism view. Furthermore, it is conducive to the identification of language and culture as 'market forces' with distinct effects within the wider process of globalization.

27

References

Anderson, Benedict (1991), *Imagined Communities: Reflections on the Origin and Spread of Nationalism* (2nd edn., Verso, London).

Assmann, Hugo (1974), 'Evaluación de algunos estudios latinoamericanos sobre comunicación masiva, con especial referencia a los escritos de Armand Mattelart', paper presented to the XI Congreso Latinoamericano de Sociología, Costa Rica, June.

Bakewell, Peter (1991), 'Colonial Latin America', in J. Knippers Black (ed.), *Latin America: Its Problems and its Promise* (2nd edn., Westview Press, Boulder, Colo.), 57–66.

Beltrán, Luis Ramiro (1978a), 'TV Etchings in the Minds of Latin Americans: Conservatism, Materialism and Conformism', *Gazette*, 24/1: 61–85.

—— (1978b), 'Communication and Cultural Domination: USA–Latin American Case', *Media Asia*, 5/4: 183–92.

Braudel, Fernand (1993), *A History of Civilizations* (Penguin Books, New York).

Bunce, Richard (1976), *Television in the Corporate Interest* (Praeger, New York).

Cardoso, Fernando Henrique (1973), 'Dependency and Development in Latin America', *New Left Review*, 74: 83–95.

—— (1977), 'The Consumption of Dependency Theory in the United States', *Latin American Research Review*, 12/3: 7–24.

Cockcroft, James (1983), *Mexico: Class Formation, Capital Accumulation, and the State* (Monthly Review Press, New York).

Collins, Richard (1990), *Television: Policy and Culture* (Unwin Hyman, London).

Crovi Druetta, Delia (ed.) (1995), *Desarrollo de las industrias audiovisuales en México y Canadá* (Universidad Nacional Autónoma de México, Mexico DF).

Crystal, David (1997), *English as a Global Language* (Cambridge University Press, Cambridge).

Dagnino, Evelina (1973), 'Cultural and Ideological Dependence: Building a Theoretical Framework', in F. Bonilla and R. Girling (eds.), *Structures of Dependency* (Stanford University, Stanford, Calif.), 129–48.

Davis, Cary, Haub, Carl, and Willette, Joanne (1983), 'US Hispanics: Changing the Face of America', *Population Bulletin*, 38/3: 1–43.

de Camargo, Nelly, and Noya Pinto, Virgilio (1975), *Communication Policies in Brazil* (UNESCO, Paris).

Dorfman, Ariel, and Mattelart, Armand (1975), *How to Read Donald Duck: Imperialist Ideology in the Disney Comic* (International General, New York).

El estado del mundo: edición 1997 (1996) (Akal Ediciones, Madrid).

Fadul, Anamaria (ed.) (1993), *Serial Fiction in TV: The Latin American Telenovelas* (School of Communication and Arts, University of São Paulo, São Paulo).

Fernández Christlieb, Fátima (1987), 'Algo más sobre los orígenes de la televisión latinoamericana', *DIA.Logos de la comunicación*, 18 (October), 32–45.

Fox, Elizabeth (1988), 'Media Policies in Latin America: An Overview', in E. Fox (ed.), *Media and Politics in Latin America: The Struggle for Democracy* (Sage, London), 6–35.

—— (1997), *Latin American Broadcasting: From Tango to Telenovela* (University of Luton Press, Luton).

Frappier, John (1968), 'US Media Empire/Latin America', *NACLA Newsletter*, 2/9: 1–11.

Galeano, Eduardo (1973), *Open Veins of Latin America: Five Centuries of the Pillage of a Continent* (Monthly Review Press, New York).

García Canclini, Nestor (1995), *Consumidores y ciudadanos* (Grijalbo, Mexico DF).

—— (1997), 'Hybrid Cultures and Communicative Strategies', *Media Development*, 44/1: 22–9.

González, Jorge (1997), 'The Willingness to Weave: Cultural Analysis, Cultural Fronts and Networks of the Future', *Media Development*, 44/1: 30–6.

Hall, Stuart (1996), 'When was "the Post-colonial"?: Thinking at the Limit', in I. Chambers and L. Curti (eds.), *The Post-colonial Question: Common Skies, Divided Horizons* (Routledge, London), 242–60.

—— (1997), 'End Notes', *Media Development*, 44/1: 54–6.

Hinchberger, Bill (1997), 'Jorge Amado Writes from Heart, Home', *Variety* (31 March–6 April), 56.

Hugh-Jones, Stephen (1995), 'Brazil: A Glass Half Full', *The Economist* (29 April), 3–5.

Huntington, Samuel (1997), 'The Clash of Civilizations?', in Foreign Affairs Agenda (ed.), *The New Shape of World Politics* (Norton, New York), 67–91.

Janus, Noreene, and Roncagliolo, Rafael (1978), 'A Survey of the Transnational Structure of the Mass Media and Advertising', report prepared for the Center of Transnationals of the United Nations, Instituto Latinoamericano de Estudios Transnacionales, Mexico DF.

Klee, Carol (1991), 'Introduction', in C. Klee and L. Ramos-García (eds.), *Sociolinguistics of the Spanish-Speaking World* (Bilingual Press, Tempe, Ariz.), 1–8.

Lent, John (1990), *Mass Communications in the Caribbean* (Iowa State University Press, Ames).

Lozano, José Carlos (1996), 'Media Reception on the Mexican Border with the United States', in E. McAnany and K. Wilkinson (eds.), *Mass Media and Free Trade: NAFTA and the Cultural Industries* (University of Texas Press, Austin), 157–86.

McAnany, Emile (1984), 'The Logic of Cultural Industries in Latin America: The Television Industry in Brazil', in V. Mosco and J. Wasko (eds.), *The Critical Communications Review, ii: Changing Patterns of Communications Control* (Ablex, Norwood, NJ), 185–208.

McClintock, Anne (1992), 'The Angel of Progress: Pitfalls of the Term "Post-colonialism"', *Social Text*, 10/2–3: 84–98.

McWilliams, Carey (1968), *North from Mexico* (Greenwood Press, New York).

Marques de Melo, José (1992), 'Brazil's Role as a Television Exporter within the Latin American Regional Market', paper presented to the 42nd Conference of the International Communication Association, Miami, May.

Martín-Barbero, Jesús (1993), *Communication, Culture and Hegemony: From the Media to Mediations* (Sage, London).

Martín-Barbero, Jesús (1997), 'Cultural Decentring and Palimpsets of Identity', *Media Development*, 44/1: 18–21.

Mattelart, Armand (1980), 'Cultural Imperialism, Mass Media and Class Struggle: An Interview with Armand Mattelart', *Insurgent Sociologist*, 9/4: 69–79.

——(1991), *Advertising International: The Privatisation of Public Space* (Routledge, London).

Mejía Barquera, Fernando (1989), *La industria de la radio y la televisión y la política del estado Mexicano*, i: *(1920–1960)* (Fundación Manuel Buendía, Mexico DF).

Mignolo, Walter (1995), 'Afterword: Human Understanding and (Latin) American Interests: The Politics and Sensibilities of Geocultural Locations', *Poetics Today*, 16/1: 171–214.

Morley, David, and Robins, Kevin (1995), *Spaces of Identity: Global Media, Electronic Landscapes and Cultural Boundaries* (Routledge, London).

Mosco, Vincent (1996), *The Political Economy of Communication* (Sage, London).

Muraro, Heriberto (1985), 'El "modelo" latinoamericano', *Telos*, 3: 78–82.

Orozco Gómez, Guillermo (1995), 'The Dialectic of TV Reception: The Audience's Structuring of TV Viewing Strategies', *Mexican Journal of Communication*, 2: 93–106.

Pasquali, Antonio (1967), *El aparato singular: un día de televisión en Caracas* (Universidad Central de Venezuela, Caracas).

Pool, Ithiel de Sola (1977), 'The Changing Flow of Television', *Journal of Communication*, 27/2: 139–79.

Read, William (1976), *America's Mass Media Merchants* (Johns Hopkins University Press, Baltimore).

Richards, Michael, and French, David (1996), 'From Global Development to Global Culture?', in D. French and M. Richards (eds.), *Contemporary Television: Eastern Perspectives* (Sage, New Delhi), 22–48.

Riding, Alan (1986), *Distant Neighbours: A Portrait of the Mexicans* (Vintage Books, New York).

Rogers, Everett, and Antola, Livia (1985), 'Telenovelas: A Latin American Success Story', *Journal of Communication*, 35/4: 24–35.

Roncagliolo, Rafael (1995), 'Trade Integration and Communication Networks in Latin America', *Canadian Journal of Communication*, 20/3: 335–42.

Rønning, Helge (1997), 'Language, Cultural Myths, Media and *Realpolitik*: The Case of Mozambique', *Media Development*, 44/1: 50–4.

Salinas, Raquel, and Paldán, Leena (1979), 'Culture in the Process of Dependent Development: Theoretical Perspectives', in K. Nordenstreng and H. Schiller (eds.), *National Sovereignty and International Communication* (Ablex, Norwood, NJ), 82–98.

Sánchez Ruiz, Enrique (1994), 'The Mexican Audiovisual Space and the North American Free Trade Agreement', *Media Information Australia*, 71: 70–7.

Schiller, Herbert (1969), *Mass Communications and American Empire* (Augustus M. Kelley, New York).

—— (1990), 'Not Yet the Post-imperialist Era', *Critical Studies in Mass Communication*, 8: 13–28.

Schlesinger, Philip, and Morris, Nancy (1997), 'Cultural Boundaries: Identity and Communication in Latin America', *Media Development*, 44/1: 5–17.

Schwaller, John (1987), 'Discovery and Conquest', in J. Hopkins (ed.), *Latin America: Perspectives on a Region* (Holmes & Meier, New York), 57–70.

Schwarz, Cristina, and Jaramillo, Oscar (1986), 'Hispanic American Critical Communication Research in its Historical Context', in R. Atwood and E. McAnany (eds.), *Communication and Latin American Society: Trends in Critical Research, 1960–1985* (University of Wisconsin Press, Madison), 48–75.

Schwoch, James (1990), *The American Radio Industry and its Latin American Activities, 1900–1939* (University of Illinois Press, Urbana).

Shohat, Ella (1992), 'Notes on the "Post-colonial"', *Social Text*, 10/2–3: 99–113.

Silva, Ludovico (1971), *Teoría y práctica de la ideología* (Editorial Nuestro Tiempo, Mexico DF).

Sinclair, John (1996), 'Culture and Trade: Some Theoretical and Practical Considerations', in E. McAnany and K. Wilkinson (eds.), *Mass Media and Free Trade: NAFTA and the Cultural Industries* (University of Texas Press, Austin), 30–60.

Sreberny-Mohammadi, Annabelle (1991), 'The Global and the Local in International Communications', in J. Curran and M. Gurevitch (eds.), *Mass Media and Society* (Edward Arnold, New York), 118–38.

Straubhaar, Joseph (1991), 'Beyond Media Imperialism: Asymmetrical Interdependence and Cultural Proximity', *Critical Studies in Mass Communication*, 8: 39–59.

—— (1992), 'Asymmetrical Interdependence and Cultural Proximity: A Critical Review of the International Flow of Television Programs', paper presented to the conference of the Asociación Latinoamericana de Investigadores de la Comunicación, São Paulo, August.

Tomlinson, John (1991), *Cultural Imperialism: A Critical Introduction* (Johns Hopkins University Press, Baltimore).

Tunstall, Jeremy (1977), *The Media Are American: Anglo-American Media in the World* (Constable, London).

Valdez, Luis (1972), 'Introduction: "La Plebe"', in L. Valdez and S. Steiner (eds.), *Aztlán: An Anthology of Mexican American Literature* (Vintage Books, New York), pp. xiii–xxxiv.

Varis, Tapio (1978), 'The Mass Media TNCs: An Overall View of their Operations and Control Options', paper prepared for a meeting of the Asian and Pacific Development Administration Centre, Kuala Lumpur.

—— (1984), 'The International Flow of Television Programmes', *Journal of Communication*, 34/1: 143–52.

Waisbord, Silvio (1995), 'Leviathan Dreams: State and Broadcasting in South America', *Communication Review*, 1/2: 201–26.

—— (1996), 'Latin American Television and National Identities', paper presented to the conference of the International Communication Association, Chicago, May.

Waisbord, Silvio (1997), 'Television in Latin America', manuscript for entry in A. Smith (ed.), *Television: An International History* (Oxford University Press, Oxford), forthcoming.

Waters, Malcolm (1995), *Globalisation* (Routledge, London).

Wells, Alan (1972), *Picture Tube Imperialism? The Impact of US Television in Latin America* (Orbis, Maryknoll, NY).

Wilkinson, Kenton (1995), 'When Culture, Language and Communication Converge: The Latin American Cultural-Linguistic Television Market', Ph.D. dissertation, University of Texas at Austin.

Williamson, Edwin (1992), *The Penguin History of Latin America* (Penguin Books, London).

2 | The Autumn of the Patriarch: Mexico and Televisa

The development of television in Mexico is synonymous with the history of how the whole of the Mexican broadcasting system has been very much formed by the entrepreneurship of two generations of patriarchs from the one family, the Azcárragas, and by the emergence of their company, Televisa, as a quasi-monopolistic, cross-media conglomerate which not only has dominated the Mexican television market, but has been actively pursuing its ambitions in most of the rest of the Spanish-speaking world. This entrepreneurship would have to be called 'dependent entrepreneurship', in the sense that the strategic growth of Televisa and its corporate ancestors has been ultimately conditioned by the subordinate position which Mexico occupies within the world system, especially relative to the US, but it has been most consequential none the less for the structures which television has assumed both in the Latin American region and, to a more restricted degree, within the US itself. In other words, while individual entrepreneurs and interest groups can only act within the structural constraints which history gives them, over time their actions come to modify the structures themselves. It is in this sense that the narrative of the development of television as an industry in Mexico can be periodized in terms of the lives of Emilio Azcárraga Vidaurreta (from the 1920s until his death in 1972), an active agent in first establishing radio and subsequently television in Mexico, and his son Emilio Azcárraga Milmo (1930–97), who then presided over Televisa for more than two decades of domestic consolidation and international expansion. The current period has been marked, amongst other great changes, by the death of the latter, and the succession of his son Emilio Azcárraga Jean (1968–), who is leading Televisa into a more competitive and globalized, and thus uncertain, future.

'The Voice of Latin America from Mexico'

The fact that radio today has become so much a taken-for-granted, unglamorous medium, incapable of rousing the passions associated with debates about television, can make us underestimate the formative influence which it has had in its time in building up the whole institutional structure upon which television was later to base itself. In the Mexican case, radio technology became available at a time when both foreign capital (at that stage, French as well as US) and Mexican entrepreneurs were looking for new investment opportunities. Significantly, the very first radio station was begun by a US-educated engineer, not in Mexico City, but in Monterrey, the industrial capital of the north-east, a city with a reputation both for its spirit of capitalism and for its responsiveness to US influences (Fernández Christlieb 1976: 240–1).

The first commercial radio station in Mexico City was CYL, opened in 1923 by Emilio Azcárraga's brothers Raúl and Luis, all sons of a Spanish immigrant from Navarre (Martínez 1996: 50). Raúl had a radio sales business, and had received technical training in Texas (Mejía Prieto 1972: 26; Fernández Christlieb 1976: 238–9). Emilio also was US-educated, reportedly at the University of Texas at Austin (Esparza 1997: 50), and managed an RCA Victor phonograph and radio dealership, the Mexico Music Company. He was married into the Anglo-Mexican banking and mining Milmo family, but his access to capital was through RCA, not the Milmos. In 1930, he too opened a commercial radio station in Mexico City, XEW, which was backed principally by the Mexico Music Company (Fernández Christlieb 1976: 241–4).

It was from this point that Mexican commercial radio entered its rapid expansion, having been more preoccupied in its earlier days with selling radio sets rather than building audiences for the sale of advertising time. Emilio Azcárraga built XEW into a chain of stations in the central and northern provinces which became affiliated with RCA's broadcasting network in the US, NBC. With an entertainment format which shrewdly commercialized popular culture genres, and the then still quite innovative practice of selling airtime to advertisers, the XEW network enjoyed great success as 'The Voice of Latin America from Mexico' (de Noriega and Leach 1979: 17).

However, Azcárraga was not bound by his links to RCA and NBC. In 1938, he opened another station in Mexico City, XEQ, this time with capital from the US network CBS, and this became the basis for another network (Mejía Prieto 1972: 61; de Noriega and Leach 1979: 170). Azcárraga had put himself into a position in which he could take advantage of both of the US networks' desire to build chains able to attract US national advertisers who had become interested in advertising in Latin America at this time. Accordingly, the US network model of operation was adopted for both the 'Tricolor' XEW-NBC and the 'Blue' XEQ-CBS chains: the network affiliates were provided with programmes from the network in return for time which the network could then sell to advertisers (Arriaga 1980: 226).

Although NBC did produce some Spanish-language programming in the 1930s (Fox 1997: 17), Azcárraga's networks were distinguished not by English-language programmes from the US, but by Mexican popular music, radionovelas, and other entertainment material being produced by Azcárraga's company, Radio Programas de México. There were also programmes they were receiving in an exchange with Goar Mestre, who was developing commercial radio in Cuba in much the same way at this time. Radio Programas de México also was active in affiliating new stations in Central America, and instrumental in assisting NBC to enter South American countries such as Colombia. Azcárraga had been quick to develop an orientation to his region, both commercially and later politically: as noted in Chapter 1, he and Mestre became the key figures in setting up AIR, the organization of private broadcasters in the region, after 1945 (Fernández Christlieb 1987; Mejía Barquera 1989: 120–9).

At this stage, a significant incursion into Mexican radio was made by another media entrepreneur, Rómulo O'Farrill Silva, who opened the station XEX in Mexico City in 1947, and took control of the major newspaper Novedades the following year, integrating it with the station. O'Farrill and his son later became involved in television, as will soon be seen, and magazine publishing as well, in both of which they were to become partners with the Alemán family (Fernández Christlieb 1987).

Both O'Farrill and Azcárraga had been lobbying the President of the time, Miguel Alemán Valdés (President 1946–52), to grant licences for the introduction of television. In 1947, Alemán appointed a commission to investigate which kind of system Mexico should adopt for the establishment of television. This consisted of Guillermo González Camarena, an engineer with a long record of successful experimentation with colour television, and a distinguished writer, Salvador Novo. While Novo dissented in favour of the European public model, González Camarena's recommendation in favour of the US commercial model was met with Alemán's de facto acceptance when he granted a licence to Rómulo O'Farrill for XHTV Channel 4 in 1949. This was the first television station not just in Mexico, but in Latin America. It began transmitting the following year, during which a second licence was granted to

Azcárraga for XEWTV, Channel 2, which first went to air in 1951. Yet a third licence was awarded in 1952 to González Camarena for Channel 5 (Sánchez Ruiz 1991: 29–30).

However, because so few people owned sets, television was not attractive to advertisers, or sponsors who would buy airtime for their own programmes, as the system then worked in the US, so Mexican television could not at first fit itself to the commercial model. With his experience in cinema as well as radio, Azcárraga was running his production studios like a theatre, charging admission for live productions so as to meet his costs in building them ('TV in Mexico' 1951). Rather than ruin each other by competing in such a small market, the three channels decided to merge in March 1955 to form Telesistema Mexicano (TSM). This was a pooling of the three licensees' operations, but firmly under the control of Azcárraga and O'Farrill: Camarena did not even get a seat on the board (Fernández Christlieb 1975: 109).

TSM immediately created a programme export arm, Teleprogramas de México, and set about extending the coverage of its channels, particularly in the north, as with radio, and differentiating the channels for particular audience segments. Azcárraga and O'Farrill ensured that the expansion of TSM was propelled by the foreign technology and investment which they needed. In 1958, a TSM station in Monterrey acquired the first of many Ampex videotape machines from the US, which were to enable TSM to extend the domestic network as well as its nascent export activities with more programmes. As a new technology, videotape permitted high-quality television recording not before possible, and hence greater distribution of programmes. The expansion of the production activities was undertaken with a direct 25 per cent investment from the third major television network in the US, ABC, to create a subsidiary, Teleprogramas Acapulco, in 1962. Under the direction of Miguel Alemán Velasco, the son of the President who had granted the original licences and who was now a partner within TSM, this company concentrated on the mass production and distribution of *telenovelas* (de Noriega and Leach 1979: 21–2; Pérez Espino 1979: 1444; Sánchez Ruiz 1991: 30–1). At the same time, Azcárraga was venturing into the US, setting up his first stations there as outlets for TSM programmes, as will be explored in more detail in Chapter 4.

Other technical innovations which enabled TSM to extend its coverage during the 1960s were the introduction of cable technology through the subsidiary Cablevisión in 1966 (Pérez Espino 1979: 1461), and the advent of colour transmission in 1967 (de Noriega and Leach 1979: 22–4). But by this time, TSM no longer had the market all to itself. In 1968, a licence was granted to a film producer, Barbachano Ponce, to open a station in Monterrey, Channel 12, which he built into a network in the north and central regions, Telecadena Mexicana. Also that year, the powerful industrial group Alfa, owned by the Garza Sada family of Monterrey, was given a licence to open Channel 8 in Mexico City. Their company Televisión Independiente de México (TIM) had been operating in Monterrey since 1960, but the move to Mexico City meant a direct competitive challenge to TSM. Also in Mexico City, the radio entrepreneur Francisco Aguirre had been granted a licence to open Channel 13 (de Noriega and Leach 1979: 23–4; Pérez Espino 1979: 1451).

The State and Television

Clearly, the political climate had changed from the days when a President could grant a company a television licence in a virtually unregulated environment, and move on to join as a partner at the end of his term. Under López Mateos (President 1958–64), the first comprehensive broadcasting regulatory regime had been introduced (de Noriega and Leach 1979: 29–33), while Díaz Ordaz (President 1964–70), as well as opening up TSM's former market monopoly to more licensees and establishing a government educational service and a cultural channel, sought to tax all television licensees in consideration for their use of the infrastructure which the state provided for them. This was in connection with the microwave network and satellite station which the government had built to broadcast the 1968 Olympic Games held in Mexico City (de Noriega and Leach 1979: 22–3). The licensees united behind TSM in resistance against the government's proposal, a compromise being reached when the licensees agreed to 'cede' a proportion of 12.5 per cent of their transmission time to the government for its use: 'fiscal time' instead of the tax. The government accepted, though it never took much advantage of the time so gained (Granados Chapa 1976: 228–30).

A more serious and consequential Mexican stand-off occurred with Luis Echeverría (President 1970–6), who was determined to secure a place for the state in television broadcasting, and to reform the industry. In 1972, as well as establishing its own specially targeted rural network, Televisión Rural de México (de Noriega and Leach 1979: 49), the government bought Aguirre's Channel 13 when it went bankrupt, and began operating it under a state agency, SOMEX (Mahan 1985: 62–4). Faced with the intervention of the state in the market, the spectre of a public broadcasting competitor, and the threat of more regulation, TSM and TIM took a historic decision: they merged their operations under the umbrella of a new company, Televisión vía Satélite, or Televisa. This was effectively a confederation of the original three licensed companies which had merged in 1955, plus TIM, at that time under the direction of Joaquín Vargas (de Noriega and Leach 1979: 25–6).

The formation of Televisa thus brought the Grupo Monterrey together with the other powerful industrial groups that were behind TSM: Grupo Alemán and Grupo Puebla (O'Farrill), tying Televisa closely to the national bourgeoisie (Bernal Sahagún 1978: 59). In terms of the politics of the state in Mexico, it typifies 'the relative autonomy of the industry in the face of state initiatives to control it' (Mahan 1985: 62). More than this, it also shows that, contrary to the common assumptions that the Mexican state has always facilitated (Rogers and Antola 1985: 27) or even lurked behind (Valenzuela 1986) the monopolistic expansion of private television interests, there is a significant dimension in which this demonstrably is not the case, and the intervention of the state has had a formative and enduring effect in shaping the structure of the industry, even if in a quite counterproductive manner. The politics of class and the politics of the state still each have their own logic and interests to pursue.

That being said, it is true that the more general framework in which relations between the state and the private television interests have been conducted has been one of mutual support and ideological consensus. Presidents have come and gone, but the same party, the Partido Revolucionario Institucional (PRI), has controlled the state throughout the entire history of commercial broadcasting in Mexico, and the broadcasters have had strong links with the PRI (Fox 1997: 37). Within a few years of the crisis with Echeverría, and even after the collapsed Telecadena Mexicana had been added to the state network in 1975, Miguel Alemán Velasco was rhetorically praising 'the Mexican formula' (Alemán Velasco 1976: 195), a kind of division of labour between Televisa and Channel 13 in which the state's endeavours were made to legitimize those of Televisa, and shore up its quasi-monopoly. In other words, the attempts at state intervention tended to reinforce the hegemony of the private interests, rather than break it down (Sinclair 1986).

Televisa's Golden Age

With TSM and TIM merged, and their former commercial competitors incorporated into a state network which never became the threat that had at first been anticipated, Televisa was set for a golden age. As it happened, Emilio Azcárraga Vidaurreta never lived to see the formation of Televisa, having died on 23 September 1972, as if with TSM, for the agreement to form Televisa was made in the following December, with formal operation under that name beginning in the new year (Sánchez Ruiz 1991: 32). The death of the older Azcárraga had both hastened the merger, and allowed Emilio Azcárraga Milmo to step into the breach as President. For almost the next two decades, Televisa was directed by a triumvirate of the sons of the founding fathers of the 1950s: Azcárraga together with the younger Alemán and O'Farrill, giving an oligarchic as well as a patriarchal cast to its control. The Garza Sada family sold its 25 per cent share in 1982, affected by the economic crisis of that year. That share was soon thereafter acquired by Azcárraga (Mahan 1985: 61–4; Sánchez Ruiz 1991: 33).

As in the years of the fathers' TSM monopoly, Televisa could segment the national market with differentiated coverage and programming on its channels: mass viewing on Channel 2; downmarket *telenovelas* and sport on Channel 4; youthful viewing on Channel 5; and ostensibly more upmarket programming of films and series on Channel 8. The majority, over 60 per cent of the programmes at first, and later more like 80 per cent, were being produced by Televisa itself. Its channels were attracting 93 per cent of the audience, and a comparable proportion of advertising revenue—the state channel also was in part supported by advertising. In all, Televisa had evolved 'the most attractive package of saturation coverage ever put together in the history of Mexican television' (de Noriega and Leach 1979: 53–7).

Thus, apart from its virtual monopoly, Televisa was consolidating its strength in the Mexican market by the vertical integration of production and distribution. There was a whole production infrastructure in place, not just the studios, but supporting activities such as talent schools, and a dubbing operation for imported programming, a longtime speciality of its corporate ancestor. As well as its broadcast television with up to full national coverage, distribution was augmented with cable. There was horizontal integration as well—with the merger, Azcárraga's radio and recording interests were brought under the Televisa corporate umbrella, while the O'Farrills' interests in magazines and the daily *Novedades* also helped the Televisa partners to ensure the cross-promotion and ever more intensive commercialization of their various media interests: publicity for television stars in the press, promotion of recorded music on television shows, and so on. Significant additions to the range of cross-media activities during this period were Televicine in 1978, a film production division, and Videovisa in 1985, under which video hardware and software was produced and distributed (Sánchez Ruiz 1991: 32–4). Televisa's conglomerated operations at their fullest extent are looked at in more detail in Chapter 3, with particular attention to the structural similarities Televisa shares with its counterpart in Brazil, TV Globo.

Televisa was one of the first media corporations in the world to see the advantages of satellites for the distribution of programmes to far-flung and dispersed audiences which were outside its borders, but which shared linguistic and cultural similarities with the programming's nation of origin. In view of the fact that the name Televisa was conceived as an abbreviation for Televisión vía Satélite, it would come as no surprise that much of the technological development which was undertaken in these years had to do with Televisa's ambitions to extend its distribution to selected audiences on an international scale. Satellite distribution has thus augmented the role of Protele, Televisa's sales division, which, as well as selling Televisa programmes to the few independent channels remaining in Mexico, exists to sell programme rights and physically distribute programmes on an international basis through its foreign offices. In 1976, Televisa commenced a venture it called Univisión, a weekly feed of its domestic programming to the US border for subsequent distribution to its stations in the US via satellite. The following year, Televisa established an office in Madrid, and began occasional satellite transmissions to Spain (de Noriega and Leach 1979: 59; Sánchez Ruiz 1991: 32). We shall see in Chapter 4 how integral Televisa's operations in the US have been for its international stagegies, and in Chapter 5 how it has persisted with attempts to establish a market in Spain. In both cases, the use of satellite transmission has played a crucial part.

Yet by far the most ambitious and consequential step made by Televisa into satellite broadcasting was in response to a further instance of confrontation with the state in Mexico. In 1982, the new President, Miguel de la Madrid (President 1982–8), mandated a constitutional change which reserved all powers over satellite development to the state, thus cutting the ground from under any move which Televisa might have wanted to make into domestic satellite development in Mexico. However, while the Mexican Government went on to engage the US satellite corporation Hughes International Communications to build and, in 1984, to launch its domestic satellite system known as Sistema Morelos, Azcárraga raised the stakes by mobilizing Televisa's associates within the US to make an application to establish an international satellite system to be based there, and capable of reaching both North and South America, as well as Europe (Fernández Christlieb 1985; Valenzuela 1986; Sánchez Ruiz 1991: 33). As is outlined in Chapter 4, within a few years this was successfully put into effect as PanAmSat.

Just as Televisa's loyalty to the ruling party did not protect it from de la Madrid's albeit unsuccessful attempt to keep satellite development out of Televisa's hands, it should also be noted that the state continued to develop its own national television network in competition with Televisa, however weak that might have been. In particular, the reach of the state's Channel 13 network was augmented in 1985 by converting most of the original Televisión Rural de México into a second network, Channel 7, with a new entity being created, Imevisión (Sánchez Ruiz 1991: 34). The two Imevisión channels lasted until the 1990s, when, under the regime of Carlos Salinas de Gortari (President 1988–94) and the prevailing ideology of privatization, the Imevisión channels were put up for sale to private owners (Mejía Barquera 1995: 85–8), a thread which will be picked up again in the next section.

In terms of programming initiatives for the international market, Televisa used Galavisión, its US satellite-to-cable subsidiary, as the base from which it began transmitting an international service of the same name. Programmes were mainly drawn from its Channel 2 schedule in Mexico, combined with an international news service also established by Televisa around this time and based in the US, ECO (Empresa de Comunicaciones Orbitales). Once again, these developments were closely linked to Televisa's strategic moves in the US in 1986 and 1987, led by Azcárraga himself, which are discussed in Chapter 4. As detailed there, Azcárraga made a serious error of judgement in attempting to bring in a Televisa executive to take control of ECO in the US. The problem was that Televisa had always been seen to lack credibility in the area of news, precisely because of the close relationship it had in Mexico to the ruling party, the PRI. This relationship had served Televisa well in the past, so long as the political benefits outweighed the negative effects upon Televisa's reputation as a news source. However, Televisa's declared political allegiance started to become a problem for it in the second half of the 1980s, not only in the corporation's international aspirations, but within Mexico itself. This was because of growing popular support for the major conservative opposition party, the PAN (Partido Acción Nacional), particularly after 1986 when the PAN's apparent win in a state election in Chihuahua, a northern province, was overturned, and Televisa chose to ignore the entire dispute, effectively assisting the PRI in a notorious cover-up attempt. Televisa's partisanship for the PRI was also made brazenly apparent in its handling of the 1988 presidential election campaign, and in Azcárraga's public declarations as a PRI supporter, not to mention Alemán's later departure to become a PRI Senator in 1991 (Zellner 1989). ECO was officially launched in 1988, with transmission to Europe (notably Spain) and parts of Africa as well as North and South America ('Alejandro Burillo's Rising Star at Televisa' 1991), but the contradiction of an international news service

41

compromised in credibility by domestic allegiance to a national government has not been resolved.

As the 1980s came to a close, the beginning of the end of Televisa's golden age, the age of domestic market domination under the 'Mexican formula', presided over by the patriarchs of three oligarchic families, was coming into view. One other international initiative of Azcárraga's which should be mentioned at this point was the setting up of an English-language sports and entertainment newspaper in the US in 1990, the *National*. This ceased publication after only sixteen months and the loss of over $US100 million (Donaton 1991), a serious loss for Televisa to deal with, and surely a strong indication that Azcárraga's strengths were in Spanish-language rather than English content, and probably more in the audiovisual rather than the print media.

Even before this disastrous folly, the costs of international expansion were taking a toll on Televisa, with a large debt to carry and substantial losses in both 1988 and 1989. The crisis appears to have brought to a head a struggle for power between the family-based factions within the management group which had been going at least since 1986, when Televisa had been obliged to divest itself of its national network of stations in the US, a significant change in corporate fortunes detailed in Chapter 4. Whatever the obscure dynamics were within the peak management, in an internal restructuring of holdings in 1991, Azcárraga and his family greatly increased their share in Televisa, while O'Farrill completely sold out his 24 per cent interest, and left. Alemán also departed, but leaving a son still within the administrative council, to whom he ceded his significant share. Azcárraga took over the video, radio, and dubbing divisions, while the cable division went to his sister Carmela (Acosta 1991: 14; 'Big Shuffle in Mexican TV Ownership' 1991; Sánchez Ruiz 1991: 35).

It transpired that this consolidation of Televisa's control under the Azcárragas was in preparation for a public float on both the Mexican and New York stock exchanges in 1992. Presumably O'Farrill and Alemán had chosen not to endure with Televisa into this new era, while Azcárraga had determined that it was the only way he could raise the capital needed to meet debt obligations and fund his further ambitions for international expansion. For as well as dealing with the immediate liquidity crisis, it became apparent that Azcárraga was eager for finance to make a return to the US market, a strategic position he had been forced to vacate in 1986, as well as to establish some presence in South American markets. These concerns can be understood in terms of the NAFTA (North American Free Trade Agreement) then imminent, in anticipation of which Azcárraga had been lobbying to have the foreign ownership provisions over US broadcasting modified in his favour (Fisher 1992). In the event, he was obliged to enter a partnership with a US majority owner and another Latin American network in order to restore some direct control over the major Spanish-language television network in the US which the Azcárragas had previously owned, by then known as Univisión. This whole history will be detailed in Chapter 4. The point here is that the float had meant that Televisa was in a strong cash position to be buying back into the US, as well as making several new investments throughout 1992 and 1993.

Thus, in July 1992, on top of the announcement of Televisa's intended return to its former network in the US, came the news that Televisa had acquired 76 per cent of Compañía Peruana de Radiodifusión, Peru's second-ranked network, for around $US7 million ('Televisa anunció oficialmente la compra de canal peruano' 1992). Already at the end of 1991, for a similar amount, Televisa had bought 49 per cent of Chile's first private channel, Megavisión, and entered an arrangement covering technical and commercial advice, programme supply and co-production, input from Megavisión to ECO and admission to the OTI (Organisación de Televisión Iberoamericana), and a seat for Megavisión's head, Ricardo Claro, on Televisa's directorate (Ehrmann 1991; 'Televisa compro 49 por ciento de Megavisión' 1991; Ehrmann 1992). Such selective direct investments in other Latin American countries were something quite new for Televisa, and perhaps also related strategically to extensions of the NAFTA agreement then mooted. Programme distribution was more clearly a priority in another deal begun that year in the Southern Cone, however, involving the state-owned ATC (Argentina Televisora Color), which agreed to take Televisa programmes ('Televisa compro 49 por ciento de Megavisión' 1991). Also in 1992, Televisa announced a non-competitive programme distribution and licensing agreement with Venevisión, its Latin American partner in the US network (Morgan Stanley 1992).

Direct investments continued in 1993, notably with Televisa paying $US200 million for a non-controlling 50 per cent share in PanAmSat, the international satellite venture it had initiated in the 1980s, but later withdrew from, as will be explained in Chapter 4. There were also some strategic alliances with international media corporations announced. Two of these did not proceed, with the US home-shopping cable channel QVC and the cable operator TCI (Tele-Communications Inc.), but an agreement to produce and distribute a Latin American version of the Discovery cable channel was put into effect, and a programme production and distribution arrangement with News Limited was commenced (Mejía Barquera 1995: 71–3). However, as the next

43

section will show, such internationalization of television services has
coincided with yet another economic reversal in Televisa's domestic
market, leaving both in a greatly weakened position.

Into the Global Era

It is ironic that it was the quincentennial year of 1992 which marked such
a high point in Televisa's development, particularly in its ability to fund
international expansion, as has just been outlined. Five years later, by
1997, Televisa was in crisis: it was almost a billion US dollars in debt and
desperately selling down prime assets; its management had become
unstable; it was facing real competition in its domestic market for the
first time; and it was being subordinated to foreign-based partners in its
international ventures. On all of these counts, Televisa was being put
through fundamental changes which, taken together, amounted to a
major downturn in its fortunes precisely at a time when the stakes
were being raised by international players in Spanish-language markets,
so it is worth looking at this transformation in some detail.

The 'Tequila Effect'

If Televisa ever needed a reminder that, for all its international ambitions, its fortunes were still tied to those of a dependent nation, this
came at the end of 1994 when the Mexican Government devalued the
peso, and then allowed it to float. From a rate of Ps 3.47 per US dollar
just prior to the devaluation, the peso fell immediately to around Ps 5.00
per US dollar, eventually stabilizing at just under Ps 8.00 per US dollar,
as of late 1996–early 1997. Over the same period, inflation blew out
dramatically from 7.1 per cent in 1994 to 52 per cent in 1995, then back
down to 27.7 per cent in 1996 and 4.3 per cent in the first quarter of 1997
(Grupo Televisa 1997: 30).

Both devaluation and inflation had drastic effects for Televisa, as for
other Mexican companies. The business magazine *Fortune* estimated
that Televisa's value dropped $US3,800 million from 1994 to 1995 (Puig
1997*c*: 16). More than this, the devaluation also plunged Televisa deep
into debt, and curtailed its ability to generate income. Largely because of
its international activities, Televisa has considerable operating costs and
expenses in US dollars, much in excess of its US dollar-denominated
sales, so it has had to earn so much more in pesos to meet its US dollar
commitments. Furthermore, because the Mexican Government's auster-
ity programme in response to the fiscal crisis was having an adverse

effect on the domestic consumer market at the same time, part of the so-called recessionary 'tequila effect', Televisa's income from new advertising revenues decreased. This drop was over 44 per cent in 1995, although net sales overall decreased less than 10 per cent, reflecting an offset from programme licensing revenues ('sales').

Most of Televisa's advertising revenues are obtained under the 'French Plan', in which advertisers pay a year in advance at an agreed rate, with an option to 'top-off', or acquire more time at the same preferential rate later. This system is most advantageous to Televisa's financial planning and liquidity. However, since the crisis, Televisa has been sorely testing the loyalty of its advertisers with steep increases each year in nominal advertising rates, up to 80 per cent in 1996 (Grupo Televisa 1997: 30–7). It is difficult to see how this method of squeezing more income from diminished sources can be sustained in the now more competitive environment to be discussed below, since the competing network, TV Azteca, is more flexible over allowing advertisers to have airtime on credit, as well as being cheaper ('Country Profile: Mexico' 1996: 5; Ramón Huerta 1997: 30).

Televisa's debt, of almost a billion US dollars in 1997, is composed of interest-bearing notes already issued before the devaluation; a 1994 loan from the Mexican bank Banamex, the largest in Mexican private-banking history, intended to hedge against the then-anticipated devaluation; 1994 and 1995 loans from the Government of Spain, used to finance the expansion of Televisa's terrestrial networks in Mexico at that time; and a Morgan Guaranty Loan, secured against Televisa's subsequently reduced interest in PanAmSat (Grupo Televisa 1997: 53–5). Much of the debt from prior to the devaluation was incurred by Emilio Azcárraga Milmo having funded the buyout of his sister Laura's interests in the company in 1993, including Videovisa before it was sold on (Mejía Barquera 1995: 82; 'Country Profile: Mexico' 1996: 5).

In order to meet its debts, and the cost of servicing them, Televisa began in 1995 to sell down its interests in some of its strategic assets. First was the sale of all of its interest in Televisa Peruana, the majority owner of the Peruvian station it had acquired in 1992. Next came the sale of 49 per cent of its cable division, Cablevisión, to a subsidiary of the privatized Teléfonos de México, or Telmex (Grupo Televisa 1997: 71). Then, towards the end of 1995, with the death of Rene Anselmo (Cosper 1995), PanAmSat was converted from a limited partnership to a public company, diluting Televisa's former half-share to 40.5 per cent. Another significant sell-down occurred in the following year, when also as a result of a public float, and the opportunity to realize $US190 million, Televisa's former 25 per cent interest in the US Univisión network and 12 per cent interest in the corresponding station group were reduced in total to a less than 20 per cent interest in the restructured Univisión (Grupo Televisa 1997: 73).

Thus, within two years of the 1994 devaluation, Televisa had given up most of what it had gained in the 1992–3 wave of expansion. Even if the Peruvian channel was not a significant loss, the reduction in its command over Cablevisión meant a weakened position in the domestic cable market with regard to its competitor Multivisión. As to the dilution of its participation in Univisión, the crucial toehold in the US Spanish-language television market which it had regained only in 1992, this meant that Televisa's position was once again weakened in this key strategic market, although its programme supply agreement continued to hold.

The PanAmSat restructure of 1995 had not been so great an obstacle in Televisa's international manœuvres, but that was not the end of it. The subsequent merger of PanAmSat with the US-based satellite division of General Motors, Hughes Electronics Corporation, in September 1996, effectively meant that Hughes acquired most of Televisa's interest in the restructured and, once again, publicly traded company that resulted, the 'New PanAmSat' (Grupo Televisa 1997: 73). The outcome of Televisa's agreement with Hughes was that it received $US650 million for its former share in PanAmSat, of which it applied 70 per cent, or about $US450 million, towards its debt of $US988 million, with the remainder being reinvested in the group's other activities. Televisa retained a 7.5 per cent interest in the restructured PanAmSat, with the rights to acquire more equity in the DTH (direct-to-home) satellite television operation Sky (Cardoso 1997; González Amador 1997).

In May 1997, this arrangement was announced formally as part of Televisa's *Televisa 2000* plan, in which the company committed itself to increasing its audience share, developing its DTH service, and improving its financial results over the three years to follow (González Amador 1997). Televisa's sell-down of its participation in PanAmSat, like its previous dilutions of interest in the other ventures, was rationalized in terms of getting back to its 'core business', to invoke the business cliché of the time, or, in the words of the announcement: 'the fundamental business of the company has always been the production of programming, and it doesn't necessarily need to be the owner of programme distribution companies' (quoted in Cardoso 1997).

Certainly, as the history of Televisa's development has shown, programme production for the domestic market has always been its stock-in-trade, but this has been augmented significantly by its vertical integration with distribution systems, principally its own networks in

Mexico, but also, if less consistently, Univisión and its predecessors in the US, and PanAmSat at the international level. It is difficult not to see *Televisa 2000* as an attempt to make virtue out of necessity, particularly when Televisa's domestic and external competitors are taken into account, as will be done here shortly. Furthermore, it will be suggested that, in the more competitive markets, the quality and range of Televisa's production itself has become a problem. As one financial analyst commented on *Televisa 2000*: 'Rather than budget cuts we would sooner see Televisa announce programme innovations which would serve to revitalize the share market' (quoted in González Amador 1997).

After 'the Tiger'

However, first it remains to consider one other great internal problem for Televisa in 1997, namely its difficulties in establishing a stable and effective management structure following the retirement of Emilio Azcárraga Milmo ('the Tiger') as President of Televisa on 3 March, and his subsequent death from cancer on 16 April. Given the degree to which Azcárraga had consolidated all power and decision over Televisa within his own person, and the patronal style of management which he cultivated, his succession was always going to be a problem. It is believed that Azcárraga had known of his illness for some years, but he seems to have vacillated in his choice of a successor. At one stage, in the 1991 reshuffle, Azcárraga Milmo had anointed his nephew Alejandro Burillo Azcárraga (Martínez Staines 1991), but he soon fell from favour (Puig 1997c), so that on his retirement it was his son Emilio Azcárraga Jean whom Emilio Azcárraga Milmo named as his successor to be President.

At the same time, Guillermo Cañedo White became the Chairman of the Board. Together with his brother José Antonio, also a member of the Board, Cañedo White had 10 per cent of Televisa shares. Their father Guillermo Cañedo de la Bárcena had been a Televisa Vice-President, whose membership of the International Soccer Federation had twice brought the World Cup to Mexico (and thus to Televisa), and who also was President of the Organización de la Televisión Iberoamericana. The father also had died in 1997, in January, so there was a major generational change taking place with the accession of both Emilio Azcárraga Jean and Guillermo Cañedo White.

However, generational transition to the sons of the dead fathers was tempered with oligarchic tradition, in that Miguel Alemán Velasco, he of the triumvirate of Televisa's golden age, and son of the Mexican President who had granted the first television licences, returned to the Board. As noted, Alemán Velasco had left Televisa in 1991 to become a PRI

Senator, but now obtained leave to assume a Vice-President's position on the Board with special responsibilities for news and DTH development. Explaining this move as the fulfilment of a promise to the late Azcárraga, Alemán took care to ensure it was on condition that the 14.8 per cent of Televisa shares held by him and his son Miguel Alemán Magnani, also on the Board, would exceed the holdings of the Burillo family at 14 per cent, and the Cañedo Whites at 10 per cent (Puig 1997a).

While the return of Alemán typifies the dynastic character not just of Televisa but of media ownership in the Latin world and beyond it, it can also be read as an attempt to balance the youthful vigour of Emilio Azcárraga Jean (who was 29 at this time) and Guillermo Cañedo White (then 37) with the maturity and continuity which Miguel Alemán represented, so as to rebuild confidence on the Mexican and New York stock exchanges. This interpretation is borne out by some other appointments to the Board in the week following Azcárraga's death, namely Claudio X. González, the President of Kimberly Clark of Mexico, one of the nation's biggest consumer goods manufacturers and advertisers; Luiz María Ansón, Televisa's close associate in its DTH venture in Spain; and David Evans, the World Director of Sky, the joint DTH venture with News Corporation and others, to be discussed more fully below. These appointments reflect the global compass of Televisa's stakeholders and their active interest in ensuring its well-being. It is significant that González is also on the board of Banamex Accival, associated with one of Televisa's major creditors (Castro Rocha 1997).

Whatever apparent stability was achieved with this arrangement was broken by June, however, when Alejandro Burillo Azcárraga, having gained an additional packet of shares from a former wife of his late uncle, was successful in having the Cañedo White brothers put off the Board (Celis Estrada 1997). Little wonder that the London *Financial Times* commented that the internal struggles of the company were coming to resemble the plot from one of its *telenovelas* ('*FT*: la batalla por el control en Televisa parece "una telenovela"' 1997). For Televisa, this is not a joke: such perceptions of 'the market' are a significant obstacle for an internationally listed company desperate to maintain the capital it needs to deal with recession and competition at both domestic and international levels.

New Players, at Home and Away

It would be evident at this stage that, for nearly all of its existence, Mexican television has been run as a virtual monopoly. In the previous sections, it was seen how the original licensees first merged to form

Telesistema Mexicano in 1955, and then, as a bulwark against government intervention in the industry, merged with a competitor to form Televisa in 1972. Thus, Televisa has been formed in an uncompetitive environment, effectively protected by the Mexican Government and its weak participation in the industry through Imevisión, its former network. This was 'the Mexican formula' until 1993 when the government sold the licences to its Channels 7 and 13 networks, together with production studios and some cinemas, to Ricardo Salinas Pliego and his partners in the Saba family, as TV Azteca.

Salinas Pliego, the majority owner, is from the Salinas y Rocha family of retail store owners. He owns Elektra, a chain of hundreds of electrical stores throughout Mexico, and some subsidiary chains, and TV Azteca is an integral part of their development. It is notable that he has been acquiring television interests also in the Central American countries to which his retail chains are now being extended ('Azteca into El Salvador' 1997). Like Televisa, this is a Mexican company with an international orientation, and it will become clear presently that there are further similarities between Televisa's strategies and those of TV Azteca (Ramón Huerta 1997).

Before the government sold it off, the former Imevisión had been obtaining around 2 per cent of the ratings (Moffett and Roberts 1992: 1). By 1995, the new TV Azteca had about 14 per cent of the audience, rising to 22 per cent in 1996 ('Avanza TV Azteca' 1997), and by the end of that year, it was claiming 37 per cent of the prime-time audience, and 23 per cent of television advertising revenue. There were also substantial increases in the amount of its own production, and in profit: 51 per cent, compared to Televisa's losses ('TV Azteca gana mayor audiencia' 1997). The following year it was claiming 33 per cent of television advertising revenue (Sutter 1998).

With the advent of TV Azteca, programming has become the basis on which competition is conducted, and quality, in the broadest sense, has become an issue. For all the wealth which Televisa's productions have generated both at home and abroad in the past, this success has been on the basis of quantity rather than quality. Many of the obituaries which appeared upon Azcárraga Milmo's death recalled this frank comment from a 1992 press conference:

Mexico is the country of a modest, very wretched class, which isn't ever going to stop getting screwed over. There is an obligation for television to bring diversion to these people and take them out of their sad reality and difficult future.... the rich, like me, are not clients because we rich don't buy a whole lot. In short, our market in this country is clear: the popular middle class. (Quoted in Puig 1997c: 15)

The kind of programme appropriate for such a target audience was made explicit by the young Azcárraga Jean on his succession: 'This is a business. The fundamental thing, the face of this company, is the production of entertainment, then information. To educate is the government's job, not Televisa's' (quoted in Puig 1997b: 30). As well as being a rationalization for the low intellectual and production values of Televisa's characteristic output, the *telenovelas* which dominate their production and programme schedules, this comment alludes to the absence of credibility which has always dogged Televisa as a news and information source. This has been the price of the close relations it has cultivated with the PRI and the state, as has been seen in the previous section, and also of its readiness to commercialize the content of its information programmes (Zepeda Patterson 1997). So long as Televisa was a virtual monopoly, audiences had no means of expressing their dissatisfaction with Televisa programmes, and Televisa could claim to be giving the people what they wanted.

At the beginning, TV Azteca's competitive strategy had been to offer a range of imported programming (Mejía Barquera 1995: 88), and although it is significant to observe that TV Azteca has since moved towards showing much more of its own productions, it is also notable in Mexico for the introduction of some of the same programmes which aided the rise of the Fox network in the US, namely *Los Simpson* (*The Simpsons*) and *La Niñera* (*The Nanny*) (Godard 1997). Although the relationship later became soured, from 1994 until early 1997 TV Azteca also enjoyed the benefit of the programme content, technology, and prestige of a formal relationship with the major US network NBC (Enríquez 1995; Ramón Huerta 1997; Rebollo Pinal 1997).

Another notable association formed by TV Azteca has been with the US Spanish-speaking network Telemundo, which is the competitor of Univisión, the network in which Televisa has an interest in the US. TV Azteca has been utilizing the studios it acquired, now known as Azteca Digital, and producing programmes in collaboration with Telemundo which each of them can show on their networks (Strover et al. 1997: 20). Thus, rather than compete on the basis of imported programming alone, as it first intended, TV Azteca now seems to be looking for the most attractive balance of imported and local programming, offering a wider and more innovative range than Televisa has done throughout its unchallenged years.

In terms of 'quality programming' as it is more conventionally understood, it is worth noting at this point that there are still state-subsidized channels: the long-standing Canal Once (11), dating from 1958, and, from 1992, Canal 22. Both are dedicated to cultural programming under the auspices of the SEP (Secretariat of Public Education) and extend only over the Mexico City metropolitan area. Canal Once accepts sponsorship, and was attracting 6 per cent of the audience as of 1995. Canal 22 is much more limited in its audience (Toussaint 1995; 1997a). More recently, Canal 40 has appeared, a niche commercial channel delivered free-to-air and via cable on a national basis, aimed at educated, affluent adults, and offering its own innovative, critical local programmes, and a news service supplied by CBS (Columbia Broadcasting Service) of the US, CBS-Telenoticias (Toussaint 1997b; 1997c).

A by-product of the competition between the networks has been competition between the ratings services in Mexico, IBOPE and A. C. Nielsen, thereby providing more intensive attention to audience measurement (Barragán 1997). This in turn has encouraged many advertisers to shift at least some of their budgets to TV Azteca, with the added incentive that not only is TV Azteca's purchasing plan more flexible than Televisa's French Plan, but their rates represent relatively much better value (Ramón Huerta 1997: 30).

To some extent, the increasing audience and corresponding advertisers' interest in TV Azteca is analogous to the increasing popular support gathered over the last decade for the PAN, the conservative opposition to the PRI, the ruling party which has monopolized Mexican politics for decades. In both cases, the attraction of the competition is not so much because it is better or even different, but just a change. One TV Azteca executive is explicit: 'We are doing what Televisa is doing—they are a terrific model' (quoted in Sutter 1996). In addition to increasing local production, their international ambitions in Central America, and the relationship with Telemundo, TV Azteca's *yo también* ('me too') strategy extends to the acquisition of soccer teams and sports promotion activities, and the launching of a recorded music division: in both cases, like Televisa. Furthermore, with these strategies, they are pursuing the same audience, aiming to build their share of the free-to-air or broadcast audience to 38 per cent by 2000, and ultimately, to an equal share with Televisa (Ramón Huerta 1997: 35).

It is important to appreciate that Televisa is facing competition not only on its traditional ground of broadcast television, but also in its cable distribution service, Cablevisión, a company it established in 1966, and in which it still maintains the 51 per cent majority share (Crovi Druetta 1995). Yet competition is not new in the cable field. In 1989, Multivisión was launched by veteran broadcasting entrepreneur (once manager of TIM) Joaquín Vargas Gómez as a subscription service delivered by MMDS (multipoint multichannel distribution service) as well as by cable, and distributed by satellite. By 1993, with 250,000 subscribers in Mexico City, it claimed to have overtaken Cablevisión. Furthermore, it had begun to make direct investments in Latin American cable providers, and to establish arrangements with US programme suppliers to package their programmes for the whole Latin American market, notably with the film channel Cinecanal (Mejía Barquera 1995: 78–9). As of the second half of 1996, Cablevisión had a total of around 450,000 subscribers, while Multivisión was well ahead with 720,000 (Olivas and Lince 1996a: 8).

Although continuing to compete with cable services, both Cablevisión and Multivisión are now looking more towards the new satellite distribution/delivery technology of DTH, and it is in this field that the Mexican services are becoming involved in strategic alliances with major US-based and continental Latin American companies. Cablevisión and Multivisión have been the vehicles through which Televisa and the Vargas camp have entered into this global league. It is worth noting that, since 1993, foreign investors have been permitted to hold up to 49 per cent of Mexican cable companies, but this has been of little consequence. As mentioned, the major US cable company TCI did not proceed with an agreement to buy 49 per cent of Cablevisión in that year (Mejía Barquera 1995: 78), and although there has since been some US investment in Multivisión ('Empresa texana comprará acciones de MVS Multivisión' 1997), the trend is towards the Latin companies participating in international joint ventures concentrated on continental Latin America as a whole, rather than them attracting investment into their domestic markets. The exception is the provincial cable operator Megacable, in which a minor US company bought a 40 per cent stake in 1995 ('Country Profile: Mexico' 1996: 7).

A final note on cable: the future of cable television as a separate delivery system has become an open question. While the participation of Telmex in Cablevisión provides for the possibility of developing sophisticated interactive fibre-optic cable services, and there is some experimental use of this technology, all the Mexican systems operate on an installed base of the older, much less versatile coaxial cable, dating back to 1954 (Crovi Druetta 1995; Olivas and Lince 1996a). Furthermore, the *Televisa 2000* plan and the emergent pattern of the international alliances suggests that all technological development, investment, and programme packaging are becoming concentrated on continental DTH, so digital satellite appears to be the preferred mode of delivery, rather than fibre-optic cable, at least as far as distributing television over large distances is concerned.

The Global League

While DTH satellite television transmission can be seen as just a new phase of development of existing satellite services and similar in concept to other kinds of 'pay-TV' systems, there are certain qualitative differences which are being emphasized by the largely US-based satellite and programming interests which are promoting the medium in Latin America and the rest of the world. These differences will be returned to at other appropriate points in the book, but suffice it to say here that digital decompression technology on the current generation of satellites now being launched permits a much greater number of channels to be carried than has been the case in the past. This in turn not only allows for a greater variety of channels dedicated to certain kinds of programme, such as films, sport, news, and music, than with cable, but, furthermore, allows the same channel to be transmitted in more than one language. Thus, there is less of a technical barrier against programmes produced in languages other than those used for transmission. The subscriber requires a small receiving dish (about 60 centimetres) and a set-top decoding box. This means that the DTH market is attractive not just to the satellite industry and programme suppliers, but also to the manufacturers and retailers of this domestic consumer hardware, such as the Salinas chain, Elektra.

While not representing so great a qualitative leap as the advent of either radio or television, there has been a similar pattern in which the new technology is developed outside the country and then introduced by local entrepreneurs. What has been more marked than with previous technologies, however, has been the kind of joint ventures which cut across national, regional, and global levels. It is in this kind of relationship that Televisa runs the dangers of being dominated by its global partners, and outflanked by its rivals as it loses its former competitive advantage as the world's largest producer of Spanish-language programming.

While the Vargas family's Multivisión already had some experience with digital compression from 1993 and an early version of DTH in 1994–5 (Foley 1995: 41; Olivas and Lince 1996*b*), the first entrepreneur to obtain a DTH licence in Mexico was neither a Vargas nor an Azcárraga, but Clemente Serna Alvaer, the owner of one of Mexico's few independent television channels, in Guadalajara, and also a major producer of radio programmes. Early in 1996, Serna entered a partnership with a Telmex-related company which took 40 per cent in the venture, to create Medcom. However, as Telmex was already involved with Televisa in Cablevisión, Medcom became allied with the same operation by

October of that year (Foley 1995: 41; 'Country Profile: Mexico' 1996: 8; García Hernández 1996; Toussaint 1996a).

Even at the end of 1995, DTH in Mexico had been assuming the character of a duopoly. In November that year, Rupert Murdoch's News Corporation Limited, which already had a programme exchange agreement with Televisa, announced that it would lead a pan-regional DTH consortium including not only Grupo Televisa, but also its counterpart in Brazil, Organizações Globo, and Televisa's would-be partner from 1993, TCI (through its international division, TINTA). News, Televisa, and Globo were to have 30 per cent each, and TCI the remaining 10 per cent. Apart from the scale and the cross-cultural links it brought about, this move was remarkable in that it represented a decision in favour of international corporate collaboration rather than competition, given that Televisa had been planning such a Latin American service in conjunction with PanAmSat, while News had previously announced, just the previous July, a similar venture in partnership with Globo (Brewster 1995; Francis and Fernandez 1997: 36).

Whatever opportunities Televisa saw in the deal for its further internationalization, it would have been motivated at the level of the domestic market by the fact that earlier that year, in May, Multivisión had announced it would join a similar pan-regional project led by the US satellite manufacturer Hughes, and incorporating also TV Abril in Brazil (Globo's main cable competitor) and Grupo Cisneros of Venezuela (which in other areas is a major collaborator of Televisa) ('Country Profile: Mexico' 1996: 7).

Thus, by the end of 1996, Multivisión was signed with the Hughes project, known as Galaxy, and had its licence to launch its service in Mexico, which was to be known as DirecTV, the same name as Hughes's DTH service in the US. It would be carried by one of Hughes's own satellites from the US. The new service added three times as many channels as Multivisión was then offering on cable. Of its thirteen exclusive channels, nine were from the US, and only one was of its own production (Toussaint 1996b). Like TV Abril, its counterpart in Brazil, Multivisión has 10 per cent in Galaxy, Grupo Cisneros has 20 per cent, and Hughes the dominant 60 per cent (Strover et al. 1997: 8).

At that same time, on 15 December, the corresponding Televisa service based on Cablevisión began transmission. This was called DTH Sky, in line with News Corporation's satellite ventures in other global regions. It began with more channels than DirecTV, including the Latin versions of US-based channels such as Discovery (as modified by Televisa) and MTV, as well as News's own FLAC (Fox Latin Channel). Again, several of the DTH channels were already available through Cablevisión. Sky also offered Televisa's terrestrial network channels (Toussaint 1996*b*; Francis and Fernandez 1997: 38). The plan was for 20 per cent of programming to be supplied by Televisa and its international partners in the venture (García Hernández 1996). While the service began on the Mexican Government's Solidaridad 2 satellite, the intention was to shift it to one of PanAmSat's new satellites when it became available. For its part, the Mexican Government had cleared the way for all this DTH development by signing an agreement with the US in November, under which Mexican and US satellites could transmit into each other's national space (Olivas and Lince 1996*b*; Francis and Fernandez 1997: 30, 36).

The company which manages DTH Sky is called Innova. As a joint venture with News, Televisa has 60 per cent of the shares of Innova. By the end of 1997, this company expected to have completely absorbed Serna's initial venture, Medcom (Grupo Televisa 1997: 74). While this formalizes the Cablevisión/Multivisión duopoly at the national level, there is a global level to be taken into account. In this regard, it is important to recall that PanAmSat, the satellite venture associated with Televisa, and Hughes, the leader of the competing Galaxy group, in fact had merged in September 1996, under the name PanAmSat, months before the launch of their respective services in Mexico. In the sense that both Galaxy and PanAmSat are owned by Hughes, DTH in Mexico at one elevated level has become a monopoly, but one which represents itself to consumers on the ground as a duopoly. Yet, it appears that the company's intention is to maintain both of these competing services—at least for the present (Francis and Fernandez 1997: 34). Put another way, there is a monopoly at the level of hardware, but apparent competition in terms of software, all under the same corporate umbrella.

The pay-TV industry association in Mexico, CANITEC, estimates that the maximum number of subscribers that the DTH industry can hope for in the medium term is two million, at least at the initial level of cost (Toussaint 1996*c*). Other estimates are lower, more like one and a half million. As of May 1997, Sky had around 25,000 subscribers, while DirecTV was well ahead with 55,000, having been able to build more off its own previous subscriber base. At that stage, Sky had just dropped its price to Ps 2,519 (about $US330) (Galván Ochoa 1997). Within two weeks, DirecTV was advertising its service at Ps 1,999, thus undercutting Sky by about $US77 ('Hoy DirecTV' 1997). Even so, DirecTV was a long way from its target of 200,000 subscribers in the first year. No doubt prices will continue to fall, with DirecTV aiming to bring the installation charge down to compare with the cost of a VCR (Olivas and Lince 1996*b*). However, the growth of DTH depends on the recovery of the

Mexican economy as a whole, and if the market proves too small to be profitable for both competing services, the company which controls the distribution of both of them at a global level, the new PanAmSat, can either close one or the other down, or oblige them to merge. Either way, Televisa has become most vulnerable to the strategies of both its global and regional partners.

This is not just a problem of its domestic market, but also affects those foreign markets where Televisa could once consider itself to have a natural constituency. Televisa's attempts to penetrate the television market in Spain, particularly with its international satellite service Galavisión, as alluded to in the previous section of this chapter, has been a dubious success (Bustamante 1990). An attempt in 1994 to acquire the Spanish terrestrial network Tele 5 marked another failure, as it would have breached ownership regulations, and because Televisa was considered to have no commitment to the public interest. Presumably, Tele 5's then owner, Silvio Berlusconi, had never been subjected to the same scrutiny. Televisa also had been seeking to strengthen its relations with RTVE (Radio Televisión Española), the public corporation which still dominates the much-privatized Spanish television system, for instance by transmitting RTVE's international service on Cablevisión in Mexico. As noted earlier, Luiz María Ansón, one of the new Board members of the restructured Televisa in 1997, is Televisa's representative in Spain, where his conservative credentials are presumed to be of great assistance in dealing with the new PP (Partido Popular) government of that colour (Martínez 1996: 48). Although it was reported during 1996 that Televisa would be joined by its Sky partners (News, Globo, and TCI) in a DTH venture with RTVE, the agreement it signed at the end of that year did not include them. Rather, Televisa was to hold 25 per cent of the group, Distribuidora de Televisión Digital, and the other major shareholders to be included were RTVE and Telefónica (the privatized Spanish telecommunications company). However, there is some likelihood of Sky partners being involved in the supply of programming to the venture, which is Televisa's responsibility, while Telefónica is the management body (Grupo Televisa 1997; Peralta 1997).

Although these connections will be returned to in more detail in later chapters, it is appropriate to make the observation here that Televisa faces the same sort of competition over DTH in Spain as it does in Mexico and Latin America.

In July of 1996, the Spanish cable network Canal Plus announced that Sogecable, the cross-owned media group to which it belonged, was entering a DTH venture, DirecTV, with Hughes's Galaxy Group, the same as in Latin America: Multivisión, TV Abril, and the Grupo Cisneros

Table 2. Televisa and its competition, 1997

Broadcast network TV	Televisa: four channels	TV Azteca: two channels
Subscription TV (cable)	Cablevisión (51% Televisa) 450,000 SUBSCRIBERS	Multivisión (Vargas Group) 720,000 subscribers
Subscription TV (DTH)	Sky (Innova: 60% Televisa) 25,000 subscribers	DirecTV 55,000 subscribers

(Martínez 1996: 50). With the creation of DTH platforms in Spain for both Televisa and DirecTV, Televisa is thus confronted with a similar kind of danger there as it can be seen to face from its friendly global rivals in its domestic market and the Latin American region. The domestic competitive situation which had emerged at the time of Televisa's 1997 restructure is summarized in Table 2.

Televisa Reconstructed

It has been shown throughout this section how the Mexican financial crisis, the death of Emilio Azcárraga Milmo, and the advent of local and global competition together have caused a major restructure of Grupo Televisa, including the sale of non-core businesses such as video distribution, and the dilution of its interests in such major assets as Univisión, PanAmSat, and Cablevisión.

The restructure has not been all a matter of contraction, however. Televisa is committed under its plan *Televisa 2000* to invest further in its DTH activities, and, as has just been mentioned in the case of Spain, it has continued to make strategic investments in foreign markets. The other case in point is the US, where in July 1996 Televisa completed the acquisition of an English-language station in Tijuana, affiliated to the Fox network, and received across the San Diego (US)/Tijuana (Mexico) border area. This was in addition to two similar stations it already owned on the border with Texas (Grupo Televisa 1997: 11). While Televisa has the abject failure of the English-language sports newspaper the *National* in its past, and there has been some criticism in the trade press about the quality of its programme offerings (including English-language *telenovelas*), this also is an area which it intends to develop.

As well, it has been engaged in the more intensive development of its domestic market. It was noted earlier that Televisa borrowed funds from the Spanish Government in 1994 and 1995: this was to acquire licences from the Mexican Government for 62 new stations for about $US60 million. While the company continues to refer to creating a new network, it appears that in fact the stations have been used to extend the coverage of existing networks, particularly Channel 9 (Mejía Barquera 1995: 74–5; Grupo Televisa 1997: 52). Thus, as of 1997, Televisa's four channels were being broadcast over 299 stations, of which Televisa wholly owned 242, with majority ownership of another 16. Televisa's traditional strategy, inherited from TSM as we have seen, has been to programme the channels so as to target different demographic segments of the population, as follows, in order of size (Grupo Televisa 1997: 10):

- **Channel 2** (147 stations, reaching 97 per cent of TV homes, and holding 32 per cent market share). 'Flagship' network targeting the 'average' family, and airing mostly first-run Televisa productions, ranging across *telenovelas* (the bulk of prime time), news, variety, game shows, and sport. This channel also constitutes the service Televisa transmits via satellite to Spain.

- **Channel 5** (80 stations, reaching 90 per cent of TV homes, and holding 18 per cent market share). Predominantly foreign-produced programming, with cartoons for children in the daytime, and films and series for an adult audience at night, as well as news and home-shopping. Televisa does most of its own dubbing of foreign programmes.

- **Channel 4** (50 stations, reaching 79 per cent of TV homes, and holding 10 per cent market share). More of a regional service for Mexico, with local programmes augmented by a mix of both Televisa productions and foreign programmes in a range of genres. Also carries Televisa's international news service, ECO.

- **Channel 9** (22 stations, reaching 64 per cent of TV homes, and holding 14 per cent market share). A more 'downmarket' service with Channel 2 reruns and sport, although it also airs the educational programmes which are produced by the Ministry of Education.

Table 3 summarizes the extent of Televisa's operations at the time of the restructure of 1997, having special regard to the balance of its activities both within and outside of television. The data comes largely from the 1996 Annual Report (Grupo Televisa 1997). Note that the report does not give the proportion of income derived from 'international investments', namely in Univisión and PanAmSat, nor for the Sky DTH venture.

Table 3. Extent of Televisa's operations, 1997

Television production and distribution (domestic and international) (60.1% of net sales, 1996)	Four domestic networks, plus foreign programme distribution, ECO, etc.
Subscription television via cable (3.8% of net sales)	Cablevisión (51%).
Publishing (17.4% of net sales)	Daily newspaper *Ovaciones* wholly owned; magazine division sold down to 65%: publishes *Tele-guía, Eres, Somos,* and Spanish-language versions of US and French titles, such as *Popular Mechanics* and *Elle.*
Audio (radio and music recording) (8.9% of net sales)	Radio production and broadcasting over 17 AM and FM stations; several recording labels: Melody, Fonovisa, etc.
Other businesses (9.8% of net sales)	Includes related cultural industries such as feature film production and distribution, dubbing, show-business and sports promotion; as well as outdoor advertising and paging, plus some wholly unrelated activities.

References

Acosta, Carlos (1991), 'Televisa, gigante en crisis de liquidez por tres años de pérdidas y por la salida de socios', *Proceso* (23 December), 14–19.

'Alejandro Burillo's Rising Star at Televisa' (1991), *Broadcasting Abroad* (February), 14.

Alemán Velasco, Miguel (1976), 'El estado y la televisión', *Nueva Política,* 1/3: 193–200.

Arriaga, Patricia (1980), *Publicidad, economía y comunicación masiva* (Nueva Imagen, Mexico DF).

'Avanza TV Azteca' (1997), *La Jornada* (16 May), 16.

'Azteca into El Salvador', *Broadcasting & Cable International* (June), 8.

Barragán, Antonieta (1997), 'La controvertida medición', *Expansión* (15 January), 50–4.

Bernal Sahagún, Víctor (1978), 'México: la publicidad', in Centro de Estudios de la Comunicación (eds.), *Televisión, cine, historietas y publicidad en México* (Universidad Nacionál Autónoma de México, Mexico DF), 49–66.

'Big Shuffle in Mexican TV Ownership' (1991), *Variety* (25 March), 66.

Brewster, Deborah (1995), 'News Links up with Latin America', *Australian* (22 November), 37.

Bustamante, Enrique (1990), 'Galavisión en España y la CEE', paper presented to international colloquium, 'La televisión en Español: una perspectiva global', University of California at Berkeley, June.

Cardoso, Víctor (1997), 'Pagan 650 mdd a Televisa por su parte de la empresa PanAmSat', *La Jornada* (17 May), 16.

Castro Rocha, Edith (1997), 'Constituirá Televisa un fondo de recompra de acciones propias', *La Jornada* (24 April), 16.

Celis Estrada, Dario (1997), 'Corporativo', *El Financiero* (26 June), 12.

Cosper, Amy (1995), 'The Tale of a Man, his Dog and the Industry they Changed: Rene Anselmo 1926–1995', *Satellite Television* (November), 27–8.

'Country Profile: Mexico' (1996), *TV International* (6 May), 5–8.

Crovi Druetta, Delia (1995), 'La industria de la TV por cable en México, antecedentes y perspectivas', in Delia Crovi Druetta (ed.), *Desarrollo de las industrias audiovisuales en México y Canadá* (Universidad Nacional Autónoma de México, Mexico DF), 117–41.

de Noriega, Luis Antonio, and Leach, Francis (1979), *Broadcasting in Mexico* (Routledge & Kegan Paul, London).

Donaton, Scott (1991), '"Ain't over till it's…"', *Advertising Age* (29 July), 5.

Ehrmann, Hans (1991), 'Chile Ends Government Broadcast Monopoly', *Variety* (25 March), 72.

——(1992), 'Democracy Remakes Chilean Pubcaster', *Variety* (23 March), 90.

'Empresa texana comprará acciones de MVS Multivisión' (1997), *La Jornada* (15 April), 48.

Enríquez, Alfredo (1995), 'Television Azteca: ¿estrategia de un esquema oculto?', in Delia Crovi Druetta (ed.), *Desarrollo de las industrias audiovisuales en México y Canadá* (Universidad Nacional Autónoma de México, Mexico DF), 105–16.

Esparza, Elia (1997), 'Life after "el Tigre"', *Hispanic* (July–August), 48–52.

Fernández Christlieb, Fátima (1975), 'Información colectiva y poder en México', unpublished professional dissertation, Universidad Iberoamericana, Mexico DF.

——(1976), 'La industria de radio y televisión', *Nueva Política*, 1/3: 237–48.

——(1985), 'Canal 7 ¿Para que? (II)', *La Jornada* (2 March).

——(1987), 'Algo más sobre los orígenes de la televisión latinoamericana', *DIA.Logos de la comunicación*, 18 (October), 32–45.

Fisher, Christy (1992), 'Azcarraga Looms as Return Player', *Advertising Age* (3 February), 25.

Foley, Theresa (1995), 'The Latin American Gold Rush: Prospecting for DTH Viewers', *Via Satellite* (February), 40–7.

Fox, Elizabeth (1997), *Latin American Broadcasting: From Tango to Telenovela* (University of Luton Press, Luton).

Francis, Greg, and Fernandez, Robustiano (1997), 'Satellites South of the Border', *Via Satellite* (February), 28–42.

'FT: la batalla por el control en Televisa parece "una telenovela"' (1997), *La Jornada* (18 June), 24.

Galván Ochoa, Enrique (1997), 'Dinero', *La Jornada* (6 May), 21.

García Hernández, Arturo (1996), 'DTH Sky: 110 canales de video y 48 de audio', *La Jornada* (24 October), 25.

Godard, François (1997), 'TV Azteca is Building an Empire', *Broadcasting & Cable International* (October), 48.

González Amador, Roberto (1997), 'Plan Televisa 2000: disminuir costos de operación por 270 mdd', *La Jornada* (22 May), 15.

Granados Chapa, Miguel (1976), 'La televisión de estado: en busca del tiempo perdido', *Nueva Política*, 1/3: 223–36.

Grupo Televisa (1997), *Annual Report 1996* (Televisa, Mexico DF).

'Hoy DirecTV' (1997), *La Jornada* (16 May), 43.

Mahan, Elizabeth (1985), 'Mexican Broadcasting: Assessing the Industry–State Relationship', *Journal of Communication*, 35/1: 60–75.

Martínez, Sanjuana (1996), 'Televisa se asocia a Radio Televisión Española, con la bendición de Aznar', *Proceso* (8 September), 48–50.

Martínez Staines, Javier (1991), 'Televisa: ¿Adios a la familia?', *Expansión* (1 May), 31–7.

Mejía Barquera, Fernando (1989), *La industria de la radio y la televisión y la política del estado Mexicano*, i: (*1920–1960*) (Fundación Manuel Buendía, Mexico DF).

—— (1995), 'Echoes of Mexican Media in 1993´, *Mexican Journal of Communication*, 2: 7191.

Mejía Prieto, Jorge (1972), *Historia de la radio y la TV en México* (Editores Asociados, Mexico DF).

Moffett, Matt, and Roberts, Johnnie (1992), 'Mexican Media Empire, Grupo Televisa, Casts its Eye on US Market', *Wall Street Journal* (30 July), 1 and 6A.

Morgan Stanley and Company (1992), 'Grupo Televisa: Company Report' (Thompson Financial Networks).

Olivas, Mireya, and Lince, Bernado (1996a), 'Competitors Race to Launch DTH Service', *Business Mexico* (August), 8–11.

—— (1996b), '15 Minutes with Ernesto Vargas', *Business Mexico* (August), 6–7.

Peralta, Braulio (1997), 'España: autorizan a Televisa para participar en la televisión digital', *La Jornada* (9 March), 53.

Pérez Espino, Efraín (1979), 'El monopolio de la televisión comercial en México', *Revista Mexicana de Sociología*, 4: 1435–68.

Puig, Carlos (1997a), 'Alemán, de regreso a Televisa, al frente de un compacto grupo de jóvenes priístas', *Proceso* (30 March), 33.

—— (1997b), 'Azcárraga Jean', *Proceso* (30 March), 30–4.

—— (1997c), 'El imperio construido por Emilio Azcárraga en México sí tuvo reveses... en el extranjero', *Proceso* (20 April), 12–16.

Ramón Huerta, José (1997) 'Noticias del otro imperio', *Expansión* (4 June), 19–35.

Rebollo Pinal, Herminio (1997), 'Crece el reclamo NBC contra TV Azteca', *El Financiero* (8 May), 24.

Rogers, Everett, and Antola, Livia (1985), '*Telenovelas*: A Latin American Success Story', *Journal of Communication*, 35/4: 24–35.

Sánchez Ruiz, Enrique (1991), 'Historia mínima de la televisión mexicana', *Revista Mexicana de Comunicación*, 18: 29–36.

Sinclair, John (1986), 'Dependent Development and Broadcasting: The "Mexican Formula"', *Media, Culture and Society*, 8/1: 81–101.

Strover, Sharon, Burkhart, Patrick, Hernández, Omar, Wilkinson, Kenton, and McAnany, Emile (1997), 'Global Media and Latin America', paper presented to the annual conference of the International Association for Media and Communication Research, Oaxaca, July.

Sutter, Mary (1996), 'Home-Grown Programming Takes Off', *Business Mexico* (August), 12–14.

—— (1998), 'Azteca Pre-sales Increase by 30%', *Variety* (22 December–4 January), 34.

'Televisa anunció oficialmente la compra de canal peruano' (1992), *La Época* (11 July), S33.

'Televisa compro 49 por ciento de Megavisión' (1991), *El Mercurio* (22 December).

Toussaint, Florence (1995), 'Los canales culturales del DF', in Delia Crovi Druetta (ed.), *Desarrollo de las industrias audiovisuales en México y Canadá* (Universidad Nacional Autónoma de México, Mexico DF), 81–8.

—— (1996a), 'DTH: alianzas y fusiones', *Proceso* (3 November), 64.

—— (1996b), 'Entre Sky y Galaxy Latin America', *Proceso* (22 December), 61.

—— (1996c), 'Los retos de la TV por cable', *Proceso* (15 December), 65.

—— (1997a), '"La televisión de Estado debe existir y ser subsidiada"', *Proceso* (6 April), 59.

—— (1997b), 'Realidades en Canal 40', *Proceso* (18 May), 62.

—— (1997c), 'Tecnologías de información', *Proceso* (29 June), 73.

'TV Azteca gana mayor audiencia' (1997), *El Financiero* (16 May), 16.

'TV in Mexico' (1951), *Newsweek* (17 December).

Valenzuela, Nicholas (1986), 'Spanish Language TV in the Americas: From SIN to PanAmSat', in J. Miller (ed.), *Telecommunications and Equity: Policy Research Issues* (Elsevier Science Publishers, North Holland, Amsterdam), 329–38.

Zellner, Mike (1989), 'Televisa as Target: The Media Empire's Credibility is on the Line', *Mexico Journal* (20 March), 16–21.

Zepeda Patterson, Jorge (1997), 'Neotelevisa', *Siglo 21* (20 April), 3.

3 | The Latin American Continent: Brazil, Venezuela, and Argentina

The Boys from Brazil

Although distinct from the rest of Latin America in its language, ethnic composition, and historical experience, Brazil still exhibits parallels with other major television nations of its region in the development and structure of its media. To take a pertinent example, we have seen how the pattern for the institutionalization of television was set by the pre-existing model of commercial network radio in Mexico, and so it was in Brazil. However, more like Argentina and Venezuela, it was also shaped by government controls and dictatorship. In spite of this, by the end of the 1920s, stations like Rádio Record de São Paulo had been established. This was linked to a record store, like Azcárraga's first station in Mexico (Ferraz Sampaio 1984: 212). Over the same period, a number of US advertising agencies were setting up their offices, such as J. Walter Thompson and SS&C-Lintas (Améndola Ávila 1982: 105). There is evidence that US corporations and their agencies, at least in the Brazilian case, took an active interest in ensuring that radio developed on the commercial model, providing entertainment programming calculated to deliver audiences to advertisers. As in Mexico, radio networks built their audiences through the exploitation of popular culture, and the cultivation of commercial entertainment genres such as the *radionovela*, the serial genre which originated in Cuba, and variety shows more on a US model (*shows de auditório*). These and other genres would later make their transition in a more visual form to television (Straubhaar 1996: 222).

After 1937, radio came under the influence of the populist dictator Getúlio Vargas (President 1937–45), who set up a Department of Information and the Press to control information and foster national culture. A leading station based in Rio de Janeiro, Rádio Nacional, was taken over and harnessed to these purposes, although there was little regulation of the commercial operations of private stations (Fox 1997: 54). Significant radio stations founded in the 1930s included Rádio Excelsior and Rádio Difusora, both in Rio de Janeiro, while the audience measurement company which has since come to set the benchmark for ratings performance, IBOPE (Brazilian Institute of Studies of Public Opinion and Statistics), set up in both major cities, São Paulo as well as Rio de Janeiro, early in the 1940s (Améndola Ávila 1982: 106). Family-owned radio stations, operated on a networked basis and connected to other media properties such as daily newspapers, became just as characteristic of media development in Brazil as elsewhere in Latin America and the world. By the end of the Vargas period, Roberto Marinho had linked Rádio Globo to his newspaper *O Globo*, the Carvalho family had put together a network of stations led by Rádio Record, and Francisco de Assis Chateaubriand Bandeira de Melo had a network of five radio stations, a dozen newspapers, and a magazine chain, Diários e Emissoras Associadas (Ferraz Sampaio 1984: 199–200, 211–13; Straubhaar 1996: 221).

While US advertisers and agencies might have lurked behind the establishment of radio, when Chateaubriand opened up Brazil's first television station, TV Tupi Difusora, on 18 September 1950 in São Paulo and the following year in Rio de Janeiro, he was acting against the explicit advice of US consultants who had told him that the advertising base was too restricted to support commercial television (Ferraz Sampaio 1984: 199; Straubhaar 1984: 222). It was good advice: in this regard Brazil was like Mexico in the 1950s—advertisers were not interested in a medium which, however novel, could only reach a small number of set-owners. There were only 300 sets in 1950, most of which Chateaubriand had imported himself (Vink 1988: 22). Even by 1956 there were only 250,000 (Straubhaar 1984: 223). Nevertheless, a number of other stations appeared in those first few years, notably those joined to the REI (Rede de Emissoras Independentes), a network of independent broadcasters: TV Record de São Paulo, TV Rio, and, later, TV Excelsior (Fox 1997: 55). In spite of various programme innovations, public exhibitions to promote the medium, and the advent of domestic manufacture of television sets, television remained in an 'elitist phase', at least until the coup of 1964, when it began to undergo the great transformations which were to be brought about under the years of military rule (Mattos 1992: 5).

There were also changes ahead in the commercial basis of television itself. Those advertisers who were attracted to television wanted it to be run very much on the basis of the 'sponsorship' system which had characterized commercial radio in the US and Latin America alike, and which then had been transplanted to the new medium. In this system, instead of buying advertising time as 'spots' within programmes provided by the network, which is the predominant commercial practice today, advertisers would actually provide the programmes themselves, complete with advertising. This was a common function of advertising agencies over this period: to produce such programmes for sponsors. This was the system under which the *telenovela*, like the *radionovela* before it in the 1940s, had come to Brazil, thanks to sponsors such as Lever and their then in-house advertising agency, Lintas (Mattelart and Mattelart 1990: 9). However, whereas the US, especially after the quiz-show scandal of 1959, abandoned the sponsorship system in favour of selling spots according to the ratings of independently produced programmes (Barnouw 1979: 55–75), it persisted in some Latin American countries, particularly Brazil, where the production of variety shows and even news programmes and *telenovelas* by advertising agencies lasted until as late as 1970 (Straubhaar 1982: 145; Mattos 1992: 4–6).

A prime example of the sponsored programme was *O Repórtero Esso*, produced for the US oil company by its international US-based advertising agency McCann Erickson, and drawing on news from the US network CBS and the now-defunct US news agency UPI (United Press International). Beginning on radio in 1941, it was put to air in a televised version by TV Tupi in 1951, and endured until the end of 1970. Other transnationals amongst the first sponsors of Brazilian television programmes were Ford and Colgate-Palmolive from the US, and Nestlé from Europe (Ferraz Sampaio 1984: 106–7; Mattos 1992: 6). These were precisely the kinds of advertisers which the Brazilian broadcasting entrepreneurs had been positioning themselves to attract, rather than the local advertisers they had first had, with their simple slides (Améndolo Ávila 1982: 31).

'Order and Progress'

Even if they needed the large foreign consumer goods transnationals as advertisers, and also the US manufacturers for their transmission equipment, the major networks of the first stage of Brazilian television were not dependent on direct investment by US interests. However, TV Globo, the network which subsequently arose in the 1960s and came to dominate Brazilian television, did have the benefit of a substantial direct investment from a US media corporation. Although it was for a limited period of time, this opened up a decisive advantage for Globo over its competitors which they have never been able to close.

The kick-start given to Globo by the Time-Life investment is just one part of the explanation for its subsequent domination of the Brazilian television market. Timing was another factor, and, above all, the relationship which Globo developed with the succession of military presidents which ruled Brazil from 1964 until 1985. In the light of all these factors, it is significant that Globo's licence was first granted in 1957 under the civilian Juscelino Kubitschek (President 1956–61), but that it was 1962 before the contract with Time-Life was signed, and the channel did not go to air until April 1965, the year after the coup (Marques de Melo 1988: 13).

TV Globo began as the television division of the integrated media holdings of the Marinho family, originally based on the Rio de Janeiro daily newspaper *O Globo*. This was founded by a journalist, Irineu Marinho, in July 1925, but he died a few weeks afterwards. He was succeeded, though after a period of six years, by his son Roberto Marinho, at the age of 26 (Organizações Globo 1992). Like Chateaubriand's Diários e Emissoras Associadas, which owned TV Tupi, the dominant network when Globo entered the market, Globo had branched into other publishing enterprises, and also had commercial broadcasting experience with the radio network it began in 1944, well before making its move into television.

Like the US television networks in the 1960s, Time-Life Inc. had shown an active interest in direct investment in Latin American television, in its case supporting entrepreneurs such as the exiled Cuban Goar Mestre in Argentina and Venezuela (in conjunction with CBS), and in a comprehensive package of support for the nascent TV Globo (de Cardona 1977: 58–60). Under the contract signed in 1962, Time-Life agreed to supply financial, technical, and management assistance, in the widest sense, covering equipment, financial controls, training, programming, marketing, and commercialization in general. In return, Time-Life would receive 30 per cent of the profits. However, a Parliamentary Investigative Committee, initiated by a federal representative who was also the head of TV Tupi, found that the contract was in flagrant contravention of a constitutional provision against foreign participation in a television licence. The National Telecommunications Council put forward a similar view. The government ignored the committee's report and the council's opinion for a time, and although in 1966 Castelo Branco (President-General 1964–7) gave Globo ninety days to regularize its situation in accordance with the constitution, no sanction was used to enforce the order. Globo's only response had been to change the agreement to a leaseback deal involving the Globo building. It was not until 1968 that the cancellation of the Time-Life arrangement began to be put into effect under pressure from the next marshal, Costa e Silva (President-General 1967–9) (Caparelli 1982: 24–30; de Lima 1988: 118; Marques de Melo 1988: 14–15; Straubhaar 1984: 239).

Globo eventually paid out its obligations to Time-Life by 1971, by which stage all the US media corporations which had been so active in Latin American television in the 1960s had become disillusioned, and were withdrawing their investments in any case (Read 1976: 80). In effect, Globo had been able to tap foreign capital and so enjoy a $US6 million interest-free loan for six years, whereas its competitors had been capitalized with no more than $1 million. This leap across the financial barriers to entry allowed Globo to establish itself by 1968 as the ratings leader in the major markets of the nation. But as well as the considerable financial advantage the Time-Life collaboration gave it in entering the industry, Globo also gained in what is sometimes still called, even in Portuguese, 'American know-how'. This came particularly in the person of Joe Wallach, who had come to Brazil as a Time-Life financial adviser, but became a Brazilian citizen in order to join Globo when the relationship with Time-Life ended in 1971 (Straubhaar 1984: 228–9). He remained on the elite management group at Globo until 1985, when he went back to the US for a position with the Spanish-language television network Telemundo, but then returned to Globo in 1991 to join its satellite-to-cable division, Globosat (Cesar Carvalho 1994).

Other key personnel who came in the initial phase and stayed to form the core management over Globo's halcyon years were Brazilians Walter Clark and José Bonifacio, both of whom were recruited from competing channels. They were successful in reorienting Globo's programming away from the elite viewers whom the Time-Life advisers were still seeking, and towards mass audiences (Straubhaar 1984: 229). As well as managerial strength, Globo attracted creative talent, notably Gloria Madagan, who brought to Globo her experience in making *telenovelas* for Colgate-Palmolive in Cuba (Vink 1988: 26). Interestingly, Clark and Bonifacio also had experience with Colgate-Palmolive, having produced programmes for them in Brazil's lingering days of sponsorship (Mattos 1992: 4).

Timing was mentioned as a factor in Globo's success. This was probably more a matter of knowing how to take advantage of opportunities as they arose, rather than strategic planning. Globo's measured entry to the market was most timely in terms of the availability of foreign investment, as we have just seen, but apart from the good fortune of coinciding with a new phase in the technical development of the medium; the decline of both major competitors, TV Excelsior and TV Tupi; the diaspora of talent from Cuba after the revolution in 1959; and the availability of videotape recording around the same time, which together enabled the export of *telenovelas* (Mattos 1992: 4)—apart from all these, the greatest lucky break that history handed to Globo was the advent in 1964 of a military regime which saw in Globo both a shining example of, and an apparatus for, its modernizing project.

The series of five military presidential regimes which commanded Brazil from 1964 until 1985 were of the 'bureaucratic-authoritarian' type, seeing themselves as progressive and modernizing, allying military authority and control with technology in the interests of a state-directed capitalism, in which foreign investment was welcome, but representative institutions were not (Guimarães and Amaral 1988: 125). The obvious reluctance to move against Globo's manifestly illegal contract with Time-Life and the good standing which Globo enjoyed for so long under the military dictators' stringent regime of media control leaves little doubt that it had secured a special place in their confidence. Changes to broadcast regulation in 1962 had strengthened the state's legal controls, that is, its rights to allocate frequencies, to bestow and repudiate licences, and to demand airtime for specific purposes, such as educational and propaganda broadcasts. There were also economic controls through permit requirements and subsidies available for the importation of equipment, and in the 1970s the government made credit available by various means as an incentive for local programme production (Mattos 1982: 41–62).

From 1968 until 1980, there was also an era of severe censorship, particularly under the extraordinary powers and 'secret laws' of Institutional Act Number 5, introduced in 1968 during Costa e Silva's presidency, although used most repressively by his successor Garrastazu Médici (President-General 1969–74), and remaining in force until 1978 (de Lima 1988: 116; Mattos 1992: 8–13). Globo knew how to take advantage of what the government could offer, and how to avoid offending it. Indeed, its own ideological sympathies seemed to be in line with the 'national security' objectives of the Brazilian Government, directed against 'labour union populism and autarchic nationalism' (Marques de Melo 1992: 5). Globo's legitimization of the government, its cooperation in the management of information and public opinion, its self-censorship, its visual style ('the Globo Pattern of Quality'), and its appeal to both the popular and the affluent classes were such that a Globo executive would later identify Globo with the motto of the nation itself:

Globo became the representative of the ideals and dreams of the miracle, of the developmental pride, of the glamour, over and above the crises of the regime ... It was affinity, it was not a Machiavellian plan ... Globo made concrete an abstraction: Order and Progress. (Quoted in de Lima 1988: 120)

The benefits for Globo in this relationship were also concrete. First, it was able to extend itself into a national network by virtue of the telecommunications infrastructure (microwave, satellite, and cable) which the government built through Embratel (Brazilian Telecommunications Enterprise) and other of its agencies in the interests of modernizing and achieving 'national integration' in Brazil (Fox 1997: 62). For Globo, this meant a mass audience which could be sold to advertisers, not just a series of metropolitan ones, and, furthermore, national networking and economies of scale in programme production. An important step in the nation-binding project which both the military and Globo had in common was the inauguration of the first national news programme, *Jornal Nacional*, which was made possible by the satellite infrastructure established in 1969, both creating a national audience for Globo and realizing Embratel's motto: 'Communication is integration' (quoted in Mattelart and Mattelart 1990: 20). Secondly, because the government, particularly under Médici, became concerned with foreign cultural influence in television programming, incentives were provided to stimulate Brazilian programme production, which became one of the factors enabling Globo to launch an export career (Marques de Melo 1992: 1–2; Mattos 1992: 10–12).

However, Globo became too much the beneficiary of government policies, relative to the other channels. By 1982, Globo was a complete national network, with an audience share which often reached 75 per cent at peak hours. By contrast, TV Excelsior had long since lost its licence, in 1970. REI, the independent network it had led, closed down in 1976, although TV Record survived, and a new network was created, Bandeirantes, under the publisher and radio network owner João Jorge Saad. TV Tupi had begun to unravel after Chateaubriand's death in 1966, and although still the market leader when Globo had come along, slowly went bankrupt, losing its licence in 1980 (Ferraz Sampaio 1984: 218; Vink 1988: 28; Fox 1997: 60).

Well before the end of the 1970s, the decade of Globo's greatest dominance, the military realized the political dangers of a monopolized television industry which could turn against it, so that when João Figueiredo (President-General 1979–85) came to power in 1979, he was committed to creating new networks 'within a competitive and balanced regime' (quoted in de Lima 1988: 121). The TV Tupi licences were cancelled, and the government redistributed them to bidders

whom they believed to be their friends, namely the broadcast enter-
tainer, producer, and show-business entrepreneur Silvio Santos who
started SBT (Sistema Brasileiro de Televisão) in 1982, and Adolfo
Bloch, owner of a magazine, *Manchete*, who began a network of the
same name in 1983 (Vink 1988: 28–9; Straubhaar 1996: 225).

Although Globo had acceded to state power and allowed successive
regimes to make the network an instrument of their efforts to legitimize
themselves and control information, this relationship was 'relatively
autonomous' and only lasted so long as Globo was deriving benefit
from it. 'In serving the regime through misinformation, TV Globo was
serving itself' (de Lima 1988: 123). The licensing of new competitors
created a breach between the Figueiredo government and Globo, so that
against the background of a monstrous inflation and debt crisis at last
giving the lie to the much-vaunted 'Brazilian miracle', when the government refused to allow presidential elections by popular vote, Globo
withdrew its support.

The government's stance provoked a series of major demonstrations
throughout the country in 1984, and whereas in the past Globo characteristically would have ignored all such manifestations of opposition,
what it did in this conjuncture was to give the campaign extensive
coverage. Furthermore, in the presidential election the following year
(which was not held by popular vote), Globo demonized the military
command's nominee, and gave a favourable image to the opposition
candidate. After some months of high political drama, José Sarney was
duly elected President of the 'New Republic' (1985–90), ushering in a
more democratic era for Brazil and a new role for Globo (Guimarães
and Amaral 1988: 128–37).

Globo and its Competitors

Although the new networks created in the 1980s have not been able to
overtake Globo's dominance of television in Brazil, it nevertheless faces
more competition now than in its heyday under the military rulers, and
more than its counterpart Televisa in Mexico does now or ever has.
Furthermore, as will be detailed below, Globo has not been able to
dominate subscription television services in quite the same way as it
has broadcast or free-to-air television.

By the early 1990s, as Table 4 shows, Globo was well ahead of its
competition on all indicators. Only SBT and, far behind it, Bandeirantes
have continued to offer meaningful competition. TV Manchete was sold
in 1992 to the financially troubled HBF group, and its market share
dropped to less than 5 per cent. TV Record came under the control of an

Table 4. Television networks in Brazil by selected indicators

	1991 profits ($US million)	Number of stations	Av. share households (%)	Audience coverage (%)
Globo	650	94	49	78
SBT	140	77	12	72
Bandeirantes	96	59	2	70
Manchete	72	45	22	63
Om Brasil	30[a]	25	n/a	n/a
Record	25	10	3	45

[a] Om Brasil commenced in 1992: profit is estimate; other information not available.

Sources: BIB 1992: A209–A210; Organizações Globo 1992; 'Por baixo do pano' 1992: 98–9.

evangelical preacher, while Om Brasil suffered through its association with the impeached President Collor de Mello (President 1990–2). Globo also had links with Collor, and had supported him, but was able to distance itself in time, and so escape any similar fate (Hoineff 1993: 50; Fox 1997: 64–5).

Because Globo's number of stations and audience coverage are not significantly greater than those of SBT, there is constant competition for audience share. In Brazil, ratings are measured by the independent private organization IBOPE, and although Globo also undertakes its own audience research, both Globo and its competitors constantly adjust their programming in accordance with each other's IBOPE scores (Mattelart and Mattelart 1990: 37–9). However, by and large, Globo maintains a considerable edge over its competitors through its capacity to provide virtually all of its own programming, much of which is tailored to suit what the market researchers call the 'A and B class' audiences (Mattelart and Mattelart 1990: 38). Globo's competitors tend more to attract the 'D and E' audiences, one reason why Globo could charge advertisers $US45,000 for 30 seconds at prime time, when the equivalent on SBT was costing $US22,500 ('Por baixo do pano' 1992: 98–9). In recent years, SBT has consistently attained an audience share of up to about 20 per cent, drawing on both imported programming (including Mexican *telenovelas*) and its own productions ('Carrossel mexicano' 1991; Paxman 1995b: 58; 'Brazil' 1996). In 1997, Globo was claiming an audience share of 74 per cent in prime time (probably more like 60 per cent over all), and a commensurate 75 per cent of all advertising revenue (Rede Globo 1997).

One other broadcast network not listed in the table should be mentioned here, not because it offers domestic competition to Globo, but because it supplies programming to the estimated 750,000 Brazilians in the US. This is CNT, which, although based in the southern provincial city of Curitiba, broadcasts nationwide in Brazil, and also provides programmes to cable services in Miami and New York (Barbosa 1994).

Although Globo's dominance of domestic broadcast television seems unassailable, it has met stronger competition in the realm of subscription or 'pay-TV' as new modes of transmission have been introduced on this basis. The first of these was the opening up of the UHF (ultra high frequency) band for broadcast-delivered subscriber services. Unlike the free-to-air broadcast channels on the VHF (very high frequency) band, the signal is sent out scrambled and requires to be decoded on equipment supplied only on subscription. The first full such service to be offered was TVA (Televisão Abril), a joint venture of a financial and industrial group, Machline, and the television division of Grupo Abril, Brazil's other major media conglomerate. Launched in 1991, TVA offers CNN and ESPN from the US, and RAI (Radio Audizioni Italiane) and Canal Plus channels from Europe. Abril had already launched a narrowcast channel prior to this, its own Brazilian version of the US music channel MTV (Abril Group 1992: 52–3; Bahiana 1994: 21; Straubhaar 1996: 233).

Grupo Abril has grown from a strong base in print media: in fact it is the largest publishing operation in Latin America. It did not enter television services until 1990, with the advent of the new distribution technologies, although it had been heavily involved in video distribution since the beginning of the 1980s. The publishing division, Editora Abril, was founded in 1950 by an Italian refugee, Victor Civita, who came from the US with the rights to publish Disney comics in Brazil. The business was built up on comics and magazines, including some foreign titles, but most important has been *Veja*, a well-regarded news magazine with the highest circulation of any publication at all in Brazil. The group is now managed by Roberto Civita, son of the founder who died in 1990, and has wholly owned subsidiaries in Portugal and Spain, and majority interests in publishing houses in Argentina and elsewhere in Latin America (Pickard 1991; Abril Group 1992: 8–10). It has been reported that, like Globo, Abril was also seeded by Time-Life capital (Mattelart and Mattelart 1990: 220). Certainly, a later alliance with HBO, the Time-Warner film channel, was helpful in giving it a competitive advantage at one stage (Glasberg 1995: 35B).

With Abril opening up subscription television as a new area, Globo soon responded, meeting Abril's MMDS (multipoint multichannel distribution service) venture with its own four-channel service, Globosat. Transmitted via Brazil's domestic satellite, Brasilsat, this could be received directly by a small satellite dish (Bahiana 1994: 22; Straubhaar 1996: 233–4). Both competitors sought out programming alliances, Abril forming HBO Brasil as just mentioned, and Globo getting access to other US film studio output, though of course also having recourse to its own programming, an asset TVA did not have. As well, sources of foreign capital were secured: Chase Manhattan acquired an interest in TVA, while Globo garnered a loan from the World Bank (Glasberg 1995: 35–6B).

Meanwhile, a number of 'hardwire' cable subscription franchises had been established in the main cities, notably by Multicanal. This was begun by a mining entrepreneur, Antonio Dias Leita Neto, and offered programming from several other Latin nations: ECO from Televisa in Mexico; TV Nacional from Chile; Telefé from Argentina; TVE from Radio Televisión Española; and RAI from Italy (Hoineff 1993: 62). With attention shifting to cable and the Brazilian Congress preparing to regulate it, in 1993 Globosat established a subsidiary to be its cable distribution arm, Net Brasil, the programming function being left with Globosat (Bahiana 1994: 22). This time it was TVA's turn to respond, which it did by offering its MMDS subscribers a free changeover to the cable service it commenced in São Paulo in 1994. In the interim, it too had begun to offer its service via satellite, also on Brasilsat (Glasberg 1995: 36[b]).

By mid-1997, subscription television had grown rapidly, so that there were 2.5 million pay-TV homes in Brazil, a nation of 34.5 million television homes in total. Of the pay-TV homes, 67 per cent were cabled, 22 per cent had MMDS, and the remainder were DTH (direct-to-home). Globo had caught up Abril's early lead and achieved pre-eminence in the subscription television market through Net Brasil, by then the largest MSO (multiple system operator) in Brazil, having 700,000 subscribers compared to TVA's 350,000. While this is not as decisive a lead over its competition as it enjoys in broadcast television, Globo also had acquired a 33 per cent stake in Multicanal, and this brought in a further 650,000 subscribers. At that time, North American investors such as the Bank of America and Bell Canada were showing interest in new cable and MMDS licences which the government had promised to auction, in the light of imminent approval for foreign investment in the cable sector, but attention was shifting yet again to another delivery technology, DTH (Cajueiro 1997: 28).

The qualitative differences between DTH and other modes of subscription television distribution, including earlier forms of satellite delivery, were outlined in Chapter 2, as were the two schemes under which DTH is being established in Latin America on a pan-regional basis. Brazil is a major market for both of these, and each of them incorporates one of the key competitors in subscription television: Globo is aligned with News Corporation, Televisa, and TCI in the Sky project; while Abril's allies are Grupo Cisneros and Multivisión in the Galaxy Latin America/DirecTV venture led by Hughes.

As with the subscription television market in general, it was Abril rather than Globo which made the first move into this new area, although the Grupo Cisneros of Venezuela has been the front-runner in the Galaxy consortium in Latin America, and Venezuela was the first nation to commence the service. Brazil followed soon after, however, ahead of Mexico and Chile, and by mid-1997, Brazil was believed to have more than half of the 200,000 subscribers in the twelve countries where Galaxy was operating. The relative importance of Brazil as a market for DTH was also reflected in the fact that half of the transponders on the Hughes satellite carrying the service were dedicated to programming in Brazilian Portuguese (Bulloch 1997: 20; Paxman 1997e).

Measuring up on the International Scale

For some years now, articles about Globo have routinely referred to it as 'the fourth largest television network in the world', after the US majors, and although the only source ever given for this factoid is an obscure 1981 newspaper article (Mattos 1984: 206), or Globo's own propaganda (Marques de Melo 1988: 23), it still makes sense if we think of it as an index of the vast size of the Brazilian audience, rather than any claim to truth, since it disregards larger audiences in Asia. With a population of 161 million ('Latin American TV & Pay TV at a Glance' 1997), virtually all of whom are reached by Globo, the Brazilian audience is almost half the estimated total number of native English-speakers (330 million), or Spanish-speakers (346 million), in the world ('The Principal Languages of the World' 1996); more than half the 300-odd million Spanish-speakers who inhabit the Americas; and about two-thirds of the approximately 250 million people who ostensibly form the audience for the major networks in the US.

As businesses, if we take annual revenue as the measure, both Globo and its Mexican counterpart Televisa would fall within the range of 1996 revenues by which the trade journal *Broadcasting & Cable* ranked the 'Top 25 Media Groups' of 1997 (Higgins and McClellan 1997). This list covers only US media corporations, but Globo, with annual revenue of $US1.9 billion (Symmes 1997: S12), and Televisa, with a gross sales figure of $US1.4 billion in 1996 (Grupo Televisa 1997), compare to the lower-ranking print companies on the list, such as the Washington Post Company, Cox, Bloomberg, or Scripps. They are well behind both the owners of the US networks (NBC, for example, is $US5.2 billion), and even further behind their global partners in Sky: News Corporation's figure is $US14.3 billion, and TCI is $US8 billion (Higgins and McClellan 1997).

In terms of output, it is Televisa rather than Globo which is the world-beater, at least by sheer volume. By the mid-1990s, Televisa was producing over 50,000 hours of programming per year (Grupo Televisa 1997: 6). This is more than that which is produced by all the US networks combined (Goldis-Pittsburg Institutional Services 1997), although the US pattern is for the networks to buy programming from independent production companies, rather than produce their own. Globo produces around 4,400 hours per year, less than one-tenth of Televisa's output, but would claim that it is all 'quality' programming (Organizações Globo 1992; TV Globo 1996). Each of them claims to be exporting to about 130 countries (de la Fuente 1997: 47; Symmes 1997: S11).

The fact that both Globo and Televisa do produce most of their own programming, that is, that production and distribution are vertically integrated, is one key characteristic they have in common, and it is instructive to make the comparison of how the two organizations structured themselves to reach their pre-eminence. Horizontal integration of other media activities is another salient characteristic, as well as participation in certain related cultural industries. Table 5 sets out the different media and other areas of business in which each of them was engaged as of the early 1990s, before Televisa commenced the sell-down of interests outlined in the previous chapter.

As was detailed in the previous chapter, Televisa has sold down and out of a number of companies not considered to be core businesses over recent years, notably Videovisa, and some of its much more peripheral activities. But what is striking in the table is that, with the exception of film production, Globo and Televisa have corresponding companies in every area of activity designated. Of these, the financial core is formed by domestic television broadcasting, which has cross-promotional synergies with radio, recording, and print. Historically, radio has been more important to Televisa, while print has been much more of a core business to Globo, and indeed to its main competitor in this area and in subscription television, Abril. Both Televisa and Globo also have their educational and cultural foundations, for the sake of their corporate social standing and legitimacy in their respective societies, and each has some more profit-oriented promotional and other commercial activities

Table 5. Comparative corporate integration of Globo and Televisa

	Globo	Televisa
Broadcast	Rede Globo de TV	Four national networks
Satellite/cable	Globosat	Cablevisión
DTH	Sky	Sky
Video	Globo Video	Grupo Videovisa
Radio	Sistema Globo de Rádio	Radiópolis
Records	Som Livre	Discos Melody, others
Newspapers	*O Globo*	*Ovaciones*
Magazines	Editora Globo	Editorial Televisa
News agency	Agência Globo de Noticias	ECO (Empresa de Comunicaciones Orbitales)
Film		Televicine
Educational television	Roberto Marinho Foundation	Televisa Cultural Foundation
Promotion	Vasglo	Promovisión
Television distribution	Department of International Marketing	Protele
Other cultural industries	TV commercials Printing and graphics Merchandising Market research Galleries	Dubbing Billboards Product distribution Galleries
Other fields	Finance and insurance Cattle farms Mining Furniture Microelectronics	Insurance Real estate Jets Maintenance Paging
Telecoms	Mobile telephony	PanAmSat

related to their media interests, as well as a series of unrelated businesses. As we have seen, they are both active in subscription television, which also draws on their domestic content production, and are even allies in Sky, one of the two major DTH ventures in the region. The other significant area in which each is active is foreign programme distribution.

Cross-media ownership, or the horizontal integration of companies in different media, is not unusual in media corporations worldwide. However, the degree to which Globo and Televisa combine both horizontal and vertical integration, in conjunction with the traditional family-owned patrilineal and autocratic mode of ownership and control, add up to an ideal type of what can be called the 'Latin American model' of media corporation. Later in this chapter, we will encounter a variation of this ideal type in Venezuela, a rising media power, and even in Argentina, where the media have followed a quite different path of development.

However, the greatest significance of this Latin American model of media organization, and of the integration of production and distribution in particular, is the strong connection it seems to bear to programme export activities, and a drive to the globalization of activities in general. These include direct investment in other countries' networks, and involvement in international satellite services. While there are certain intrinsic features of their domestic markets which provide both Globo and Televisa with incentives to internationalization, as will be explored in the final chapter, the integration of production and distribution for the domestic market appears in both instances to have become a powerful motive force for the expansion of international activities.

In Globo's case, internationalization began with the celebrated export of one of its *telenovelas* to Portugal in 1975. Globo certainly did not invent the Brazilian *telenovela* as a genre—TV Tupi and TV Excelsior had been successful with developing them during the 1960s—but it was Globo that commercialized the *telenovela* as the staple of domestic programming, and built it into an export product in the 1970s (Mattelart and Mattelart 1990: 14–17). The lusophone world, that is, the number of countries where Portuguese is spoken, is far smaller than the Spanish-speaking world, as there are fewer people in fewer countries, and they are also more dispersed and less affluent as markets. Thus, Globo and the other Brazilian television producers have had fewer and more difficult options in developing overseas markets than Televisa, or the Venezuelan companies to be discussed in the next section. Brazil might be the biggest lusophone country in the world, and absolutely the biggest country in Latin America by both area and population, but since it is the only one in its region that speaks Portuguese, it has been more oriented to Europe in its export efforts than to its Spanish-speaking neighbours. As well as being dubbed into Spanish, Brazilian programmes for the Latin American market have to be transcodified into the transmission standard used everywhere else in the Americas, the US system, NTSC. This adds a level of costs its Spanish-language competitors do not have, some of whom in any case discriminate even against each other's programming, let alone the Brazilian material (Marques de Melo 1988: 41–3).

As will be examined further in Chapter 5, Portugal has assumed a strategic significance for Globo, much more than Spain has correspondingly for Televisa. Consequently, the success of *Gabriela*, the *telenovela* which Globo sold to the then only television network in Portugal in 1977, the nationalized RTP (Rádio e Televisão Portuguesa), was decisive. In spite of it being very expressively Brazilian in idiom, characterization, narrative, and setting, based as it was on a novel by Brazil's most popular writer, Jorge Amado (Hinchberger 1997), Portuguese audiences received it well. Encouraged that such 'colonialism in reverse' could work, Globo sold several more *telenovelas* to RTP over the next decade, and also cultivated the rather more limited television markets of the former Portuguese colonies in Africa (Marques de Melo 1988: 40).

In spite of some success in Latin America in the late 1990s with *O Bem Amado* (Mattos 1992: 13), Globo concentrated on those European countries which were culturally similar, by virtue of a common Latin heritage, and which were also more accustomed to watching dubbed programmes. After its Department of International Marketing was set up in 1980, Globo sold *Escrava Isaura*, a romantic historical *telenovela*, to Italy, and this began a vogue in that country for Brazilian and other Latin American *telenovelas* for the next few years. In 1985, Globo also sold *Escrava Isaura* to Canal Plus in France, and then more *telenovelas* to other French channels. Interestingly, these sales were made on the basis of very narrow margins, a strategy to keep down the price, and so open up more markets in the French-speaking world (Marques de Melo 1988: 42–3). Indeed, one Globo executive calls this 'the drugs strategy: first you practically give, wait for success and later you sell for the best price' (quoted in Sousa 1997: 5). Thus, Globo's practice is to set different prices for different markets, and at different stages, just as US exporters always have done, but in general it is able to charge more in European than in Latin American markets (Marques de Melo 1992: 9). Significant in this respect is that its overseas offices are in Paris and London. In the 1980s, Globo was earning only 20 per cent of its 'offshore income' from the Latin American market, the bulk of it being derived from Europe, so in this respect it is 'more international' than Televisa (Mattelart and Mattelart 1990: 12).

While linguistic and cultural similarities might have helped to open up some initial markets for Globo, and, it should be added, for some much smaller Brazilian producers such as Manchete and Bandeirantes, the sale of Brazilian *telenovelas* certainly has not been restricted to what Roncagliolo calls the 'Latin-European countries' (1995: 340). By the end of the 1980s, *Escrava Isaura* and other *telenovelas* were being discovered by audiences in such culturally and geographically remote countries as the former Soviet Union, Poland, and China, as well as the UK, Australia, and New Zealand. Although international sales at the beginning of this decade were only 3 per cent of total revenue (Marques de Melo 1992: 8), an even smaller proportion of income for Globo than for Televisa, Globo has continued to seek to develop programme exports as a major area of activity, and it continues to be a production-driven organization. This is evidenced by its $US120 million investment in Projac, a consolidated production complex outside of Rio de Janeiro, opened in 1995, with the expectation of making costs more competitive (Paxman 1995*b*).

The importance of European markets to Globo has been apparent in the selective direct investments it has made. In the wake of starting the craze for Latin American *telenovelas* in Italy, Globo bought TMC (Telemontecarlo) in 1985, a minor regional channel which it planned to use as a base for satellite broadcasting in Europe. Unable to challenge the dominance of the Italian Government's RAI and Berlusconi's RTI networks, Globo sold out of TMC in 1994, having lost $US120 million (McCarter 1990: 22; 'News in Brief' 1994; Paxman 1995*b*: 58). By that time, Globo had made a more significant investment in Portugal, the opportunity for which was the creation of two private competitors to RTP in the early 1990s. Globo secured a 15 per cent interest, the maximum allowable for a foreign investor, in one of these, SIC (Sociedade Independente de Comunicação), and has since helped to build it up to become the leading network in Portugal (Sousa 1997). Because Globo has a particular relationship to Portugal the same way as Televisa does to Spain, this will be taken up again later in Chapter 5. Similarly, Globo's participation in the Sky consortium, as already outlined, will be taken up in more analytic perspective in Chapter 6.

It remains to consider the current state of Globo. Just as Televisa has had to face a crisis of succession with the death of Emilio Azcárraga Milmo, the question must be asked as to how Globo will fare after the death of Roberto Marinho, now in his nineties. However, because Globo's management has been less dominated by Marinho alone than Televisa reportedly was by Azcárraga, there should be less of a crisis of transition. Long-serving Globo executives responsible for successful strategies in the past are still there, such as José Bonifacio de Oliveira Sobrinho ('Boni'), the programming specialist, or have returned, as is the case with Joe Wallach at Globosat. Roberto Marinho has three sons, each of whom is a Vice-President of a separate major division of the organization—television, radio, and the newspaper—although one of them, Roberto Irineu, has been designated the 'heir apparent'. This would indicate that more of a basis for succession has been laid than at Televisa, but some well-placed observers predict the outbreak of tense rivalries between the brothers, particularly as Globo faces ever stronger competition from SBT (Paxman 1995*b*). On the other hand, an American communications journalist who visited Globo in 1997 reported:

My requests to interview Marinho were ignored, and one Globo official told me ... that at age 92 the man was no longer transmitting on all channels ... day-to-day control of the private company has passed to his three sons ... Now the next generations of Marinhos ... have accepted that Globo will lose its near monopoly on Brazilian media as multinationals move in, and are counter-attacking by going global: Globo has courted deals with AT&T for cellular phones, Ted Turner for cable, and Rupert Murdoch's NewsCorp for satellite television. (Symmes 1997: S14)

The question then becomes, who is globalizing whom?

The Venezuelans are Coming

The backwardness of dictatorship and military government in Venezuela prior to 1945 meant that radio began later there than elsewhere in Latin America, although when it did, it was less subject to regulation. This circumstance allowed commercial radio companies to thrive and, at least in the case of Venezuela's oldest-surviving network, Radio Caracas Televisión (RCTV), to make an unhampered transition to television in the early 1950s (Giménez Saldivia and Hernández Algara 1988: 168; Fox 1997: 67–8).

Television broadcasting in Venezuela today is dominated by two strong and internationally active networks—a virtual duopoly, with weak domestic participation by the state. However, the pre-eminent network is not RCTV, but Venevisión, which did not begin until 1960 when one of the pioneering channels, Channel 4, formerly known as Televisa, was purchased by an industrial corporation owned by a Cuban immigrant, Diego Cisneros, with the help of an initial investment of almost 43 per cent from the US network ABC. A similar late arrival in the 1960s was Cadena Venezolana de Televisión (CVTV) Channel 8, owned by another of Venezuela's industrial groups, in conjunction with the then-exiled Cuban entrepreneur Goar Mestre, and with the participation of US capital from Time-Life and the CBS network. However, Channel 8 was subsequently acquired by the state in 1974, and made into its national network. As such it is in a preferential position to receive government advertising, but it is still a losing concern, with inadequate production facilities and a heavy reliance on imported programmes (Giménez Saldivia and Hernández Algara 1988: 196 and 212–13; Fox 1997: 72 and 78).

Diego Cisneros was the founding patriarch of the industrial group which until recently still bore his name, as Organización Diego Cisneros (ODC). This had its origins in the 1940s, when it was based on refrigeration, food, and drink, notably bottling franchises for Pepsi Cola (Giménez Saldivia and Hernández Algara 1988: 189–90), although Venevisión is now the most profitable division of the group. We have seen how Emilio Azcárraga Milmo restructured Televisa in the 1990s and trimmed the scope of its activities: just so did Gustavo Cisneros, the son who succeeded Diego on his death in 1980, undertake a major restructure at that time, in the process renaming the group as Companías Grupo Cisneros (CGC). One notable divestment was the Spalding sporting goods company which it had owned in the US, while another major move was to drop the long-standing Pepsi Cola franchise in favour of Coca-Cola, making it one of the largest outside the US. At its greatest extent, the group's activities ranged over mining, supermarket chain operation (in the US and Puerto Rico as well as Venezuela), electronic goods manufacturing, and telecommunications—it has joint ventures with Motorola, Sprint, and Bell South. While CGC still retains a strong base in several industries, it has been media and communication where it has now concentrated its efforts (Bamrud 1994; Paxman 1997d).

Like Grupo Televisa and Organizações Globo, CGC is a conglomerate in which media are integrated both vertically, notably through the television network and an international sales arm serving as distribution outlets at home and abroad for its programme production, and horizontally, incorporating companies ranging across a number of media fields. These include radio broadcasting, publishing, sound recording, and film production. Other more vertical activities are television commercial production, video distribution, and talent and live-show management. They also have their own advertising agency in Miami. The group's value is estimated to be over $US 5 billion (Walley 1994; Fox 1997: 77). When compared to Televisa and Globo, we see the familiar corporate profile of the Latin American model, although one significant difference is that both Televisa and Globo are almost exclusively involved in the communication industries, whereas even if Venevisión is 'the jewel in the crown' (Paxman 1995a), CGC also has its strong bottling, retailing, and other industrial divisions which can provide a source of liquid assets and something of a buffer against economic downturns (Paxman 1997a).

CGC also clearly fits a similar pattern of patriarchal control and continuity apparent in the history and structure of Televisa and Globo. Gustavo Cisneros was one of Diego Cisneros's eight sons. Educated in the US, he sits on the boards of US businesses and universities (Bamrud 1994: 88), enjoying an international standing which Azcárraga Milmo's conspicuous consumption of yachts and women was not destined to achieve for him (Esparza 1997: 52; Puig 1997: 12). Yet while Azcárraga was always in a more defined relation within the domestic political structure of his country than Cisneros has been in his, it is ironic that because Gustavo Cisneros and his brother Ricardo became involved with a plan of former President Carlos Andrés Pérez (President 1973–8, and 1989–93) to finance greater media concentration in return for political support, they were discredited when the scheme was exposed (Paxman 1997b: 78; Fox 1997: 75–6).

In terms of international activities, CGC entered the 1990s already deriving about half its earnings outside of Venezuela, much more than the corresponding level for Televisa and Globo, but much of that was attributable to its non-media divisions (Bamrud 1994: 26). Venevisión since has been active in acquiring direct interests in television networks in other Spanish-speaking countries. In this respect, it mirrors Televisa, with whom Venevisión entered the deal to purchase Univisión in the US as equal partners, while Televisa's 49 per cent share of the former government channel Megavisión in Chile is matched by Venevisión's 49 per cent share in the university channel RTU, now Chilevisión. Venevisión also has a 25 per cent interest in a channel in Puerto Rico (where it competes with the US network Telemundo), and a stake in a Caribbean media group, CCN (Smirnoff 1994b; Paxman 1995a; 1997d: 74).

It was noted in Chapter 2 that Venevisión is the largest of the Latin American partners in the Hughes Galaxy DTH consortium, also known as DirecTV. Its 20 per cent share involved an investment of $US250 million. There is a separate company, Miami-based Cisneros Television Group (CTG), which has been developing programming packages both for cable services and for the Galaxy venture, exploiting Venevisión's low-cost production facilities in Caracas. Venevisión launched an international channel in 1997 which carries 70 per cent of programming it produces itself, while it hopes to bring the corresponding percentage on the domestic network up to 80 per cent in 1999. Accordingly, the production facilities have been expanded, and Cisneros has made known to Hughes his ambitions to become involved with them in Japan, India, and Spain (Paxman 1997*a*; 1997*c*; 1997*d*: 75). It was also noted in the previous chapter that while Venevisión was competing with Televisa in DTH, they are partners in the US with Univisión, and in Latin America they collaborate in a mutual programme distribution arrangement. Clearly, there is potential for conflict of interest in this situation, so the ambitions both of them have for developments with DTH might well undermine the stability of their collaboration. Cisneros is forging ahead with extending the Galaxy DTH DirecTV service, having secured an agreement in 1997 to bring it to Argentina, which has been Latin America's largest cable market (Swan and Jose 1997*a*).

In its domestic market, Venevisión faces much more substantial competition than do either of its counterparts in Mexico or Brazil. While Televisa worries about the build-up of TV Azteca's share, as of 1996 it still had over three-quarters of the audience, and similarly Globo had a 68 per cent audience share, compared to its closest competitor SBT's 18 per cent ('Brazil' 1996). Venevisión, however, has more like a half of the Venezuelan audience, while around 30 per cent watch RCTV, and the government channel and other smaller competitors share the rest ('Venezuela' 1996). Very much like Venevisión, RCTV is owned by a family-based industrial group, Phelps, which has several other horizontally and vertically integrated media and communications companies, as well as interests in property, construction, and manufacturing. These industrial activities mark the Venezuelan variation on the Latin American model. Phelps's media companies include radio networks, a daily newspaper, and book publishing and distribution companies, as well as an advertising agency (Giménez Saldivia and Hernández Algara 1988: 180–1). In addition, they have divisions in video and sound recording, production, and distribution, and also in talent management (Fox 1997: 77).

RCTV's domestic network consists of four national channels, while its international activities are centred on programme production and distribution through Coral Pictures Corporation, and participation in the GEMS international cable channel. This is a joint venture with International Television Inc. Oriented towards a global market of women in the Spanish-speaking world, GEMS carries much of RCTV/Coral Pictures' fare. Both Coral and GEMS are based in Miami, the virtual media capital of the Spanish-speaking Americas (GEMS 1993; Shackelford 1995).

Just as RCTV offers strong competition to Venevisión in the domestic market, this is also the case in programming export activities. Coral is a major distributor of programming, with its number of hours sold annually comparable to that of Televisa and Globo. Seventy per cent of what it sells is RCTV/Coral programming, much of the rest coming from European producers. Coral was responsible for opening up Spain to Venezuelan *telenovelas* in 1991, although Venevisión was also quick to cash in on the vogue which its competitor so began. Both became involved in co-productions with networks in Spain at that time ('Coral Looks for New Frontiers' 1992; 'Venevisión Strikes Gold in the Webs of Spain' 1992).

One other Venezuelan television corporation with an international dimension is Omnivisión. Though operating as a domestic subscription cable service since 1986, Omnivisión's distinction in the globalization of Latin American television is to have been the Latin American partner in one of the first US-based cable channels available in the region, the Time-Warner cinema channel in Spanish, HBO Olé. As well as this and other US channels, Omnivisión also carries the national services from Latin Europe, Spain's TVE and Italy's RAI ('En busqueda de la integración latinoamericana' 1991; 'HBO Plans Pay TV Launch in Latin America' 1991).

Argentina: Cable and Convergence

Even more so than in Venezuela, a jagged history of military intervention and populist dictatorship in Argentina prevented the development of a mutually supportive relationship between the state and private television owners of the kind which has characterized Mexico and Brazil. There were three private channels set up in the late 1950s, each in conjunction with investment from one of the US networks. These included Channel 13, established by the ubiquitous Goar Mestre in association with Time-Life and CBS. The channels were prohibited from forming networks, so joined their affiliates to their production companies, which in Channel 13's case was Proartel. However, all of the channels were subsequently nationalized under Perón in the 1970s, and although they continued to be run on a commercial model, it was not until the 1980s that Argentinian television became free from very direct government control. Since state-owned television had thus become associated with decades of military and civilian dictatorship, the democratically elected regimes of Alfonsín in 1983 and Menem in 1989 have progressively turned television over to private ownership (Fox 1997: 101–6).

Thus Argentina is different from the other television industries considered in this book, which have been built on dominant national broadcasting networks. Within the Argentinian industry, the historical absence of networks and the relative recency of liberalization have given a special importance to the satellite-to-cable mode of distribution. More than 60 per cent of all television households in Argentina are cabled, making a total of over 5 million pay-TV homes, almost 45 per cent of all pay-TV homes in the entire region, and well ahead of Mexico, the next most cabled nation, with just over 2 million pay-TV homes (Goyoaga and Paxman 1997: 27; 'Latin American TV & Pay TV at a Glance' 1997; Waisbord 1997: 18). The incidence of cable links Argentinian television into the convergence of the media and telecommunications industries and their technologies on a global scale. Thus, quite apart from the fact that it is one of the more active exporters and co-producers of programming amongst the Latin American countries, Argentinian television deserves attention here also because of the relationship which it bears to regional and global telecommunications corporations.

Although Argentina has had no networks as such, the privatization process has put television channels into the hands of companies which were either in print media, or have since been able to diversify into other media. It was not only the auctioning of the licences, but the removal of a previous restriction on cross-media ownership which has created the new media corporations. In 1989, Channel 13 was awarded to Grupo Clarín, owners of the newspaper with the largest circulation in the Spanish-speaking world, *Clarín*. As has been characteristic of media ownership elsewhere in the region, Clarín is owned by a family company, but unlike the patrilineal succession which we have seen at work in the Mexican, Brazilian, and Venezuelan dynasties, the Noble family is headed by the widow of the founder (Paxman 1996: 40), not unlike the way in which María Perón took over on the death of her husband Juan Perón (President 1945–55 and 1973–4). In addition to the television division, called Artear (Arte Radiotelevisivo Argentina), Clarín has added radio stations to its other interests. These include a news agency and newsprint production, vertically integrated with *Clarín*, as well as unrelated activities such as real estate (Fox 1997: 106).

As Waisbord observes (1997: 22), Argentinian television owners, having been hampered by the prohibition on networks, have tended not to vertically integrate production with distribution in the way their counterparts elsewhere have done, but they have vertically integrated cable with broadcasting. In Clarín's case, they bought a cable company in 1992, Multicanal. Facilitated by government liberalization of foreign investment in the telecommunications industry, and particularly by a trade agreement with the US that became effective in 1994, Clarín sold 30 per cent of Multicanal that same year to an Argentinian investment group which is backed by Citicorp. In 1996, Clarín sold a further 25 per cent share to TISA (Telefónica Internacional Sociedad Anónima), the international division of the private Spanish telecommunications company which controls half of Argentina's telephone duopoly through Telefónica de Argentina, and which also has cable investments in Peru and Chile (Paxman 1996: 40; Waisbord 1997: 20).

The Channel 11 licence was awarded to Telefé (Televisora Federal), formed by a book and magazine publisher, Editorial Atlántida; a group of ten independent television stations; and industrial conglomerates Grupo Soldati and Grupo Zanón (Fox 1997: 106; Waisbord 1997: 11). In addition to two satellite radio networks, Telefé also purchased a cable division, Megacable, but sold this and its 200,000 subscribers to Multicanal in 1996, giving Grupo Clarín 52.5 per cent and its partners 22.5 per cent each in the new Megacable (Waisbord 1997: 19–20).

The other private channels are Channel 2, América TV, owned by Eduardo Eurnekián, also an owner of cable television and other media; and Channel 9, owned by entertainment and media entrepreneur Alejandro 'El Zar' Romay and operated as Libertad, the same name as his radio network. Romay too has interests in cable television (Goyoaga 1997; Swan and Jose 1997b; Waisbord 1997: 11). This leaves ATC (Argentina Televisora Color), Channel 7, as the only remaining channel owned by the state, yet this too is in the process of privatization (Besas 1993). ATC is the Argentinian channel mentioned in Chapter 2 as having a programming distribution deal with Televisa (Fox 1997: 106).

The privatization of the television channels gave a strong stimulus to advertising expenditure, so that by 1996, Argentina had the highest advertising expenditure per capita in the region. The channels which have attracted the greatest advertising revenues are also those which are most engaged in programme production and distribution, namely Artear, Telefé, and Libertad. Given the persistence of the traditional structure in which television channels in Buenos Aires have formed production companies to make programmes that could be distributed to their provincial affiliates, and the strong preference of audiences for Argentinian programmes, privatization has encouraged an overall increase in the proportion of domestic production from 55 to 65 per cent. Furthermore, there has been a strong drive to establish distribution arrangements and co-production partners abroad, not just in other Latin American countries, but in Asia, the Middle East, and Europe. Telefé has been particularly active in these areas (Waisbord 1997: 12–15). In addition, Telefé has been a 20 per cent partner with Peru's leading network, Panamericana, in mounting a cable channel in Spanish, SUR, which is transmitted to both North and South America (Mendosa 1994).

The growth of cable which so distinguishes Argentinian television can be attributed to the mandated absence of networks in the development of broadcast television. While first used to distribute the signal from terrestrial antennae to remote towns in the 1960s, the liberalization of satellite transmission in the 1980s facilitated the take-up of cable television in the cities. Thus, from serving as a mere rural relay system for broadcast channels, cable came to offer an untiered mix of domestic and international programming to wealthier urban dwellers. It is significant that while broadcast television prospers on advertising revenue, there is negligible advertising on cable television. The source of revenue is subscription fees of around $US 30–40 per month (Pasquini Durán and Uranga 1993: 26–7; Waisbord 1997: 18–20).

At one stage, there were as many as 1,700 cable operators, that is, the local companies which subscribers pay to be connected to the signals they downlink, but a 1996 figure puts them at 1,183. This is indicative of a shake-out in the industry, wherein the small operators are being squeezed out by larger ones, particularly after foreign investment was allowed into the industry after 1994, and the zoning of cable companies was deregulated (Smirnoff 1994a; Waisbord 1997: 19). It has been noted how Multicanal, which includes US and Spanish partners, made itself the biggest of Argentina's cable operators, with 1.3 million subscribers. The other two major MSOs are VCC (Video Cable Communication) and Cablevisión, which have a similar number between them. Both were formerly family concerns which have attracted major US partners, and a merger between them has been the object of trade speculation in recent years.

The attraction for the foreign telecommunications companies is that Argentina's two private telephone companies are not permitted to deliver television services, but, as of 1997, MSOs have been allowed to offer basic telephone and data services. From 1994 until 1997, VCC was 50 per cent owned by Continental, a subsidiary of the telecommunications company US West, while the major US cable operator TCI (actually through its international division, TINTA) had 51 per cent of Cablevisión. In 1997, US West raised its share in VCC to 90 per cent, but TCI sold half of its share in Cablevisión to Citicorp Equity Investments, thus giving Citicorp 64.5 per cent while retaining 25.5 per cent. Cablevisión was founded by Channel 2's owner, Eduardo Eurnekián, who retains a 10 per cent interest (Goyoaga and Paxman 1997: 30; Swan and Jose 1997b; Waisbord 1997: 20, 24–5).

Citicorp Equity Investments is owned by Citibank of the US, and Banco República and the Wertheim Group in Argentina. As well as its majority interest in Cablevisión, it has a strong indirect interest in

Telefónica de Argentina and hence in Multicanal. Furthermore, it is expected to buy out half of US West's share in VCC, the addition of which will then give it more than half of all Argentina's cable subscribers. Apart from such a strong presence in all the major MSOs, Citicorp Equity Investments has acquired interests in both the terrestrial network Telefé and the publisher Atlantida (Arias 1997).

As to the US cable corporation TCI, if we recall that it is a partner with Televisa, Globo, and News in the Sky DTH venture outlined in Chapter 2, this raises the question of the future of DTH in a country so heavily committed to cable. TCI's sell-down of its cable interest and a simultaneous announcement that it was going to 'boost its programming presence in the region' suggests a shift towards DTH (Swan and Jose 1997b). Apart from that, all that can be noted on present indications is that Gustavo Cisneros of Venevisión, representing the opposing Galaxy Latin America DirecTV consortium, concluded a deal with President Menem in July 1997 to permit DirecTV to be made available in Argentina. On the same visit, he also bought a 90 per cent interest in Imagen Satelital, the country's largest programme procurement and packaging company. This is expected to work with Grupo Clarín, which Galaxy had already signed as its collaborator in Argentina (Swan and Jose 1997a). Sky had not at that time commenced any service to Argentina; however, it has since been announced that Sky will be offering its service through a partnership with Citicorp, Telefónica de Argentina, TCI, and Cablevisión (Swan and Jose 1998). It is not clear how Galaxy's arrangements will affect the DTH plans of Nahuelsat, a new satellite system for the Southern Cone of the continent launched in 1997, and owned by Argentinian interests in conjunction with GE Americom of the US and three European aerospace companies (Bulloch 1997: 22). For a nation already so committed to cable distribution, there seems to be an excessive capacity of DTH services on offer.

References

Abril Group (1992), *The Abril Group* (São Paulo, Editora Abril).

Améndola Ávila, Carlos Rodolfo (1982), *A teleinvasão: a participação estrangeira na televisão do Brasil* (Cortez Editora/Editora UNIMEP, São Paulo).

Arias, Carlos (1997), 'Latin America Watch', *International Cable* (October), 32.

Bahiana, Ana Maria (1994), 'Brazil', *Television Business International*, February: 21–2.

Bamrud, Joachim (1994), 'Premio Internacional de la Excelencia da NATPE a Gustavo Cisneros', *Producción y Distribución* (February–March), 26, 28, and 88.

Barbosa, Phydias (1994), 'Se consolida red de TV brasileña en Estados Unidos', *Producción y Distribución*, 5/24: 86.

Barnouw, Erik (1979), *The Sponsor: Notes on a Modern Potentate* (Oxford University Press, Oxford).

Besas, Peter (1993), 'Snappy Private Nets Give Argentine TV a Facelift', *Variety* (29 March), 48.

BIB (1992), *BIB World Guide to Television and Programming* (North American Publishing Company, New York).

'Brazil' (1996), *Broadcasting & Cable* (22 January), 106–7.

Bulloch, Chris (1997), 'DTH in Latin America', *International Cable* (July), 18–22.

Cajueiro, Marcelo (1997), 'Brazilian Investors Play Waiting Game', *Variety* (21–7 July), 28.

Caparelli, Sergio (1982), *Televisão e capitalismo no Brasil* (LP&M Editores, Porto Allegre).

'Carrossel mexicano' (1991), *Veja* (12 June), 78–84.

Cesar Carvalho, Mario (1994), 'Globo seria igual sem Time-Life, diz Wallach', *Folha de São Paulo* (22 January).

'Coral Looks for New Frontiers' (1992), *Variety* (23 March), 78.

de Cardona, Elizabeth (1977), 'American Television in Latin America', in G. Gerbner (ed.), *Mass Media Policies in Changing Cultures* (John Wiley, New York), 57–62.

de la Fuente, Anna Maria (1997), 'Endless Love', *TV World* (January), 45–7.

de Lima, Venicio (1988), 'The State, Television, and Political Power in Brazil', *Critical Studies in Mass Communication*, 5: 108–28.

'En busqueda de la integración latinoamericana' (1991), *Comunicación*, 75: 136.

Esparza, Elia (1997), 'Life after "el Tigre"', *Hispanic* (July–August), 48–52.

Ferraz Sampaio, Mario (1984), *História do radió e da televisão no Brasil e no mundo* (Achiamé, Rio de Janeiro).

Fox, Elizabeth (1997), *Latin American Broadcasting: From Tango to Telenovela* (University of Luton Press, Luton).

GEMS (1993), press release.

Giménez Saldivia, Lulú, and Hernández Algara, Angela (1988), *Estructura de los medios de difusión en Venezuela* (Universidad Católica Andres Bello, Caracas).

Glasberg, Rubens (1995), 'Bringing up Brazil', *Multichannel News International* (April), Supplement, 6ᵇ AND 346ᵇ.

Goldis-Pittsburg Institutional Services (1997), 'Grupo Televisa SA: Company Report', Investext Group.

Goyoaga, Beatriz (1997), 'Romay Fights for his Libertad', *Variety* (31 March–6 April), 68.

—— and Paxman, Andrew (1997), 'Cabled up in Argentina', *Variety* (21–7 July), 27 and 30.

Grupo Televisa (1997), *Annual Report 1996 (Televisa, Mexico DF)*.

Guimarães, Cesar, and Amaral, Roberto (1988), 'Brazilian Television: A Rapid Conversion to the New Order', in E. Fox (ed.), *Media and Politics in Latin America* (Sage, London), 125–37.

'HBO Plans Pay TV Launch in Latin America' (1991), *Broadcasting Abroad* (March), 4.

Higgins, John, and McClellan, Steve (1997), 'When Media Moguls Collide', *Broadcasting & Cable* (7 July), 4–5.

Hinchberger, Bill (1997), 'Jorge Amado Writes from Heart, Home', *Variety* (31 March–6 April), 56.

Hoineff, Nelson (1993), 'Globo Dominates Brazil's $1.3B TV Scene', *Variety* (29 March), 50 and 62.

'Latin American TV & Pay TV at a Glance' (1997), *Variety* (21–7 July), 28.

McCarter, Michelle (1990), 'TV Net Grows in Italy', *Advertising Age* (17 December).

Marques de Melo, José (1988), *As telenovelas de Globo* (Summus Editorial, São Paulo).

—— (1992), 'Brazil's Role as a Television Exporter within the Latin American Regional Market', paper presented to the 42nd Conference of the International Communication Association, Miami, May.

Mattelart, Michèle, and Mattelart, Armand (1990), *The Carnival of Images: Brazilian Television Fiction* (Bergin & Garvey, New York).

Mattos, Sérgio (1982), *The Impact of the 1964 Revolution on Brazilian Television* (Klingensmith Independent Publisher, San Antonio).

—— (1984), 'Advertising and Government Influences: The Case of Brazilian Television', *Communication Research*, 11/2: 203–20.

—— (1992), 'A Profile of Brazilian Television', paper presented to the 18th Conference of the International Association for Mass Communication Research, Guarujá, August.

Mendosa, Rick (1994), 'SUR Focuses and Expands for Latin American Pay TV', *International Cable* (January), 42–3 and 49.

'News in Brief' (1994), *TV International* (24 January), 4.

Organizações Globo (1992), *Organizações Globo* (Central Globo de Comunicação, Rio de Janeiro).

Pasquini Durán, José, and Uranga, Washington (1993), 'Future Options for Satellite Use in Latin America', *Media Development*, 3: 25–8.

Paxman, Andrew (1995a), 'Cisneros Views World as Oyster', *Variety* (27 March–2 April), 46.

—— (1995b), 'Globo Relies on Projac for Lift', *Variety* (27 March–2 April), 43, 48, and 58.

—— (1996), 'Quiet Clarin Making Moves', *Variety* (25–31 March), 40 and 60.

—— (1997a), 'Economy, B'casters Rebound in Venezuela', *Variety* (27 January–2 February), 32.

—— (1997b), 'Cisneros Back to 1st Love', *Variety* (31 March–6 April), 74 and 78.

—— (1997c), 'CTG Embraces Group Philosophy', *Variety* (31 March–6 April), 74 and 77.

—— (1997d), 'Globally Mobile', *Variety* (31 March–6 April), 74–5, 78.

—— (1997e), 'Satcasters Transmit Signs of Success', *Variety* (21–7 July), 28.

Pickard, Christopher (1991), 'Abril in Rio: "I Want My Pay TV"', *Rio Life* (October).

'Por baixo do pano' (1992), *Veja* (17 June), 96–9.

'The Principal Languages of the World' (1996), *The World Almanac and Book of Facts* (World Almanac Books, Mahwah, NJ), 642–3.

Puig, Carlos (1997), 'El imperio construido por Emilio Azcárraga en México sí tuvo reveses...en el extranjero', *Proceso* (20 April), 12–16.

Read, William (1976), *America's Mass Media Merchants* (Johns Hopkins University Press, Baltimore).

Rede Globo (1997), 'History of the Company', http://www.redeglobo.com.br/inst/english/inst2.html

Roncagliolo, Rafael (1995), 'Trade Integration and Communication Networks in Latin America', *Canadian Journal of Communication*, 20/3: 335–42.

Shackelford, John (1995), 'Miami: Launch Pad for Latin America', *International Cable* (April), 20–8.

Smirnoff, Miguel (1994*a*), 'Argentina', *Television Business International* (February), 23.

—— (1994*b*), 'Chile', *Television Business International* (February), 24–5.

Sousa, Helena (1997), 'Crossing the Atlantic: Globo's Wager in Portugal', paper presented to the conference of the International Association for Mass Communication Research, Oaxaca, July.

Straubhaar, Joseph (1982), 'The Development of the Telenovela as the Preeminent Form of Popular Culture in Brazil', *Studies in Latin American Popular Culture*, 1: 138–50.

—— (1984), 'Brazilian Television: The Decline of American Influence', *Communication Research*, 11/2: 221–40.

—— (1996), 'The Electronic Media in Brazil', in R. Cole (ed.), *Communication in Latin America: Journalism, Mass Media, and Society* (Jaguar Books on Latin America, Wilmington, Del.), 217–43.

Swan, Alex, and Jose, Andy (1997*a*), 'Latin America Watch', *International Cable* (August), 50.

—— —— (1997*b*), 'Latin America Watch', *International Cable* (September), 62.

—— —— (1998), 'Latin America Watch', *International Cable* (February), 54.

Symmes, Patrick (1997), 'The Hacker Tourist Maps Brazil', *Wired* (October), S11–15.

TV Globo (1996), display advertisement, *Variety* (25–31 March), 45.

'Venevisión Strikes Gold in the Webs of Spain' (1992), *Variety* (23 March), 78.

'Venezuela' (1996), *Broadcasting & Cable* (22 January), 116.

Vink, Nico (1988), *The Telenovela and Emancipation* (Royal Tropical Institute, Amsterdam).

Waisbord, Silvio (1997), 'The Market Deluge: Privatization, Concentration and New Technologies in the Argentine Media Industry', manuscript prepared for forthcoming publication in A. Alberran and S. Chan-Omsted (eds.), *Global Media Economics* (Iowa University Press, Iowa City).

Walley, Wayne (1994), 'NATPE to Honor Venevision's Cisneros', *Electronic Media* (24 January).

4 | 'The Wealthiest Hispanics in the World': Spanish-Language Television in the United States

When the first Spanish-language television network in the US was initiated in San Antonio, Texas, in 1961, 'Hispanics' were fewer than 7 million, less than 4 per cent of the national population (Brischetto 1993a). By the 1990 Census, there were two national networks broadcasting to an estimated 26 million of them, by then almost 10 per cent of the population, and predicted to outnumber African-Americans as the largest ethnic minority in the US by 2020 (Brischetto 1993b: 6).

As a label for a category of persons, the term 'Hispanic' is of quite recent coinage, legitimized by the US Census Bureau's use of it since 1980, and fostered by media and market research companies with a commercial stake in the creation of an audience, and hence a market, of 'Hispanics' (Flores-Hughes 1996; Rodriguez 1997a). However, both the Census Bureau's interest in being able to identify the population of Latin American origin in the US, and the media's interest in cultivating them as an audience, go back to the late 1920s, the first years of Spanish-language radio. At that time, Spanish-speakers in the US were almost all of Mexican origin (Rodriguez 1997b). What has been different in the period since the Second World War is that immigrant inflows from Puerto Rico and from Cuba since the 1960s, and more recently from Central and South America also, have diversified the Spanish-speaking population to the extent that, although the people themselves tend to identify with their national origin, a more generic term has been needed both for demographic monitoring and for marketing communication purposes.

Thus, the population of Spanish-speaking origin is now regularly referred to by the collective term 'Hispanic' in these contexts, and also in the Spanish-language media, such as television news. However, another generic term preferred by many would be 'Latino' (Rodriguez 1996), which has the advantage of including all people of Latin American origin, including the otherwise invisible Portuguese-speaking Brazilians, who like to point out that, 'Although all Hispanics are Latinos, not all Latinos are Hispanic' (Hector Guadalupe, quoted in Margolis 1994: 254).

Certainly, the current generation of communal activists call themselves Latinos, or, as is now often the case, Latinas. It is worth remembering that Spanish-speakers in the US have become conscious of themselves and mobilized politically as a group over much the same period that television has been in the process of cultivating them as a market. Their activism began with the Chicano movement amongst Mexican-Americans in the Southwest in the 1960s, and subsequently has shaped itself in response to wider movements, notably feminism and multicultural identity politics. Thus, although many people of Spanish-speaking origin in the US are comfortable with the term 'Hispanic', for others it is redolent of official control and ethnic discrimination.

Of all those who identified themselves as being of 'Hispanic Origin' in the 1990 Census, 13.5 million, or 60 per cent, said they were either 'Mexican', 'Mexican American', or 'Chicano'. This remains the largest group by far, numbering more than 17 million amongst the total of 26,646,000 Hispanics estimated in 1994 (US Census Bureau 1997), and over 50 per cent larger than it had been in the 1980 Census, although the fastest-growing category measured in 1990 was 'Other Hispanic'. This included more than a million descendants of the original Spanish settlers of the territories subsequently annexed by the US, but predominantly it was composed of people of Central and South American origin (3.2 million), and totalled over 5 million. Next in both size and rate of growth were Puerto Ricans (2.7 million, an increase of over 35 per cent since 1980), and more than 1 million Cubans, who had increased by 30 per cent since the previous Census (Brischetto 1993a; 1993b).

The high rates of growth are significant not just because of the ever-greater proportion of Spanish-speakers in the population which they represent, but because almost half of the growth is due to immigration (Brischetto 1993b: 7). That is, the Spanish-speaking population of the US grows almost as much from a continual influx of immigrants, both legal and undocumented, as it does from its own natural increase. So, while the number of people who speak Spanish at home (at least 7.5 per cent of the whole US population over 5 years old) might be rather smaller than the number who claim Hispanic origin (Brischetto 1993a), the flow of Spanish-dominant new arrivals feeds substantial communities resistant to assimilation, and ensures that Spanish remains next only to English as the most widely spoken language in the US. In this respect, the US Spanish-speaking population resembles the huge diasporic over-seas populations of Chinese, Indians, and Arabs, which also have been cultivated as international markets for television in their own languages and cultures (Sinclair et al. 1996).

While the actual extent of the nature and use of Spanish by Hispanics remains contested, it is clear that it is the only language other than English sufficient to sustain television networks in the US on a national basis. Even before the television era, Spanish-language radio was able to keep its support, while broadcasting in other languages died out, given the constant cultural renewal in Spanish-speaking communities, as contrasted to the gradual assimilation experienced by other immigrant groups (Rodriguez 1997a; 1997b). On the other hand, it would be a mistake to think of Spanish-language television as the medium of a culturally and linguistically segregated stratum of the population. Although the dominant network claims to be reaching the 87 per cent of Hispanics who speak Spanish at home, the network knows from its own commissioned research that a third of this group is actually bilingual, and, furthermore, that while 31 per cent of Hispanic house-holds do watch Spanish-language television, 69 per cent watch only English-language television (Rodriguez 1997a). Spanish-language tele-vision is on a continuum with mainstream television, an integral part of the television industry in the US, not a marginal alternative for a socially alienated minority. As the CEO (Chief Executive Officer) of one of the Spanish-language networks once put it, his was not a Latin American network, but 'an American television network that speaks Spanish' (Blaya, quoted in Subervi Vélez et al. 1994: 340).

Although natural increase is exceeded by immigration as a cause of growth, it is also important to take into account that US Hispanics tend to be younger, to form households sooner, and to have larger families than the rest of the population. In fact, their rate of increase was seven times that of the general population in the decade to 1990 (Brischetto 1993b: 6–8). These demographic characteristics could be expected to make Hispanics attractive to the marketers of consumer goods and services, and a powerful motive for the establishment of Spanish-language television in the US therefore has been to attract and build a Hispanic audience which could then be commercialized by being 'sold' to such potential advertisers.

Indeed, as Astroff has argued (1997), since the early 1980s at least there has been a discourse about US Hispanics, or, to use the preferred term, Latinos, developed by such 'cultural brokers' as market researchers, advertising agencies, and, by extension, the Spanish-language media. As well as their demographic characteristics, Latinos are said to have several more cultural tendencies inclined to endear them to marketers. To take one instance, they are allegedly 'brand loyal': that is, they establish preferences for well-advertised brands and continue to favour those brands (Adams-Esquivel 1988).

The protagonists of this discourse are themselves Latinos:

> most contemporary Hispanic marketers and audience researchers are US Latinos. Hispanic audience research is constructed by one class of Latinos, college educated and professionally salaried, symbolically reproducing a saleable product out of the 'mass' of US Latinos, more than half of whom have not completed high school, and whose median household income is roughly three quarters that of the general US population. (Rodriguez 1997a)

Thus, the responsible agents who are commercializing the Latino population as the Hispanic market include this elite, as well as the Latin American media moguls and Wall Street finance capitalists who have been running the television networks. This commercialization is happening because in spite of the generally lower socioeconomic indicators for Latinos relative to the mainstream US population, the commercial interests can see that its Latino population makes the US at least the sixth (Strategy Research Corporation 1986: 38), and more likely the fifth (Avila 1997: 40) largest Spanish-speaking country in the world, and, furthermore, the richest, particularly in comparison to Latin America (Rodriguez 1996: 62). 'Hispanics in the United States are the wealthiest Hispanics in the world', as one early study enthused (Guernica and Kasperuk 1982). More recently, the Census Bureau has been tracking the growth of a Hispanic 'middle class', households with an annual income between $US30,000 and $US120,000 (Douglas 1996).

The size and relative wealth of the Latino population in the US has major implications for the continued viability of Spanish-language media there, and for the strategic significance of the US television market within the Spanish-speaking world as a whole. This is a point which Latin American broadcasters were quick to grasp, and which eventually has become recognized by US mainstream programme providers, investors, and also advertisers, as we shall see.

Thus, the Spanish-language television industry has been one of the most active agents and also beneficiaries of the mode of capitalist ethnography with which a Hispanic audience has been constructed for sale to advertisers. For example, it was the Spanish International Network (SIN), the first Spanish-language television network in the US, which commissioned the comprehensive *Spanish USA* report in 1979

(Yankelovich, Skelly, and White 1981). Aided by the decennial censuses, the industry has an interest in the production of 'Hispanics' as a category of persons, not just because it is the 'natural' constituency which it seeks to create for itself as an audience for Spanish-language programming, but because it has had to convince potential advertisers that such an audience exists, and that it is worth their while to spend money with Spanish-language television in order to reach it. It is worth noting that although Spanish-language television's share of all US television advertising is not proportionate to the size of its audience, as will be documented below, and that advertising specifically directed to Latinos is less than 1 per cent of all US advertising expenditure, Spanish-language television takes half of that, with about one-third of it going to the dominant network, Univisión (Avila 1997).

The advertisers have taken some convincing. As will be demonstrated in this chapter, the Spanish-language television industry in the US has had a precarious existence, depending on external subsidization in the case of one network, and the narrow avoidance of bankruptcy in the case of the other. At least in 1992, Nielsen ratings were instituted, and the networks could document the claims which they had been making to the hitherto sceptical large national advertisers. Yet even five years after this, Spanish-language television had not been able to achieve a share of total television advertising expenditure in proportion to its audience: although it was attracting 4 per cent of viewers, it was receiving only 1.7 per cent of all television advertising revenue (Alex Brown and Sons 1997). Nevertheless, in spite of this disproportionate share, the value of advertising on Spanish-language television has increased at a rate of 11 per cent each year since 1990, compared to 4 per cent for all broadcast television advertising (Merrill Lynch 1997). Furthermore, while the size of the mainstream viewing population remains fairly static, the audience for Spanish-language television has continued to grow (Coe 1995: 46).

At no stage to date have advertisers directed the development of US Spanish-language television: as in Latin America, it has been the initiative of particular entrepreneurs, in this case both Mexican and US, which has formed Hispanics into a television audience, in anticipation of being able to sell this audience to advertisers as a market. It has been an audience difficult to sell, although the roll-call of national advertisers on Spanish-language television now looks much the same as that of the biggest advertisers overall in the US: the major retailers, and all the prominent food and drink, automobile, and cleaning products transnational corporations, are there (Zate 1996). In 1996, seven of the top ten advertisers at both networks were the same: Procter & Gamble, AT&T,

Sears, McDonald's, Anheuser-Busch, Ford, and Colgate-Palmolive (Mendosa 1996a).

Through SICC and SIN

Television broadcasting for a Spanish-speaking minority in the US did not spring up from nothing, but, as in Latin America and elsewhere, it was built up from the institutional and industrial base already laid down by radio. It is worth remembering that most of the south-western US, where much of the Spanish-language population, particularly that of Mexican origin, is concentrated today, was part of Mexico until 1848. Thus, even before radio, there were newspapers which dated back to that time. Spanish-speaking radio began in the 1920s with immigrant radio producers broking time on mainstream stations, but did not become established until the 1930s, by which time Emilio Azcárraga Vidaurreta, the progenitor of Televisa, was broadcasting across the border from his Mexican stations, and relaying programmes within the US by arrangement with a station in Los Angeles (Rodriguez 1997b). This began a long involvement by the Azcárraga dynasty in the development of Spanish-language broadcasting in the US, and established the model whereby entertainment programming generated for a commercial audience in Mexico, and already paid for and proven there, could do double service by attracting a culturally and linguistically similar audience on the other side of the border.

However, Azcárraga's move to broadcasting from within the US itself did not happen until the days of television. As it happened, the first Spanish-language television station in the US was not established by Azcárraga, but by a US Latino, Raúl Cortez, who opened up Channel 41 in San Antonio, Texas, on the newly created UHF (ultra high frequency) band in 1955. This venture was based on his experience with his radio station KCOR, which had been the first full-time, Latino-owned, Spanish-language station in the US. However, Cortez found programming costs could not be matched by advertiser support, and sold Channel 41. It was subsequently acquired in 1961 by the Spanish International Communication Corporation (SICC) (Subervi Vélez et al. 1994: 335–6; Rodriguez 1997b).

SICC was the corporate vehicle through which Azcárraga built up his chain of stations in the US. Like most countries, the US restricts broadcast station ownership to its own citizens. Under Section 310b of the Communication Act, 'aliens' or persons acting for them cannot control more than 20 per cent of the stock in a television station, although the ownership of the networks which supply programmes to and sell advertising time for the stations is not so restricted (Gutiérrez 1979: 141–4). For this reason, the fact that Spanish-language television in the US for its first twenty-five years was a virtual extension of Mexico's predominant network, and run from there, had to be concealed behind a legal fiction. Azcárraga had 20 per cent of SICC, with the other stockholders being employees or associates who were US citizens. Notable amongst them was Rene Anselmo, a US citizen of Italian and Chilean parentage from Boston, and a graduate of the University of Chicago, who had been working for Telesistemo Mexicano (TSM), Azcárraga's network in Mexico, in charge of the export marketing arm which Azcárraga set up for it in 1954, Teleprogramas de México (Gutiérrez and Schement 1984: 243; Subervi Vélez et al. 1994: 335; Cosper 1995).

Anselmo was to become *prestanombre* (borrowed name) for the Azcárragas in the US for the next twenty-five years, after which he would lead the sometime joint venture with Televisa, PanAmSat, the world's first private international satellite system. Other shareholders in SICC included Edward Noble, owner of an advertising agency active in Mexico and Central America; the Frank Fouces, both father and son, who owned a chain of Spanish-language cinemas in Los Angeles; and Raúl Cortez, former owner of the San Antonio station (Bagamery 1982; Maza 1986: 22).

Anselmo had first tried to sell TSM's programmes to the major US networks, but had been rebuffed with their view that such specialized 'ghetto time' programming was not appropriate to the mass medium which they then saw television exclusively to be (de Uriarte 1980; Bagamery 1982). The acquisition of the station in San Antonio represented Azcárraga's strategy in response: to distribute TSM programmes via his own niche network in the US. Thus, at the same time, the Spanish International Network (SIN) was created as the network management vehicle, wholly owned by Azcárraga, which was there to supply the stations with programmes and sell time to advertisers (Maza 1986: 20).

San Antonio is the oldest Mexican-American city, and one of the largest, currently seventh on the list of what marketers now call DMAs (dominant market areas) for Hispanics (Zate 1996). Stations in other major cities on that list also were acquired by SICC over the next decade: KMEX Channel 34 in Los Angeles in 1962; WXTV Channel 41 in New York in 1968; and WLTV Channel 23 in Miami in 1971. In the 1970s, two stations in California (Fresno and San Francisco) were added, then one in Phoenix, through related companies. As well, affiliates were established at that time in Albuquerque, Chicago, Corpus Christi,

Houston, and Sacramento. Prior to 1976, programmes would be physically transported from Mexico to Los Angeles, then 'bicycled' to San Antonio and all these other stations in SICC (Subervi Vélez et al. 1994: 336).

Rene Anselmo was made President of both SICC and SIN, although he was paid by SIN and Teleprogramas de México, the arm of TSM in Mexico which he had headed, and which was the corporate vehicle through which TSM supplied SIN with most of the programmes shown on the SICC stations. In 1971 he was given 25 per cent of SIN in recognition of the role he had played over its first decade. With the death of Emilio Azcárraga Vidaurreta, his succession by Emilio Azcárraga Milmo, and the creation of Televisa at the end of 1972, the new Televisa export entity Protele became the programme conduit, and SICC and SIN underwent some consolidation, notably amongst the various related companies under the SICC umbrella (Maza 1986: 22; Valenzuela 1986: 330–1).

However, it should not be assumed that the arrangements between TSM/Televisa and SICC/SIN were profitable. On the contrary, even though it controlled both programme supply and advertising sales, SIN did not make a profit for its first seven years, nor was it paying for the programmes it was receiving from Mexico. In effect, the Azcárragas had been heavily subsidizing their US operations through allowing them to run up debts and continuously deferring the payments due for programming (Valenzuela 1986: 330). When, at the end of 1975, the debt was approaching $ 2 million, the Televisa partners pressured Azcárraga to demand that it be settled. However, the share issue with which Anselmo was authorized to achieve this caused a rift with the younger Frank Fouce, by this time the Chairman and majority stockholder in SICC. Fouce brought a civil suit against Anselmo and SICC, charging them with breach of fiduciary duty, self-dealing, and mismanagement (Critser 1987: 28).

Over the next ten years, the Fouce action brought the relationship between SICC and SIN and the Azcárragas into the open, triggering a further legal action which brought them under investigation by the US broadcast regulatory agency, the Federal Communications Commission (FCC). If the FCC had been turning a blind eye to the real state of ownership of Spanish-language television in the US, it could no longer after 1980, when the Spanish Radio Broadcasters' Association, a since defunct Latino media interest group, filed a charge that SICC was under foreign control (Critser 1987; Wilkinson 1991). These and other legal suits, but particularly the FCC investigation, brought to light the whole corporate culture of SICC/SIN, which, in the words of one former employee, was like 'the Mexican feudal system' (quoted in Critser 1987: 28).

This is a reference to the peculiarities of the Azcárragas' management style, perpetuated by Anselmo, of dealing with associates and employees within a system of personal obligations created through loans and gifts. More damaging were revelations of how SIN had eventually achieved its profitability at SICC's expense, through its control of the pricing structure for programmes, and by billing SICC for more programmes than actually were supplied (Gutiérrez 1979: 145–7; Critser 1987: 28–9).

Yet in the same decade through which the court actions dragged on, SICC/SIN built itself into a truly national network through astute application of new signal distribution technologies as they became available. Already an innovator with its use of the UHF band, SICC/SIN's greatest technological distinction was in 1976, when it fully interconnected all its stations and affiliates via satellite so that they could air the same programming at the same time—programming which itself was being transmitted via satellite from Mexico on a weekly basis. This put SICC/SIN ahead of the mainstream networks, ABC, CBS, and NBC, in being the first network to be fully interconnected via satellite. On the other hand, SICC/SIN was pleased to follow the commercial practice of the mainstream networks in the following year when it instituted a 'must carry' regime with its affiliates. This meant that instead of SICC paying SIN for receiving bicycled (physically transported) programmes, SIN began paying the SICC stations, as a national network, to carry the by then daily satellite feed, including commercials, transmitted from Mexico. This early satellite link arrangement was named Univisión, a name Televisa continued to use later for a venture which aimed to extend its reach into Latin America, and so create an intercontinental audience for sale to transnational advertisers, but the first Univisión was subsequently abandoned with the Mexican currency crisis of 1982 (de Noriega and Leach 1979: 59; Gutiérrez and Schement 1981; Maza 1986: 24; Valenzuela 1986: 332).

In 1979, SIN also began to pay cable franchise operators, at the rate of 10 cents for every subscriber with a Spanish surname, to carry its satellite feed, thus adding cable distribution to its network. Then, after 1981 when it secured FCC approval to develop LPTV (low power television—stations with a radius of up to 20 kilometres), it was able to add such stations to the network in several smaller cities across the US. Thus, neither the size of the communities reached nor their distance apart mattered, as satellite coverage (whether received by broadcast, cable, or LPTV) meant that they could be reached, formed, and sold to advertisers as a national audience. Together, the commerciotechnical innovations allowed SICC/SIN to cover the vast majority of the US Spanish-speaking population by the end of 1983 (Valenzuela 1986: 332–3; Subervi Vélez et al. 1994: 337).

Thus, by 1986, when the legal actions concluded with SIN being obliged to sell off its stations to US interests, it could claim 409 outlets reaching 82 per cent of Hispanic households, or 15 million viewers (Univisión 1987). Furthermore, the impact of national networking on advertising revenues had been spectacular: from $US6 million in 1977, to $US10 million in 1978, then $US20 million in 1980, rising to over $US32 million in 1983 (Valenzuela 1986: 334). However, an FCC-appointed judge had determined that Anselmo was 'the representative of aliens' (quoted in Wilkinson 1995: 145), and that SICC was thus in breach of the foreign ownership provision. He ordered that the licences of thirteen SICC stations therefore should not be renewed, and were to be transferred to US owners. This put SICC 'in play' amongst a number of bidders, some of them Latino, but notably also mainstream (sometimes referred to, misleadingly, as 'Anglo') interests who had become alerted to the value of a Spanish-language national network.

Into the Mainstream

The divestment and sale of the SICC stations marked the end of a long period in which the Mexicans had been able to develop a television network in the US without either regulators or commercial competitors caring much what they were doing, though it also showed the ultimately self-destructive consequences of their monopolistic, centralized, and patronal style of management. Above all, the legal decision and its timing meant that Spanish-language television had become too much of a potentially profitable business to be left to aliens and Latinos: it was moving uptown from the ghetto, delivered by the FCC to the corporate mainstream of industrial and financial capital.

Yet it was not as if mainstream corporate interests had not become aware of Spanish-language television as a business prior to the outcome of the SICC/SIN court cases in 1986, nor even that SICC had had a total monopoly of the Spanish-language television market. Already in the previous year, Saul Steinberg and Henry Silverman of Reliance Capital, part of a Wall Street investment group, had bought an independent station in Los Angeles. Under the name KVEA and managed by Joe Wallach, a former executive with TV Globo in Brazil, it soon built up enough of an audience to encourage Steinberg and Silverman to look for more stations. They went on to buy John Blair and Company, which owned Spanish-language television stations in Puerto Rico and Miami, and then WNJU, a New York station owned by Norman Lear in partnership with A. Jerrold Perenchio and run by Carlos Barba, which was at the centre of a loose cooperative arrangement of Spanish-language independents called Netspan. Other stations and affiliates were acquired in Chicago, San Francisco, and elsewhere, all of which Reliance developed into a major competitor to SICC/SIN in the form of the Telemundo network (Sinclair 1990: 48; Subervi Vélez et al. 1994: 341–3).

The FCC-appointed judge's decision against SICC/SIN in January 1986 launched a number of appeals and a bidding competition, in which Reliance joined other mainstream bidders, including an associate of Azcárraga, John Gavin; producers Norman Lear and A. Jerrold Perenchio; and Hallmark Cards, acting with a 25 per cent partner, First Capital Corporation of Chicago. The Hallmark Cards/First Capital bid of $US301.5 million was the one which the court's sale committee accepted. In spite of their having no experience with Spanish-language television, the greeting card/financial services consortium's bid eventually won out over a higher bid from a Latino group, TVL Corporation, because the Hallmark bid was considered more financially sound. Furthermore, it was considered as a 'friendly' bid, unlike that of Reliance, because Azcárraga had been able to negotiate terms with the bidders.

These included an arrangement under which the SIN network would continue to operate in the immediate term, supplying programmes to its former stations for the first two years, during which time SIN was to take 37.5 per cent of the stations' income, and the stations would retain their existing management. This gave the new owners an established source of programming, at the same time as it enabled Azcárraga to minimize the disastrous impact which a hostile bidder might otherwise have wreaked upon the market which he had built up for Televisa's programming in the US. The decision to award the stations to Hallmark was contested by some of the unsuccessful bidders, and by Latino organizations concerned that Spanish-language television was being taken over by the mainstream, but although all these problems were not finally resolved until 1991, they did not prevent the FCC from giving immediate effect to the sale (Sinclair 1990: 48–9; Wilkinson 1991: 41–51; Subervi Vélez et al. 1994: 338–9).

Over the next year, Hallmark went on to acquire more of the former SICC stations, those that had not been included in the divestment deal, and in February 1988 also bought the SIN network itself. By that stage, SIN was fully owned by Televisa, since Anselmo's business interests had been separated out from Televisa in the sidewash from the court decision, though both the former SICC stations and the SIN network were known as Univisión (not to be confused with the intercontinental venture of the same name abandoned by Televisa in 1982, nor with Univisa, the name which Televisa chose for its reconstituted interests in the US after the divestment). Presumably, without the integration of the stations with the network, and knowing how in the past the network had been made profitable at the expense of the stations, Televisa soon formed the view that there was no value in hanging on to just the network. Thus, a new deal was negotiated under which Televisa could continue to derive several of the benefits which it had previously enjoyed through integrated ownership: Hallmark Cards Inc., as the new owner of the Univisión network, would have first option on Televisa-produced programmes for the following ten years, giving Televisa a secure long-term distribution outlet; and Televisa would have free advertising time on the Univisión stations for all its products and services (Sinclair 1990: 55; Subervi Vélez et al. 1994: 339).

As well as being obliged to sell its stations and ultimately its network, Televisa was having to absorb the shock of a more competitive market emerging in which it was no longer good enough to treat the audience as a mere extension of Mexico. This was brought home in 'the Zabludovsky affair'. It should be explained that news always had been a weakness in Televisa's practice of transmitting programming direct from Mexico, because of the close relationship which Televisa had with the Mexican Government and ruling party, as was discussed in Chapter 2, which was seen to compromise its credibility. To its credit, SIN had recognized the resistance which Mexican-Americans as well as other kinds of US Hispanics, notably Cuban-Americans, showed towards Mexican news and current affairs programmes, and in 1981 established its own US-based news programme, *Noticiero Nacional SIN*, to replace the programme previously fed directly from Mexico, *24 Horas*. The US service was being run out of Miami by a professionally respected team of journalists under the directorship of a Cuban-American, Gustavo Godoy.

Immediately following the sale of the SICC stations, Azcárraga came to the US in order to take charge of the crisis in Televisa's international activities. One of his strategies was to attempt to integrate the *Noticiero Nacional SIN* staff into the international Spanish-language news service ECO (Empresa de Comunicaciones Orbital) initiative which he was mounting at that stage. However, his mistake was to bring in Jacobo Zabludovsky to do it. Zabludovsky is a Televisa executive, but best known as the anchor of *24 Horas* over its many years, in which role he is the person most closely identified with Televisa's political partisanship.

Accordingly, there were strong protests from viewers, and Godoy and half of the *Noticiero Nacional SIN* staff resigned. Within six months, Zabludovsky was returned to Mexico; the SIN service was renamed *Noticiero Nacional Univisión* and relocated to Los Angeles under a new director; and Godoy and his colleagues, as the Hispanic American Broadcasting Company, were producing *Noticiero Telemundo*, a news programme for the competing network, Telemundo, in Miami (Marín 1986; Sinclair 1990: 46–7).

The Zabludovsky affair showed up Azcárraga's insensitivity to the different political and cultural formation of US Latinos, expecting that a very Mexican solution would do to solve a problem in the US, but it also was indicative of the changing composition of the US Hispanic population over the 1960s and 1970s. The relatively greater numbers of Cubans and Puerto Ricans on the East Coast, particularly in Miami and New York, made for a more heterogeneous, less captive audience than the traditional Mexican-origin population of the Southwest. It was not as if SICC/SIN had been oblivious to the differences within the total target audience, but its economics were such that it had an interest in glossing over them. Thus, while Anselmo could declare that his 'mission' had been 'to unite the Puerto Rican in New York, the Cuban in Miami, the Mexican in San Antonio and the Chicano in Los Angeles through their common Spanish heritage' (quoted in Bagamery 1982: 99), clearly SICC/SIN had sought to do that on the basis of the predominantly Mexican programming to which they had access. When Hallmark became the owners of the new Univisión, as the name implies, they too sought to play down the differences within their potential audience with a consensual approach that they called 'Walter Cronkite Spanish', a mode of address and house style of programming which minimized national cultural and linguistic differences (Univisión 1987).

It was in this context of the dubious hegemony which Mexican programming was claiming over the Hispanic audience as a whole that the Telemundo network emerged and, for a time, initiated a competition for audience share on the basis of programming it was producing specifically for US Latinos. Telemundo's New York capital backing and Puerto Rican connections perhaps gave it more of an orientation towards East Coast Latinos, or, at least, less of a vested interest in providing imported programming from one major source. Just as audiences in most countries of the world will be responsive to programming which expresses their own culture, many US Latinos turned on to Telemundo's news service already mentioned, *Noticiero Telemundo*, which began in 1987, and, in the following year, *MTV Internacional*, based on the Viacom youth music channel, as well as a *telenovela* which combined Mexican, Puerto Rican, and Cuban immigrant families into the one narrative (Subervi Vélez et al. 1994: 343).

Under Hallmark's ownership and with Chilean-born former SICC executive Joaquín Blaya as President, Univisión also became involved in domestic US production. Blaya's approach was to adapt US formats into Spanish, his most notable successes being a three-hour Saturday-night variety show, *Sábado Gigante*, and an *Oprah*-style talk show, *Cristina*. In his time at Univisión, Blaya lifted the percentage of domestic programming from 6 per cent in 1987, its level when he joined, to 44 per cent in 1992, when he left to head up Telemundo, largely because of this local production issue. At that time, however, Telemundo was still ahead, with 55 per cent domestic production, most of which was coming out of the extensive studios near Miami which it acquired in 1988, as well as from its Los Angeles and Puerto Rico stations. Significantly, Univisión also shifted its production activities to Miami in 1991, leaving its former owner to consolidate its operations in Los Angeles as Univisa (Coto 1991; '"Foreign Programs Work Fine for Us", Rival Says' 1993; 'Network is Pushing its Domestic Identity' 1993; Subervi Vélez et al. 1994: 344). These moves have consolidated Miami as the media centre both of the Spanish-speaking US and of Latin America (Shackelford 1995). As one executive has it, 'Miami is the capital of Latin America' (quoted in Whitefield 1997: 21).

Because ratings measurement at this stage was unreliable, it is difficult to assess the relative preference which audiences might have shown for domestic over imported programmes, or the claims made by the networks at that time, such as Telemundo's assertion that even audiences of Mexican origin preferred US-produced programmes. What is clear is that, regardless of audience response, the networks found themselves in a war of attrition so far as the business side was concerned. The high costs of US domestic production, between $US13,000 and $US24,000 per hour, could not be recouped at the level at which advertisers were prepared to pay for commercial spots: a maximum of $US6,500, but more typically $US2,000, and down to as little as $US100. At this rate, both networks were making heavy losses (Besas 1990). One response was to attempt to export programmes to other countries in the region, the proven Televisa tactic, but although Univisión had some success in this regard, with satellite transmission of *Sábado Gigante* in particular, Telemundo found it more difficult. One reason for this was that some of its most successful programmes were being produced in conjunction with US companies such as CNN (Cable News Network) and MTV (Music Television), who not only controlled the foreign licences but were themselves interested in becoming established in Latin America, thus capitalizing on their Spanish-language ventures in the US (Silva 1991).

Indeed, just as the investment of Hallmark in Univisión and of Reliance in Telemundo had marked an influx of mainstream capital to the US Spanish-language television industry at the national level over this period, at the international level, from the end of the 1980s onwards, there developed a corresponding move by US cable channels into Latin American markets. CNN showed an early interest in exploiting the linkage between US Hispanic television and Latin American cable markets, first with dubbed entertainment programming, and subsequently with a news service in Spanish. This was *Noticiero Telemundo-CNN*, which, from May 1988, it produced for Telemundo to broadcast in the US, since the *Noticiero Telemundo* formerly produced by Godoy's company in Miami had proved too costly. When CNN opened a satellite-to-cable channel for Latin America in January 1989, *Noticiero Telemundo-CNN* became part of the service (Wilkinson 1992: 16 and 26).

Also attracted by the prospect of building up the demand for cable in the region, another US channel to begin a service to Latin America in these early days was ESPN (Entertainment and Sports Programming Network). Following a decade of rapid expansion in the US, it began satellite transmission of its ESPN International Network to cable systems in six nations of South America in April 1989, although a Spanish-language soundtrack was not added until 1991. Also in 1989, the Time-Warner premium cable channels HBO (Home Box Office) and Cinemax began to offer 'Selecciones', a special Spanish-language audio track option on particular programmes for interested subscribers in the US. By the end of 1991, it had launched a full channel for Latin America, HBO Olé, in conjunction with a Venezuelan partner, Omnivisión ('HBO Plans Pay TV Launch in Latin America' 1991; Wilkinson 1992: 13–15). As will be shown in the next section, US companies in satellite service provision have since joined these and the several other US programme providers now active in Latin America. Some of the new Spanish-language services were readily created by using secondary audio programme (SAP) technology: specifically, the provision of a Spanish-language soundtrack (Haley 1997: 42), easily accommodated on the new generation of satellites with their multiple channels.

However, before moving on to the present era, it remains to take account of how Televisa dealt with its exclusion from US Spanish-language television broadcasting during the years in which Hallmark was running Univisión. It was noted how Televisa was continuing to supply programming to Univisión through one of its subsidiaries grouped in Los Angeles under the Univisa umbrella. As well as the programme division, Protele, managed by Marcel Vinay, Univisa included video manufacturing and distribution companies, and a cable television network, Galavisión. The whole operation was under the control of Fernando Diez Barroso, Azcárraga's son-in-law. As soon as the two-year non-competitive clause in the sales contract with Hallmark expired, Univisa relaunched Galavisión. This had begun as a premium subscription cable service in 1979, but it had only ever attracted a small number of subscribers—160,000 by 1988. In that year, Univisa began to accept advertising on Galavisión, and to convert it to a basic cable service: that is, cable subscribers would receive it as part of their basic package of channels with no additional premium. This move enlarged the number of at least nominal subscribers to 2 million ('Galavisión Makes Bid for the TV Pie' 1990; Subervi Vélez et al. 1994: 345).

As well, several broadcast stations were affiliated to form Galavisión into a regional free-to-air network, concentrating on the south-western states where most Latinos are of Mexican origin, and offering a modified version of programming from Televisa's most popular channel in Mexico. Televisa's output is so great that it could do this without compromising its ongoing programming supply deal with Univisión (Arrarte 1990). At a later stage, in 1992, Galavisión was to incorporate Televisa's international Spanish-language news service ECO, to provide a stream of programming that was transmitted via satellite throughout Latin America and across to Europe (Subervi Vélez et al. 1994: 346). Thus, more than just a means of compensating for the loss of its former network in the US, Galavisión became a key link in Televisa's internationalization strategies.

One other major strategic business connected to Televisa and integral to its internationalization was also building strength from its US base over this period: PanAmSat. Although it had had its initial impetus in the politics of satellite development in Mexico, as was noted in Chapter 2, PanAmSat had come into existence only through Azcárraga having connections in the US, and it was a US company. As the world's first privately owned international satellite system ever authorized to compete with Intelsat, the intergovernmental agency under which all international satellite development had hitherto taken place, PanAmSat has been of enormous significance, both for the spread of Televisa's international activities, and for the US cable channels mentioned above that have entered Latin America, carried by PanAmSat, but also for the globalization of television more generally.

In response to a number of applications, the US had opened the way for commercial competitors to Intelsat in November 1984, a move then explained as 'required in the national interest'. Proposals had to be assented to by the President, at that time Ronald Reagan, whose initiative this was. PanAmSat's proposal, lodged in May, was for a satellite to serve both North and South America. The company listed Rene Anselmo as chair, and other SICC/SIN associates as directors (Valenzuela 1986: 329 and 335). This followed the stage at which SICC/SIN had achieved interconnection of its US network via satellite, and although Televisa had abandoned the former intercontinental project called Univisión in 1982, the prospect of having a private international satellite would have seemed to give it attractive new opportunities for commercializing the hemisphere with its programming. There was speculation at the time that John Gavin, the former US ambassador to Mexico and both a friend of Azcárraga and a member of Reagan's inner circle, had been influential in securing the subsequent presidential decision in favour of PanAmSat. Gavin later was to become President of Univisa's satellite division (Fernández Christlieb 1987).

However the decision was made, PanAmSat and its 'end-to-end' operating company Alpha Lyracom (incorporated in Greenwich, Connecticut) also received the subsequent FCC approval in 1987 to launch its PAS1 'Simøn Bolívar' satellite early in 1988. It thus became the only one of the five original proposals to be realized, and in spite of resistance from Intelsat and initial doubts about the financial substance of the company ('FCC Gives OK to Private Satellite Launch' 1987; Goldschmidt 1988: 393–5). At first Peru was the only Latin American country to be coordinated with PanAmSat, but agreements were subsequently concluded with eighteen countries, both in Europe and Latin America, giving it transatlantic as well as pan-American coverage ('Separate Systems: New Era for Global Communications' 1989).

Yet by that time, SICC and SIN had been sold to Hallmark, and the FCC had forbidden Anselmo to engage in any business dealings with his former mentor Azcárraga. Furthermore, in the course of the divestment proceedings, Anselmo and Azcárraga had fallen out: Anselmo had wanted to diminish Televisa's holding in conformity with the law, while Azcárraga had decided to let the stations go to a friendly bidder, rather than permit Televisa's interest in them to be diluted. Azcárraga then sacked Anselmo, and bought out his 25 per cent share of SIN. Anselmo in turn invested the proceeds in PanAmSat, thus overcoming the barrier of FCC concerns about its financial viability, and committed himself to the development of PanAmSat as an independent venture (Klink 1987; Maza 1987; Cardenas 1993; Cosper 1995).

Restructure and Global Integration

Spanish-language television in the US entered a new phase in the quincentennial year of 1992, marked by the sale of Univisión, bankruptcy at Telemundo, and the implementation of Nielsen audience measurement for this sector of the industry. The sale of Univisión was distinguished not so much by Hallmark's exit as such, but by the return of Televisa, which, in conjunction with partners from the US and Latin America, reintegrated Univisión into its international strategies. Closely watched by the FCC, and over the protests of Latino social activists, Televisa this time was careful to keep its participation in Univisión within the bounds of ownership regulation. The majority owner was A. Jerrold (Jerry) Perenchio, the Hollywood producer who also had owned Spanish-language stations in the past, as has been noted, and who in fact had been one of the unsuccessful bidders for the old SICC/ SIN when those operations had been acquired by Hallmark. Ownership of the new Univisión was structured so that Perenchio had 50 per cent of Univisión Network Partnership, and 76 per cent of Univisión Television Group, which was the actual stations. Televisa had 25 per cent and 12 per cent respectively, the remaining share being held by Venevisión, which is Televisa's counterpart in Venezuela, owned by the Cisneros Grupo de Companías (CGC) of Caracas, and directed by Gustavo Cisneros. The sale was announced in April and concluded in December, with Hallmark receiving a net $US509 million for the whole operation, compared to the total of $US748 million it has been estimated to have lost, including its annual losses as well as all outlays. It was a 'highly leveraged' transaction: that is, mainly financed through borrowing (Mendosa 1992: 26; 'The Secrets behind Univisión's Sale' 1993; Subervi Vélez et al. 1994: 348–9).

For both Televisa and Venevisión, the attraction of acquiring an effective share in Univisión was not just the base it offered them in the US market, but also the outlet it made for their programmes, as had been in place previously with Televisa's relation to SICC/SIN. The flow of programmes from Mexico and Venezuela would minimize costs, enabling the Latin networks to meet the debts incurred in the purchase as well as earn royalties (actually 15 per cent of Univisión's advertising revenue) for their home companies. The return of Televisa to the US was signalled by the appointment of Jaime Dávila as CEO of Univisión Network Partnership, with former Univisión CEO Ray Rodriguez as President and COO (Chief Operating Officer), reporting to Dávila. True to his reputation as a hatchet-man for Azcárraga, Dávila set about sacking staff, mostly those involved in Univisión's own productions, and prompting fears amongst Latino groups that Televisa and Venevisión planned to drive out local production in favour of their own programmes. Indeed, this was one key factor which prompted Joaquín Blaya, the former President of Univisión who had been responsible for fostering US production there, to resign and cross over to take up the leadership of Telemundo as CEO (Lopes 1993). Another reason was that his own management buyout offer had been refused (Mendosa 1992).

Executive appointments at Univisión Television Group were Perenchio as Chair and CEO, with Carlos Barba as President and COO. Barba was a Cuban-American who had first worked for the Cisneros family in Venezuela and most recently for their international distributor, Venevisión International. He also had had experience with Univisión's opposition network, having been with Telemundo from 1986 to 1991, and had worked for Perenchio in New York prior to that. He had been instrumental in bringing together Azcárraga, Perenchio, and the Cisneros brothers, Gustavo and Ricardo, and brokering the deal under which Univisión had been acquired by them (Mendosa 1992; 1993a; Lopes 1993).

For its part, Telemundo's financial situation had become so bad that in 1992, it could no longer keep up payments on its debt and went into default. Founding owner Saul Steinberg was unable to develop a restructuring plan before creditors forced the company into formal 'Chapter 11' bankruptcy. This brought in Steinberg's financial backers, Leon Black and Arthur Bilger, the principals of a Los Angeles-based investment company which was Telemundo's largest creditor, Apollo Advisers. Steinberg's companies agreed to surrender all but 3 per cent of their interest in Telemundo in return for a \$US207 million reduction of their debt, an 'equity for debt' solution (Mendosa 1993b).

However, because Apollo was backed in turn by Crédit Lyonnais, Europe's largest bank, and because FCC regulations restrict foreign ownership of television stations to 25 per cent, it was necessary to bring in also Bastion Capital, which took up a 9.4 per cent interest. One of the partners in Bastion was Daniel Villanueva, who had had a long career in Spanish-language television management. This included an extended time with SICC/SIN, where he had become associated with Joaquín Blaya, the new Telemundo CEO who had left Univisión when the new owners reverted to their imported programming.

By the time it was ready for FCC approval at the end of 1994, Telemundo was a public company, but controlled by Apollo and Bastion together, with Steinberg's companies regaining 17.5 per cent of the reorganized company's stock (Mendosa 1994). Thus, while Univisión had regained its links with Latin American interests in its change of ownership, notably Televisa, Telemundo was still under the control of mainstream finance capital, now from both coasts of the US, with Black as Chair. A Latino connection had been established, however, through Villanueva and his partner in Bastion (Mendosa 1996b).

In the same period as these changes in ownership were taking place, another major transition was being made with the establishment of a ratings service for Spanish-language television. Prior to this, the network owners had not been able to provide the figures needed to convince potential advertisers of the nature and extent of Spanish-language television's reach. This had been a major disadvantage in their competition, not with each other, but with the mainstream networks, because many national advertisers believed that it was sufficient to advertise with the mainstream networks alone, particularly if the audiences for Spanish-language television were unknown.

So, in order to provide the hard data needed to sell the Hispanic audience which they had created to the major advertisers whom they sought, both the Spanish-language networks collaborated in commissioning Nielsen Media Research, the major US audience measurement company, to set up a ratings measurement service for Spanish-language television. This became the Nielsen Hispanic Television Index, involving an investment of $US38.5 million, and an extensive pilot study in Los Angeles, by far the largest 'DMA' (dominant market area) in the US for Hispanics. The first national figures were produced in October and November of 1992, and documented Univisión's commanding position, with 16 of the 20 most popular programmes (Lopes 1993: 32), and an overall 61 per cent share of the prime-time audience (Mendosa 1993b).

In the ratings war that ensued, Telemundo continued to lose ground steadily. In 1993–4, it could sustain a total audience share of around 40 per cent, but by the second half of 1996, it had settled at 23 per cent (Mendosa 1996a; Avila 1997). In spite of Telemundo's former successes with US-produced programming and CEO Joaquín Blaya's commitment to it, Telemundo has never been able to compete with Univisión in the crucial 7–9 p.m. time slot. Blaya has conceded that this was 'directly attributable to our lack of access to Mexican telenovelas' (quoted in Coe 1995: 48). That is because Televisa dominates all Mexican television production. More generally, in fact, Telemundo is unable to obtain material from either the world's largest or even its second largest producer of Spanish-language programming, because they are its competitors: Televisa and Venevisión (Avila 1997: 42).

The solution attempted was a co-production arrangement with TV Azteca under which TV Azteca would produce up to four telenovelas a year at its new Azteca Digital facility in Mexico, with the costs and distribution rights shared. This gave Telemundo its access to Mexican *telenovelas*, and at a slightly reduced cost compared to that little which was available on the open market, but these *telenovelas* in fact have not been successful against those of Univisión (Alex Brown and Sons 1997). Another fruitless programming initiative was a joint venture for a twenty-four-hour news cable channel, TeleNoticias, with Reuters of the UK, Antena 3 TV of Spain, and Artear of Argentina. This was commenced at the end of 1994, but by June 1996 had been sold to CBS, the major broadcast network now owned by Westinghouse Electric, in the wake of ownership deregulation brought in by the Telecommunications Act of that year (Mendosa 1994: 60; 1996*b*: 41).

By August 1997, Telemundo's market share had fallen to 18 per cent, and the company announced that it was engaging an investment bank, Lazard Freres and Company, to help it find 'strategic programming partners'. Business analysts interpreted this to mean that Telemundo was in fact in play and looking for a major investment partner, or offering itself for a takeover. The asking price was $US600 million. All the major US broadcasting networks showed interest, in anticipation of deregulation of restrictions on their ownership of UHF stations, and also Fox and Sony, both of whom would have been able to integrate Telemundo into their wider activities in the Latin American region (Margolis 1997; McClellan 1997). Thus, in spite of its continual losses and dismal performance against Univisión, Telemundo is still seen as attractive to such investors because of the now-measurable growth in the size and value of the Spanish-language television market, in conjunction with recent ownership deregulation within the US, and because some of them are well placed to make strategic use of such a network within their regional or global plans.

In both historical and structural terms, it was the strategic link with Mexico which enabled Spanish-language television to become

Table 6. Univisión versus Telemundo, 1997

	Univisión	Telemundo
Number of owned and operated stations	12 full-power; 7 low-power, plus affiliates	7 full-power; 13 low-power, plus affiliates
Coverage of market	92%	85%
In-house production	94%	40%
Share of market	77%	23%

Source: Alex Brown and Sons 1997; Merrill Lynch Capital Markets 1997; Avila 1997.

established and built into a national network in the first instance, as this chapter has demonstrated. Conversely, Telemundo's lack of such an external connection, apart from its Puerto Rican station, is the principal explanation for its lack of success, particularly in terms of access to programming. Thus, even though the Spanish-language television market in the US has become more commercially attractive to mainstream investors, advertisers, and networks, it appears to reach its greatest value when it can be integrated into other television ventures outside the US. This seems to hold true both for Televisa's stake in having some kind of assured US distribution for its Mexican production, regardless of its level of ownership of the outlet, as well as for those US cable services which have turned their products for US Hispanics into services for the whole Latin American region, such as Viacom's MTV Latino (Brown 1995).

With this hypothesis in mind, the chapter will conclude by looking first of all at how Televisa is now conducting its business in the US, and then at the most recent moves made on the Latin American market by US satellite, cable, and network companies, and the implications which this regional and ultimately global integration has for the US domestic market.

It might be recalled from Chapter 2 that Televisa's interest in Univisión was diluted to 19.9 per cent in the process of the corporate reorganization and public float of September 1996. What remains crucial for Televisa is not its level of ownership as such, but its capacity to ensure that Univisión continues to provide it with an extensive distribution outlet for its programming. There seems no doubt that it is achieving this. Televisa has a programming arrangement with Univisión under which Univisión has first option over all Televisa (and Venevisión) programmes in exchange for which the Latin partners have been receiving first 9.4, then 13.5, and ultimately 15 per cent of Univisión's advertising revenue. This arrangement, which is meant to prevail until 2017, is actually benefiting Televisa more than Venevisión, because more than half Univisión's programming comes from Televisa, given the preponderance of Mexican-Americans in the US Latino population (Merrill Lynch Capital Markets 1997; Paxman 1997). Furthermore, from a level around 55 per cent of imported programming, when Perenchio and the Latin partners acquired Univisión in 1992, within five years the amount reached 94 per cent (Avila 1997: 40), realizing the worst fears of the US Latinos who had opposed the sale at the time (Andrews 1992), yet gaining even more market share in the subsequent ratings war against Telemundo, as we have seen.

There was a potential conflict between Televisa and Univisión at the time of the acquisition of the latter from Hallmark. As was noted in the previous section, Televisa's US subsidiary at that time, Univisa, had been building up a broadcast network from their formerly cable-only service, Galavisión, and in the same DMAs as Univisión. With Televisa once more a partner in Univisión, the conflict was avoided by Galavisión being converted back to cable-only (Mendosa 1992: 24). Galavisión was subscribed to by 1.5 million Hispanic households at the time of the acquisition (Mendosa 1994; Brown 1995). It continued to expand as a cable-only service under Univisión management, with new channels being added, all sourced from Televisa in Mexico. By 1997, Galavisión had 2.4 million subscribers, and had been sold to Univisión, thus entirely resolving Televisa's conflict of interest in that respect (Tobenkin 1997: 42), although Televisa still produces its channel packages in Mexico for distribution outside the US. In addition to ECO, the news channel, these include a *telenovela* channel, and video-hit music channels (Haley 1997: 45).

In addition to Univisión, Televisa's interests in the US include PanAmSat, for although it became completely separate from Televisa immediately after the SICC divestiture of 1987, in 1993 Televisa invested $US200 million in PanAmSat to become a non-controlling 50 per cent partner with Anselmo (Cardenas 1993; 'PanAmSat: Change in Corporate Status' 1995). With the death of Anselmo in 1995, PanAmSat was floated as a public company, reducing Televisa's interest to 40.5 per cent (Cosper 1995). As explained in the previous section, Televisa's participation in the new PanAmSat, following the merger with Hughes, is 7.5 per cent. The Hughes merger came about as an unpleasant surprise for PanAmSat, since Hughes was the main contractor building the series of PAS satellites with which PanAmSat was realizing its plans to cover the globe. However, in 1994, Hughes filed its own plan to launch a DTH (direct-to-home) service to Latin America, in direct competition with a similar initiative from PanAmSat ('Decision on PanAmSat Follow-on Spacecraft Said to be Imminent' 1994).

While Hughes was already involved in offering its DirecTV DTH service in the US, and the Latin American initiative was an extension of it, that in itself was a significant step, because it meant that a major hardware corporation had crossed the line to begin integrating content and service supply with its traditional manufacturing activities. As the 1990s unfolded, Turner's CNN and the other cable networks which had begun Latin American services early in the decade were joined by Spelling's TeleUno and the Miami-based US–Venezuelan venture GEMS ('US TV Trio Gets the Latin Beat' 1994); USA Network (Besas 1994); and Discovery, in conjunction with Televisa ('Latin Launch for Discovery' 1994). Film channels from the US included Cinecanal (incorporating Fox, Paramount, MGM, and Universal) and Cinemax ('Latin Debut for Cinemax' 1994), while Sony Picture Entertainment bought a share in the established HBO Olé (Guider 1994).

As far as the US broadcast networks were concerned, Fox opened a Latin American entertainment channel in 1993 ('Fox Fact Sheet' 1994), while others were testing the water with news services. It was noted above how CBS turned Telemundo's news programme *Telenoticias* into a cable channel after its takeover, while NBC for its part was looking to mount a Spanish-language version of its MSNBC news and information service, a joint venture with Microsoft (Brown 1997). After their rift with Azteca, NBC subsequently came to an arrangement with Televisa and the Sky DTH service, for both MSNBC and a Spanish-language business news service, Conexión Financiera ('Televisa, NBC Ink Biz News Pact' 1997). More recently, some of these services have turned their attention to providing also for the Portuguese-speaking Brazilian population, not just in the US, but, much more substantially, in Brazil. These include GEMS, Discovery Channel, and CBS Telenoticias (Whitefield 1997).

This raises the wider issue of the degree to which the growth of the Latino market in the US, the cultivation of it by mainstream corporate interests there, and the advent of international satellite distribution systems and services (whether satellite-to-cable or DTH) have now combined to allow these interests to secure domination over those markets which previously language and cultural difference had allowed the regional broadcasters, notably Televisa, Venevisión, and Globo, to monopolize. This question will be taken up in the last chapter—it is more appropriate here to look at the ownership and control of Spanish-language television within the US, and other related issues which concern the organized Latino community, in the context of regional and global integration.

Both times that Univisión has changed hands in this decade, and in the court actions against SICC/SIN in the 1980s, the ethnicity of owners and of senior management has been a matter of concern amongst US Latino groups such as the National Hispanic Media Coalition and the National Council of La Raza. This is a complex issue—US Latinos want to see US Latino owners and managers, not Latin Americans or mainstream Anglos. If anything, US mainstream owners have met with less resistance from Latinos than the Latin Americans behind Televisa and Venevisión, because the former have a better record of producing and showing US domestic programmes, one of the related issues. There also has been some tension amongst Latinos themselves on the ethnic control question, revealing the differences between US Spanish-speaking groups which both the politically correct term 'Latino' and the more commercial/ethnographic category 'Hispanic' for their different reasons gloss over—in particular, between Mexican-Americans and Cuban-Americans (Cantu 1991). Clearly, so long as which kind of Latino still matters, this will be a cause of dissatisfaction.

Just as nations perceive that their media should be owned and managed by their own nationals, so there is a perception amongst US Latinos not only that Latino owners and managers are more likely to provide them with US domestic production in programme content, but also that there will be more opportunities for the expression of communal issues, and more acceptable representations of themselves than either foreigners or mainstream owners and managers could give. Ethnic representation in the media is a further issue in itself, also of long-standing concern to Latinos (Wilson and Gutiérrez 1985; Subervi Vélez et al. 1994: 305–17).

Until 1997, Telemundo was seen as being more Latino in its control, with Roland Hernández as President and CEO, Joaquín Blaya having resigned in March 1995 (Mendosa 1996b; Avila 1997: 42). However, in January 1997, Univisión announced the appointment of Henry Cisneros as President and COO of the parent company, Univisión Communications. Henry Cisneros, it should be understood, is no relation to the Venezuelan owners of that name, but one of the best-known and, in spite of the pall of a continuing investigation, respected Latinos in the US. Another senior Latino at Univisión is Ray Rodriguez, President and COO of the network group (H. Cantu 1997; T. Cantu 1997). Carlos Barba left in October 1994 (Mendosa 1994: 58). With a strong public profile from his time as Mayor of San Antonio and a member of Clinton's first cabinet, the appointment of Cisneros is a strategic one expected to address the various concerns of Latinos about Univisión (T. Cantu 1997: 24).

However, given the economics and demographics of Univisión's market dominance, including its links not just to Mexican and Venezuelan minority owners, but also to their substantial programming supplies, Cisneros would be defying commercial logic if he sought to revert to more US domestic production.

For all the public objections, the Mexican-dominated programme schedule seems to be attractive enough to US audiences, and incurs only a mild cultural discount, particularly given that the majority of US Hispanics are of Mexican origin. Even in Cuban-dominated Miami, a clutch of Televisa *telenovelas* on Univisión made commercial television history in 1997 by out-rating the English-language mainstream networks in prime time (de la Fuente 1997: 45). Univisión usually runs a distant fifth in size behind the mainstream networks, with Fox in fourth slot (T. Cantu 1997). Thus, the commercial success of Univisión does not appear to have been dented by the campaigns of the organized Latino community. This illustrates one of the contradictions between citizenship and consumerhood (García Canclini 1995) produced by the entrepreneurial cultivation of a Hispanic market for television, one which can only become more complex as that market becomes integrated into the regional and global strategies of US and Latin American corporations alike.

References

Adams-Esquivel, Henry (1988), 'Hispanic Brand Loyalty: Myths and Realities', White Paper No. 6, Market Development Inc., San Diego.

Alex Brown and Sons Inc. (1997), 'Telemundo Group Inc: Company Report', Investext Group.

Andrews, Edmund (1992), 'FCC Clears Hallmark Sale of Univision TV Network', *New York Times* (30 September).

Arrarte, Anne Moncreiff (1990), 'And Galavisión Makes Three', *Advertising Age* (12 February), S-2.

Astroff, Roberta (1997), 'Capital's Cultural Study: Marketing Popular Ethnography of US Latino Culture', in M. Nava, A. Blake, I. MacRury, and B. Richards (eds.), *Buy this Book: Studies in Advertising and Consumption* (Routledge, London), 120–36.

Avila, Alex (1997), 'Trading Punches', *Hispanic* (January–February), 39–44.

Bagamery, Anne (1982), 'SIN, the Original', *Forbes* (22 November), 97.

Besas, Peter (1990), 'Mexicans Ride Again in Hispano TV Sweeps', *Variety* (11 April), 41 and 58.

—— (1994), 'USA Joins Latino Fray', *NATPE Daily* (26 January).

Brischetto, Robert (1993a), 'Hispanic Population has Tripled in Three Decades', *Hispanic Business* (June), 180.

—— (1993b), 'Marking a Milestone', *Hispanic Business* (October), 6–10.

Brown, Rich (1995), 'Programers' Message: Add Cable Services, Subscribers Will Follow', *Broadcasting & Cable* (9 January), 50.

—— (1997), 'NBC Kills Spanish Network', *Broadcasting & Cable* (27 January), 11.

Cantu, Hector (1991), 'The Gathering Storm in Broadcasting', *Hispanic Business* (February), 14–18 and 64.

—— (1997), 'Henry Cisneros Joins Univision', *Hispanic Business* (March), 7.

Cantu, Tony (1997), 'The Adventures of Superlatino', *Hispanic Business* (April), 19–24.

Cardenas, Francisco (1993), 'The Gamble of the Decade', *Hispanic Business* (December), 54.

Coe, Steve (1995), 'Boom Year for Hispanic TV Networks', *Broadcasting & Cable* (9 January), 46–8.

Cosper, Amy (1995), 'The Tale of a Man, his Dog and the Industry they Changed: Rene Anselmo 1926–1995', *Satellite Television* (November), 27–8.

Coto, Juan Carlos (1991), '"Hispanic Hollywood": Univision's Hub is on a Roll', *Variety* (25 March), 74.

Critser, Greg (1987), 'The Feud that Toppled a TV Empire', *Channels* (January), 24–31.

'Decision on PanAmSat Follow-on Spacecraft Said to be Imminent' (1994), *Satellite News* (15 August), 1–3.

de la Fuente, Anna Maria (1997), 'Endless Love', *TV World* (January), 45–7.

de Noriega, Luis Antonio, and Leach, Francis (1979), *Broadcasting in Mexico* (Routledge & Kegan Paul, London).

de Uriarte, Mercedes (1980), 'Battle for the Ear of the Latino', *Los Angeles Times* (14 December), Calendar 5.

Douglas, Nick (1996), 'Purchasing Power at $223 Billion', *Hispanic Business* (December), 48.

'FCC Gives OK to Private Satellite Launch' (1987), *News* (Mexico City) (1 October).

Fernández Christlieb, Fátima (1987), 'Azcárraga–Gavin ¿y Alemán?', *La Jornada* (6 May).

Flores-Hughes, Grace (1996), 'Why the Term "Hispanic"?', *Hispanic* (September), 64.

'"Foreign Programs Work Fine for Us", Rival Says' (1993), *Variety* (18 January).

'Fox Fact Sheet' (1994).

'Galavisión Makes Bid for the TV Pie' (1990), *Variety* (11 April), 40 and 60.

García Canclini, Nestor (1995), *Consumidores y ciudadanos* (Grijalbo, Mexico DF).

Goldschmidt, Douglas (1988), 'Pan American Satellite and the Introduction of Specialized Communications Systems in Latin America', in D. Wedemeyer and M. Ogden (eds.), *Telecommunications and Pacific Development: Alternatives for the Next Decade* (Elsevier Science Publishers, North Holland, Amsterdam), 393–9.

Guernica, Antonio, and Kasperuk, Irene (1982), *Reaching the Hispanic Market Effectively: The Media, the Market, the Methods* (McGraw-Hill, New York).

Guider, Elizabeth (1994), 'Sony Buys into HBO's Latin America Cable', *Variety* (27 January), 17.

Gutiérrez, Félix (1979), 'Mexico's Television Network in the United States: The Case of Spanish International Network', in H. Dordick (ed.), *Proceedings of the Sixth Annual Telecommunications Policy Research Conference* (Lexington Books, Lexington, Mass.), 135–59.

—— and Schement, Jorge Reina (1981), 'Problems of Ownership and Control of Spanish-Language Media in the United States: National and International Policy Concerns', in E. McAnany, J. Schnitman, and N. Janus (eds.), *Communication and Social Structure: Critical Studies in Mass Media Research* (Praeger, New York), 181–203.

———— (1984), 'Spanish International Network: The Flow of Television from Mexico to the United States', *Communication Research*, 11: 241–58.

Haley, Kathy (1997), 'Cable Channels Seek Promise of Hispanic Market', *Broadcasting & Cable* (6 October), 44–5.

'HBO Plans Pay TV Launch in Latin America' (1991), *Broadcasting Abroad* (March), 4.

Klink, Teresa (1987), 'Ten to Watch in 1987: Rene Anselmo', *Channels Field Guide* 87, 26.

'Latin Debut for Cinemax' (1994), *TV International* (24 January), 3.

'Latin Launch for Discovery' (1994), *TV International* (24 January), 9.

Lopes, Humberto (1993), 'Bad Vibes but Good Business?', *Hispanic Business* (February), 30–2.

McClellan, Steve (1997), 'Majors Line up for Telemundo' *Broadcasting & Cable* (4 August), 6.

Margolis, Dan (1997), 'Telemundo Group Braces for World of Change', *Variety* (28 July–3 August), 25 and 34.

Margolis, Maxine (1994), *Little Brazil: An Ethnography of Brazilian Immigrants in New York City* (Princeton University Press, Princeton).

Marín, Carlos (1986), 'A Zabludovsky no se le cree por considerarlo vocero del gobierno', *Proceso* (27 October), 20–5.

Maza, Enrique (1986), 'A la vista, la telaraña del poder de Azcárraga en Estados Unidos', *Proceso* (14 July), 20–5.

—— (1987), 'Rene Anselmo, motor del imperio de Azcárraga en Estados Unidos, eliminado', *Proceso* (19 January), 22–3.

Mendosa, Rick (1992), 'Univision: Still for US Hispanics?', *Hispanic Business* (May), 24–6.

—— (1993a), 'A New Vision for Univision', *Hispanic Business* (August), 10–16.

—— (1993b), 'The Television Wars, Part II', *Hispanic Business* (December), 52–4.

—— (1994), 'The Year Belongs to Univisión', *Hispanic Business* (December), 56–60.

—— (1996a), 'A Clear (TV) Picture', *Hispanic Business* (December), 50.

—— (1996b), 'A Matter of Media Ownership', *Hispanic Business* (December), 40–4.

Merrill Lynch Capital Markets (1997), 'Univisión Communications Inc', Investext Group.

Moody's Investor Service (1997), 'Univision Communications Inc', Investext Group.

'Network is Pushing its Domestic Identity' (1993), *Variety* (18 January).

'PanAmSat: Change in Corporate Status' (1995), *Via Satellite* (May), 74.

Paxman, Andrew (1997), 'Numero Uno', *Variety* (31 March–6 April), 59–60.

Rodriguez, América (1996), 'Objectivity and Ethnicity in the Production of the *Noticiero Univisión*', *Critical Studies in Mass Communication*, 13: 59–81.

—— (1997a), 'Commercial Ethnicity: Language, Class and Race in the Marketing of the Hispanic Audience', *Communication Review*, in press.

—— (1997b), 'Creating an Audience and Remapping a Nation: A Brief History of US Spanish Language Broadcasting 1930–1980', *Quarterly Review of Film and Video*, in press.

'The Secrets behind Univisión's Sale' (1993), *Hispanic Business* (February), 32–4.

'Separate Systems: New Era for Global Communications' (1989), *Broadcasting Abroad* (September), 6.

Shackelford, John (1995), 'Miami: Launch Pad for Latin America', *International Cable* (April), 20–8.

Silva, Samuel (1991), '¡Buenos días, Latinoamérica!', *América Economía* (July), 52: 10–14.

Sinclair, John (1990), 'Spanish-Language Television in the United States: Televisa Surrenders its Domain', *Studies in Latin American Popular Culture*, 9: 39–63.

——Jacka, Elizabeth, and Cunningham, Stuart (eds.) (1996), *New Patterns in Global Television: Peripheral Vision* (Oxford University Press, Oxford).

Strategy Research Corporation (1986), *1987 US Hispanic Market Study* (Strategy Research Corporation, Miami).

Subervi Vélez, Federico, Ramírez Berg, Charles, Constantakis-Valdés, Patricia, Noriega, Chon, and Wilkinson, Kenton (1994), 'Mass Communication and Hispanics', in F. Padilla (ed.), *Handbook of Hispanic Cultures in the United States: Sociology* (Arte Público Press and Instituto de Cooperación Iberoamericana, Houston), 304–57.

'Televisa, NBC Ink Biz News Pact' (1997), *Variety* (2–8 June), 33.

Tobenkin, David (1997), 'Univision vs. Telemundo', *Broadcasting & Cable* (6 October), 34–42.

Univisión (1987), publicity materials.

US Census Bureau (1997), 'Hispanic Population from the March 1994 Current Population Survey', http://ftp.census.gov/population/www/socdemo/hispanic/html

'US TV Trio Gets the Latin Beat' (1994), *Variety* (1 February), 47.

Valenzuela, Nicholas (1986), 'Spanish Language TV in the Americas: From SIN to PanAmSat', in J. Miller (ed.), *Telecommunications and Equity: Policy Research Issues* (Elsevier Science Publishers, North Holland, Amsterdam), 329–38.

Whitefield, Mimi (1997), 'Latin-Aimed TV Biz on Growth Curve', *Variety* (19–25 May), 21 and 27.

Wilkinson, Kenton (1991), 'The Sale of Spanish International Communication Corporation: Milestone in the Development of Spanish-Language Television in the United States', unpublished MA dissertation, University of California at Berkeley.

——(1992), 'Southern Exposure: US Cable Programmers and Spanish-Language Networks Enter Latin America', paper presented to the 18th Conference of the International Association for Mass Communication Research, Guarujá, August.

——(1995), 'When Culture, Language and Communication Converge: The Latin American Cultural-Linguistic Television Market', unpublished Ph.D. dissertation, University of Texas at Austin.

Wilson, Clint, and Gutiérrez, Félix (1985), *Minorities and the Media: Diversity and the End of Mass Communication* (Sage, Beverly Hills, Calif.).

Yankelovich, Skelly, and White (1981), *Spanish USA: A Study of the Hispanic Market in the United States* (Yankelovich Skelly and White Inc., New York).

Zate, Maria (1996), 'Media Buyers Raise the Stakes', *Hispanic Business* (December), 46.

5 | From Latin America to Latin Europe: Spain and Portugal

The television industries of the Iberian metropolitan nations of Spain and Portugal are incorporated into the same geolinguistic wholes as their respective postcolonial worlds, although each in a different manner. While that proposition is the principal rationale for this chapter, both nations deserve attention for their intrinsic interest. They share great similarities in the development of their television industries, but also in the particular deviations which they exhibit from the common pattern of transition found in recent decades in Europe. At least in the case of Spain, there are also strong corporate connections to the rest of what have been referred to already as 'the Latin-European countries' (Roncagliolo 1995: 340), while the privatization of television in Portugal has led to a renewal of its links with Brazil, both corporate and cultural.

Both Spain and Portugal are still consolidating themselves as democracies after the long periods of dictatorship during which their television systems were first established. Both of these systems were two-channel monopolies—of the government in the Spanish case, and a government–private consortium serving the functions of church and state in the case of Portugal—but neither had deep commitment to the public service ideal prevalent in most other European countries, and both were principally funded through the sale of advertising time. This in turn meant these systems, even before the privatization which was introduced in both cases under the auspices of leftist governments in the late 1980s to early 1990s, had a strong trend towards entertainment programming, with a consequent opening to international sources of such material. Both countries are highly centralized politically, and retain an instrumental approach to television as a communication medium. With privatization and deregulation, relations in each country between governments and media groups, notably newspaper-based conglomerates, have been decisive in the subsequent shape of the systems. Also in both cases, there have been instances when corporations unable to have their way with the national government have appealed to the EU (European Union) supranational authorities.

However, it would be a mistake to overemphasize these similarities, fundamental as most of them are, or to assume that Portugal is just a smaller and backward version of its peninsular neighbour. This chapter will show how the Spanish television industry is linked in much more to the rest of Europe, particularly France and Italy, and, although it has some interaction with Spanish-speaking Latin America, its Portuguese counterpart is much more connected to Brazil, and indeed other countries of its former empire. The most striking instance of this difference will be apparent in the contrast between the difficulties experienced by Televisa in gaining some foothold in Spain, and the quite disproportionate influence which Globo has achieved in Portugal. Also of interest is the attention which Portugal gives, as a nation of emigrants, to its diasporic populations in France, Brazil, and its former colonies in Africa and Asia.

Spain

'Premature Commercialization'

With all the turmoil of *laissez-faire* in which the Spanish television industry has found itself over the last two decades, it would be easy to overlook its previous history as a strictly controlled and monopolized enterprise of the Spanish Government. From its commencement in 1956, during the long era of the dictatorship of General Francisco Franco (1939–75), Televisión Española (TVE) was firmly harnessed to that regime's ideological project. A more surprising distinction is that, almost from the start, TVE was made reliant on the sale of advertising time, as in the US commercial model, instead of being like the state-supported systems elsewhere in Europe. Such a fusion of state control and private enterprise had its roots in the institutional basis established for radio in 1924 by a previous dictator, General Miguel Primo de Rivera. This had asserted the absolute power of the state over the airwaves, including the right to exploit them commercially, or to grant concessions to private interests to do so. On the latter basis, the initial commercialization and development of the medium proceeded under Unión Radio, a group linked to several major international electrical equipment manufacturers. Converting itself to SER (Sociedad Española de Radiodifusión) in 1942, this went on to become, in 1984, part of one of Spain's, and Europe's, most important media conglomerates, Prisa (Franquet 1988:

77–80). The state did not have a network of its own until 1937, but soon after, Franco gave state radio a monopoly over broadcast information, maintaining strict oversight of the private stations. Right up until two years after his death, only the state's Radio Nacional de España was allowed to carry national and international news. That was 1977, the year in which the state radio networks were absorbed into the then newly constituted broadcasting entity RTVE (Radio Televisión Española) (Franquet 1988: 81–3).

Television in Spain had begun in Madrid in 1956, not late by European standards, but six years after Brazil and Mexico. Timed to coincide with a Catholic holy day and the anniversary of Franco's movement, the Falange, the first broadcast offered a mass, followed by a speech from Gabriel Arias Salgado, the Minister for Education to whose portfolio broadcasting had been assigned (García Jiménez 1980: 230–1). Although this combination of militarism, Catholicism, and authoritarian paternalism was constitutive of the new medium as an institution in Spain, within two years, even before the single channel had been extended to Barcelona, a department was set up within TVE to liaise with advertising agencies, and the first commercials were being broadcast. In the ten years following the establishment of its administrative authority, ARE (Administración Radiodifusora Española), in 1957, the initial system under which television was financed was allowed to lapse. This had been based on a licence fee payable by set-owners, the system for financing public broadcasting which became a mainstay in other countries, notably Britain. Its early abandonment in Spain in favour of ever-greater dependence on commercial advertising serves to underscore how very different state-owned television has been as an institution in Spain compared to the other nations of Europe, though with the significant exception of Portugal (Bustamante and Giu 1988: 123).

Under Manuel Fraga Iribarne as Minister for Information and Tourism during the 1960s, Spanish television experienced more emphasis on professional and technical development than in its earliest years, with the extension of TVE to achieve national coverage, as TVE 1, and the addition of a second network, TVE 2, both in 1965. The second network was aimed at providing more cultural programming (García Jiménez 1980: 380–3), perhaps an acknowledgement that the system was even then losing sight of the public service objectives which, in a peculiar way, still legitimized it. However, Bustamante and Giu argue that while the rest of Europe was consolidating public service broadcasting as a social ideal, Spain was already on the way to a 'premature' commercialization and internationalization of its television system, but under the auspices of state enterprise, not a response to the external pressures and unleashed 'market forces' which were later so influential elsewhere (1988: 122). The Spanish experience underscores the point that public service is not to be equated with mere state ownership and control: there are social ideals in public service which never had a chance to become established in the political culture in Spain (Bustamante 1989: 71).

On the contrary, the motivation for the commercial trend in Spain has been the state's policy of requiring RTVE to fund itself to an ever greater degree from the sale of advertising time. This has caused it to behave like a commercial network, particularly in the relative freedom it found in the period after Franco's demise, and the formal autonomy from the state it was granted in a statute of 1980. Detailed evidence from the decade 1976–86 shows an effective doubling of hours given over to advertising, largely achieved through a progressive increase in hours of transmission time (Bustamante and Giu 1988: 127–31). The pursuit of audiences attractive to advertisers also had its impact on programming, of course: there was a downgrading in documentary and information programmes relative to entertainment such as films and series over this same period. According to RTVE's own reports, this meant an increase in the proportion of imported programming, particularly films from the US, and the displacement of Spanish productions from prime time (Bustamante and Giu 1988: 132–47). Thus, by the time the Spanish Government opened up television to private interests in 1988, its television system had well and truly developed the same tendencies which characterized the crisis in public broadcasting and the transition to privatization and deregulation by then familiar elsewhere in Europe. However, whereas other governments in Europe had sought to protect their national public service television systems, government policies in Spain had actually precipitated the system's breakdown. It is particularly ironic that this was presided over by a Socialist government, for reasons to be discussed later in this chapter.

Before turning to consider the current era of privatization and deregulation, and the subsequent rise of the cable and satellite contenders, one further and quite unique feature of Spanish television as it emerged in the 1980s must be mentioned: the regional community stations on the 'Third Channel'. Under Franco, there had been little interest in encouraging programming for the major linguistic minorities of Spain. On the contrary, only after the end of the dictatorship could the Catalan, Basque, and Galician regions assert themselves as the 'Autonomous Communities' now recognized by the Spanish Government. Those regions which had enjoyed some independence in the era before the Civil War of the 1930s were recognized in the 1978 constitution as 'historical nationalities' with the right to their own language and broadcasting provision, amongst other things. The law of the Third Channel effect-ively legitimized channels which were already established in Cataluña and the Basque country in 1983, although because the parties in power in these autonomous regions were opposed to the national government, this was done with reluctance. Thus, when the original channels of the first two communities mentioned above began to expand beyond their regional limits, and were joined by a Galician channel in 1988, the Socialist government retaliated with the establishment of further regio-nal channels in areas which they controlled: Madrid, Andalucía, and Valencia. Of these, only Valencia has a distinct language, so the political motivation was obvious, and the legitimacy of the concept behind the regional channels compromised (Bustamante 1989: 71; Sampedro Blanco and van den Bulck 1995: 245–6).

Although the regional languages are flourishing, the autonomous community channels have not been successful in the regionalization of television production and distribution at which they were ostensibly aimed. Much of their own production is actually in the national language, with local language input mainly being confined to dubbing and subtitling the non-regional programming which dominates prime time. The third channels are funded by the state to a much greater degree than is RTVE, but this still seems not sufficient to overcome the inherent economic problem in producing for relatively small regional audiences—there are 6 million Catalans, for example, in a Spanish nation of 39 million (Sampedro Blanco and van den Bulck 1995: 246–8). Just like RTVE, on which they were obliged to model their organizations, and against which they have been put into competition, the third channels' solution has been to sell time to advertisers: hence, the practice of scheduling national and imported programming in prime time, dubbed or subtitled into the respective languages. In-dications are that, as for RTV, the US is the biggest single source of programmes, although, interestingly, the third channels have also been an important point of entry for Latin American *telenovelas* into the Spanish market (Bustamante and Giu 1988: 147–50; Madinaveitia 1991).

Impact of Privatization and Deregulation

It was the PSOE (Partido Socialista Obrero Español) government of Felipe González which eventually responded to the pressures for privat-ization which had been building up over the 1980s, exerted both through the parliament and the courts ('the Italian way'). Parliament introduced legislation in 1987 affirming television as an 'essential public service, the operator of which is the state' (quoted in Bustamante 1989: 79–80). Three national private channels were to be established under ten-year licences. The conditions were the same as had been applied in France (and similar to those adopted later in Portugal), mainly that no one shareholder could hold more than 25 per cent of the company, and foreign (that is, non-European) ownership was to be restricted to 25 per cent (Vilches 1996: 185). Other restrictions concerned programme content. In addition to being expected to observe the 50 per cent EU quota of commercial film broadcasts, licensees were obliged to maintain a 40 per cent quota of European-originated material, half of it from Spain, and a 15 per cent quota of material produced by the networks themselves ('Spanish TV the Latest to Go Private' 1989; 'Country Profile: Spain' 1994: 5).

Two of the new channels which were subsequently licensed in 1989 and 1990 were linked to companies that had come to the fore in the processes of privatization already undertaken in two of the neighbouring countries of Latin Europe: France and Italy. These were Canal Plus Spain, with the maximum of 25 per cent being held by Canal Plus France, both of which services are terrestrial subscription; and the free-to-air network Tele 5, in which the key non-Spanish shareholder, also with the maximum allowed, has been Fininvest. The French Canal Plus has the most extensive subscription television interests in Europe, while Fininvest is the company of Silvio Berlusconi, Italy's dominant network owner and one-time President. Another major European investor in Tele 5 is the German media group Kirsch, with the maximum 25 per cent as well ('Country Profile: Spain' 1994; Godard 1997).

The domestic partners in these two channels are the Prisa group, Spain's biggest media conglomerate already mentioned above, which has 25 per cent of Canal Plus, along with the Banco de Bilbao y Vizcaya and a Madrid financial group, March, which hold 15 per cent each. Tele 5's original major partner was the public institution and radio and press owner ONCE (Organización Nacional de Ciegos—National Organization for the Blind) but it sold most of its original 25 per cent share in 1993 to financial interests based in Belgium (Davis 1993a; 'Country Profile: Spain' 1994).

The licence for the remaining private channel in Spain, the free-to-air Antena 3 TV, first fell under the control of the *La Vanguardia* and Antena 3 Radio group of Javier Godó, but a 1992 coup organized by the Spanish bank Banesto, which also had a 25 per cent share, delivered the effective control of Antena 3 TV to companies owned by Antonio Asensio of the Grupo Zeta, a Spanish press group. At that time, Rupert Murdoch's News Corporation was a partner in these companies. Both News and

Grupo Zeta had been unsuccessful bidders for a licence in 1989 (Larraya and Beaumont 1992; 'Country Profile: Spain' 1994: 7).

One other unsuccessful contender of note had been Televisa of Mexico. Televisa virtually disqualified itself at the start in being unwilling, or perhaps unable, to join with Spanish partners in a joint bid, contrary to the guidelines. In any case, although it is said to have developed an association with the Prisa radio chain, SER, at some stage, Televisa had not found favour with the PSOE government. Televisa made a later attempt to buy into one of the licensee companies, but this also failed. As first mentioned in Chapter 2, Azcárraga's 1994 attempt to buy Berlusconi's share of Tele 5 was rejected because Televisa was not considered to fit in with the Spanish public television model—as if Fininvest and News Corporation did (Martínez 1996: 48). As will be examined further below, Televisa compensated its initial failure in 1988 by bringing its satellite service Galavisión into Spain (Hernández Lomeli 1992–3: 94). More recently, in conjunction with Telefónica and RTVE, with the latter of which it has developed a working relationship in recent years ('like the hen and the fox', according to one PSOE politician), Televisa has become a partner in Vía Digital, one of the digital television ventures now competing in Spain (Peralta 1997). Galavisión now forms part of the Vía Digital 'bouquet' (package of channels offered). The emergence of satellite-to-cable and DTH satellite services during the 1990s is the next stage of development which Spain has experienced, but before introducing the complexities which this most recent step has brought with it, it is worth assessing the impact which privatization and deregulation have had as the end of their first decade looms.

With well over 11 million television households, Spain is the third largest television market in Europe ('Country Profile: Spain' 1994: 5; Hopewell 1998). Furthermore, the Spanish watch a lot of television. While Spain is second last to Portugal in terms of newspaper readership within the EU (Vilches 1996: 175), their average of 211 minutes per day (up more than 25 per cent since 1989) puts the Spanish amongst Europe's heaviest viewers (Nosty 1996: 161). Yet these avid viewers are oversupplied with television. In spite of the increase in viewership over the period since the private channels appeared, the new channels have taken audiences away from TVE. However, their gains are out of proportion to TVE's loss. TVE's last good year was 1989, the year in which the first private channels arrived. Although it appears to have retained its pre-eminence in terms of both ratings and advertising revenue for the first couple of years thereafter (*Anuario El País* 1992), what was a 72 per cent audience share in 1990 slipped to below 40 per cent in 1993. Although still holding at 37 per cent in 1996, clearly TVE has lost almost half its audience over that period. At the same time, the private channels increased their share from just over 10 to 46 per cent, most of which went to Antena 3 TV, with the regional community channels holding steady at around 15 per cent (Nosty 1996: 162).

TVE's financial decline has precipitated a crisis. Before the private channels appeared, the state subsidy had dropped to a negligible level— less than 2 per cent in 1986 (Bustamante and Giu 1988: 126). So long as TVE had a monopoly on national television advertising, it was virtually self-supporting, but competition has now produced massive deficits in TVE's budget, around a third of its expenditure in 1996, leaving it effectively bankrupt and dependent upon a government which has no commitment to public service broadcasting, and could easily let TVE go to the private sector (Vilches 1996: 188–9). The Conservative government which came to power in 1996 had threatened to 'thin out' TVE, perhaps by the privatization of one of the networks (Martínez 1996: 50). In these circumstances, the lack of a public service tradition, and its convergence with the other channels or lack of 'consistent brand image' ('Country Profile: Spain' 1994: 6), make TVE difficult to defend.

Canal Plus, in spite of a small audience share, has a profitable relationship with its mostly young, upper-middle-class subscribers, claimed at almost 1,400,000 in 1997 (Hopewell 1997*b*). Antena 3 TV started building more of a mass audience after Asensio came into it, though at the cost of high debt levels; while Tele 5, in spite of being outstripped by Antena 3 TV since 1993 in audience share, is still profitable for Berlusconi because it is integrated with his programme distribution and advertising sales businesses. The greatest beneficiaries of the new regime have been the advertisers. With the advent of the private channels, the resultant glut of advertising time pushed down the price of advertising spots such that, in the first few years, advertisers were able to get four times more airtime for the same amount that they had been paying before privatization ('Country Profile: Spain' 1994). A recent list of the top twenty advertisers included global US-origin corporations such as Procter & Gamble, Coca-Cola, and Ford; plus European-based ones such as Nestlé, Henkel, and Citroën; with Spanish corporations just in the minority (Nosty 1996: 185). Such advertisers and their agencies were amongst the principal interest groups which had agitated for the privatization and deregulation of television. At least in the case of Spain, they have been given what they wanted, but at massive cost to television as an institution.

At this point we should look at the implications which privatization and deregulation have had in this regard, and then move on to the implications for programming production and distribution. From its origins as perhaps the most controlled and centralized of the state television regimes in Europe, Spanish television now lacks any government agency with the legal competence to deal with the consequences of privatization and deregulation. While other European nations have not seen any contradiction in setting up regulatory authorities to moderate the impact of liberalization, such as the British Broadcasting Standards Council, the French Conseil Supérieur de l'Audiovisuel, or even the Portuguese Alta Autoridade para a Comunicação, in Spain 'there is no moral or legal authority sufficiently empowered to ensure either diversity of scheduling or minimum standards of programme content' (Vilches 1996: 186).

One major reason for the regulatory vacuum is that neither the succession of PSOE governments under Felipe González from 1982 until 1996, nor the PP (Partido Popular) centre-right government of José María Aznar elected in March 1996, have had the political will. On the contrary, echoing the tradition of Franco's Spain but not unknown in other democracies, the media are seen as valuable instruments of ideological influence and political patronage, and there is no desire on either side to set up a tribunal which would put television 'at arm's length' from government. For example, the awarding of licences is fairly openly regarded, not in a cynical but a matter-of-fact way, as a major means by which governments can shore up political power. It was no surprise that the consortium led by the group Prisa was granted one of the initial terrestrial licences. Prisa is based on the newspaper *El País*, begun by Jesús de Polanco, 'the Hispanic Howard Hughes behind the Prisa Group's media empire', and others, soon after Franco's death. As noted, Prisa was subsequently allowed to acquire the SER radio network in 1984 (Holland 1997). The name Prisa, incidentally, began as an acronym for Promotora de Informaciones SA, or 'Information Promotion Inc.'

Although *El País* might be seen as no more than the kind of modern, liberal newspaper one would expect to find in a democratic nation, it has become closely associated with the PSOE. This explains a lot about why an ostensibly Socialist government would have permitted the degree of concentrated horizontal and vertical media ownership which Prisa has achieved, putting it on a par with other major European conglomerates such as Havas in France, Berlusconi in Italy, or Kirsch in Germany, all of which are involved also in Spanish television. On the other hand, because some of the initial owners of Antena 3 TV were causing the network to take an anti-government stance, the PSOE is believed to have sanctioned the boardroom coup mentioned earlier which led to the Godó group's interest in the network being replaced by that of Antonio Asensio. Not surprisingly, now that the PP is in power, the Prisa group's activities are being actively obstructed by the government.

Indeed, there will be cause to return soon to this question of the political patronage of media development in the next section, where the fraught shift from cable into satellite and digital television will be considered. It remains to take note of the impact which privatization and deregulation have had on television programme production. Given the long-term trends begun by TVE, and accelerated in the era of private competition, towards more entertainment-oriented programming, and the concomitant increase in the importation of films and series, Spanish television production has been in a poor position to withstand the additional blow dealt by the decline in network revenues. As noted earlier, because Spain is now over-supplied with television, in the sense that the offer is out of proportion to the advertising revenues available, the economics of programming are such that the increase in the number of channels has meant less rather than more Spanish production. Although TVE in its time has been an acknowledged producer of quality programming, and once the sole client for Spain's independent producers, production has been one of the few areas in which it has been able to make cutbacks to deal with its financial crisis. Apart from the consequent withering of an audiovisual production sector which has depended so much upon television, the 'savage competition' of the 1990s has been encouraging both TVE and the private channels alike to bid each other up for costly and disadvantageous 'output deals' with US distributors so as to secure their sources of imported programming ('Country Profile: Spain' 1994: 5–6; Contreras 1996: 286–8).

Into the Post-Broadcast Era: Cable, Satellite, and DTH

The first step into post-broadcast television technologies was a grassroots movement into cable in the late 1980s. Because cable was a marginal technology in Spain, and not covered by the private television legislation (Bustamante and Giu 1988: 159), small operators could, with equanimity, connect entire apartment buildings to cable, and charge the recipients for the programming they supplied, mostly films downlinked from satellite services, or even hired videos. By 1993, there were an estimated 700,000–800,000 subscribers to such services. The only legal restraints were that the operators became obliged to pay royalties on the programmes shown, and were not permitted to extend their service areas beyond particular building clusters (Davis 1993*b*: 41; Bustamante 1989: 82).

While this movement helped to create an audience for post-broadcast services, cable has not since become established as a major technology. An attempt to mount cable on a large-scale commercial basis was made in October 1995, with a joint venture of Telefónica, the privately owned telecommunications monopoly in Spain, and Sogecable, a previously formed joint venture of Canal Plus and Prisa. Called Cablevisión (and unrelated to any Latin American company of that name), Telefónica and Sogecable aimed with this venture to provide forty cable channels through local operators, but by June 1996 Telefónica's right to be in the cable business was successfully challenged in court, effectively closing down Cablevisión (Williams and Hopewell 1997).

Since then, Sogecable and Telefónica have become engaged in a bitter and highly politicized competitive battle over digital satellite television. To provide some context for that, it is useful to look briefly at the background of satellite television development in Spain. Until the 1990s, direct satellite television delivery was as marginal as cable. A Spanish–European venture (which included Canal Plus) mounted such a service in 1987, Channel 10, but this was not successful (Bustamante 1989: 82–3). Nevertheless, because Channel 10 had established the legal feasibility of satellite delivery from a foreign country, and also the beginnings of an audience with satellite reception equipment, and given the fact that Televisa already had a service, Galavisión (incorporating ECO), which it could with relative ease transmit across from Mexico, Televisa commenced transmission of that service unscrambled into Spain in 1988. This began on Eutelsat, and was relayed via London, where the signal was converted from the American NTSC to the European PAL transmission standard. After 1990, it came direct via PanAmSat. Advertising time was sold very cheaply through the subsidiary set up for that purpose in Spain, Iberovisa, while Televisa's European umbrella organization, predictably called Eurovisa, maintained offices in London and Amsterdam (Hernández Lomeli 1992–3: 93–5).

Although it had announced 'the conquest of Spanish-speaking space in Europe' when it arrived in 1988, the same year, probably not coincidentally, that it had been obliged to sell off its stations in the US, it was difficult for Televisa to conceal the venture's failure by 1992. The offices of Galavisión, Iberovisa, and also Televicine in Spain had been rolled into one (Hernández Lomeli 1992–3: 96), and the London office of Eurovisa and the programme sales arm Protele closed (Kinnane 1991). All this suggests that in spite of the comparative advantages of its programme supply and satellite access, and hence its competitive advertising rates and relatively low costs in gaining market entry, Galavisión was not able to gain an adequate audience. According to independent estimates, in 1992 there were 50,000 satellite reception dishes installed in Spain (Hernández Lomeli 1992–3: 97). This figure would include the thousands which Televisa had installed free (Bustamante 1990: 11–13). Adding in the numbers of people connected to community video dishes as well, Televisa research claimed to reach a total of 3,757,100 viewers, or '18 per cent of Spanish television homes' (quoted in Hernández Lomeli 1992–3: 97–8). However, Televisa publicity wilfully confused its potential audience (those that could obtain the signal) with its actual viewers. By this time, satellite dish owners already had about twenty channels to choose from, including European and US-based services, so they could have been watching much more than Galavisión (Hernández Lomeli 1992–3: 95–7).

By contrast, Canal Plus and Prisa, as Sogecable, were able to build on the strength of their Canal Plus Spain terrestrial subscription service as a basis for mounting a satellite-delivered analogue subscription service of an initial two, and then five channels, Canal Satélite, on the European Astra satellite in 1993 (Williams and Hopewell 1997). Then, early in 1997, Canal Satélite Digital (CSD) was launched by Sogecable, also on Astra. The ownership of Sogecable is the same as for Canal Plus Spain (Canal Plus, Prisa, and the banks named earlier), and Sogecable in turn has 85 per cent of CSD, the remainder being held by the leading free-to-air network Antena 3 TV. In addition to its terrestrial, analogue, and digital subscription television services, Sogecable also embraces Sogepaq, a major film and television rights sales and management organization; and Sogetel, a film production arm active in both Spanish-language and English-language international co-productions. Sogecable is the wealthiest and most powerful film conglomerate in Spain, which is the world's seventh-largest film market, and a country which likes to see films on television—over half of Canal Plus Spain's programming is films.

Sogecable's mode of integration is such that it can maximize the commercialization of films, both in cinemas (it has entered exhibition as well as distribution, and has major links with Time-Warner and the Portuguese Lusomundo in this regard), as well as in its three kinds of television subscription services. Being integrated with Prisa's publications, it is also able to generate publicity support for its films (Alvarez 1997; Hopewell 1997a; 1998; Seymour 1997). Furthermore, with the launch of CSD, Sogecable was able to kick off with an offer of free digital decoder boxes to the analogue service's 100,000 subscribers, so as to provide an incentive for them to migrate to digital (Hopewell 1997b).

However, the CSD initiative was a major provocation to the PP government, which had aligned itself with a rival project, DSD (Distribuidora de Televisión Digital), trading as Vía Digital. This was being mounted by the government's allies, but they had been beaten to the launch by CSD, in which, as has just been noted, the motive force is the government's *bête noire* in the media, Grupo Prisa. By contrast, the DSD consortium was led by Telefónica, with a 35 per cent share. Apart from its traditional institutional role as a private company with quasi-government standing, the President of Telefónica is reportedly a long-standing personal associate of the Prime Minister (Hopewell 1997b). Next in DSD came the state-owned RTVE with 25.5 per cent, and, with a similar proportion, Televisa. It has been mentioned how Televisa's previous ambitions in Spain had been frustrated by the former PSOE government's negative attitude towards it. However, in addition to its recent association with RTVE, Televisa had been cultivating excellent relations with the PP government, particularly through Luiz María Ansón, a Televisa board member who is also the director of *ABC*, the Spanish newspaper most supportive of the PP, and the Right in general (Martínez 1996: 48). The shareholders with the remaining 14 per cent at the initial stage included DTH Europa; a radio chain, Cope; a magazine, *Época*; and another conservative newspaper, *El Mundo* (Peralta 1997).

Even before the CSD launch, the government was 'thinking up ways to block, delay or punish Sogecable', according to the interpretation of the trade press (Hopewell 1997a: 197). This is probably true, but the issues on which the government was bound to intervene inevitably attracted charges of partisanship. First, there was the question of soccer rights. Next to films, soccer is the most popular form of programming on television, with top games commanding up to a 50 per cent audience share (Alvarez 1997). Thus, when Sogecable made an arrangement with Antena 3 TV (the free-to-air network which also owns 15 per cent of CSD) to share soccer rights such that CSD would have exclusive rights for subscription television, the government retaliated by initiating legislation to protect soccer rights from such monopolization 'as a national patrimony' (Schweid 1997).

A second issue had to do with the technical standard upon which digital television reception in Spain was to be based. CSD had launched their service using a 'simulcrypt' system for the subscriber's conditional access set-top decoding box, which, while widely used also by Canal Plus for its DTH services in France, Belgium, and elsewhere in Europe, is proprietary to them. Just as the government could justify its legislation against the monopolization of soccer rights on the objective grounds of defending the national cultural heritage, the decoding box question was represented as an issue of anti-competitive practice. The government argued that the CSD box could only decode the CSD digital signal, and not any other competing digital signal. Accordingly, legislation was also initiated to enforce a common 'multicrypt' standard for digital decoding boxes. While this action certainly had the effect of buying time for Vía Digital to develop such equipment further and prepare for its subsequent launch in September, as CSD charged, it was also popularly welcomed in the mainstream press as being in the public interest (Hopewell 1997*b*; Schweid 1997).

However, CSD have maintained that, although proprietary, their system is open: that is, able to receive signals other than its own, including that of Vía Digital, and that the government is acting against them and in favour of its corporate allies on this issue. With these arguments, CSD took the matter to the EU, which accepted them and adjudicated that the Spanish Government would have to change its digital decree to bring it into line with EU free trade laws. This matter was still not resolved by the time of the subsequent Vía Digital launch in September 1997. In the event, Vía Digital announced that they would transmit free-to-air for the first three months, ostensibly to entice subscribers to the service, but with strong suspicions that they still had not sorted out the technical problems with their multicrypt system (del Valle 1997*a*; 1997*d*).

As the soccer rights issue would indicate, there has been intense competition between the rival services to secure sources of programming for DTH. While both TVE and Televisa bring their own programming with them into the DSD consortium, it remains to be seen how well their characteristic kinds of programme, especially Televisa's *telenovelas*, will fare in competition with CSD's offerings, particularly given Sogecable's strength in films, and the demonstrated popularity of that kind of programming in Spain. As well as signing up Spanish-language versions of such US-based global channels as Discovery and Disney, CSD has obtained an exclusive ten-year contract with Warner Brothers International for its films and series. The company also has been discussing Spanish-language co-productions with Warner Brothers, which would have the side-effect of assisting the latter's Latin American ambitions (Hopewell and Guider 1997). In addition, CSD will carry CNN International and the other Turner global channels, and has made further long-term deals with Hollywood studios for the supply of films for its pay-per-view channel ('Big Deals and Rating Roundup' 1997*a*; 1997*b*).

For its part, the leading DSD/Vía Digital partner Telefónica has bought a one-third share in Lola Films, one of Spain's leading independent audiovisual producers (Hopewell 1997*d*). This was a strategic strike, as Lola Films has been an important supplier to Sogetel, the competitor's film arm (Seymour 1997: 202). DSD is aware that it will need more than

Televisa's supply of *telenovelas* to catch up with CSD's lead. Indeed, there is evidence that the vogue for *telenovelas* in Spain has passed. A trade journal survey in 1996 found that only TVE1 was still showing *telenovelas*, and not in prime time. Three of the five of these were Venezuelan: none was Mexican. Local productions, particularly of comedy, were the most popular form of programming. Contrasting this situation to a similar survey in 1994 when Latin American *telenovelas* were the best-rating kind of series, in Italy as well as Spain, the journal quotes a private television source who says *telenovelas* 'are no longer seen as culturally relevant to the Spanish public', particularly in the role models they present for women (quoted in Akyuz 1997: 52). In response to CSD's initiatives in securing US output deals, DSD has engaged a US agent to procure $US2–3 billion worth of programming over the next ten years ('Big Deals and Rating Roundup' 1997*b*).

However, both the decoder face-off and the competition for programme sources were overshadowed completely on 23 July 1997, when Telefónica announced that it had acquired the maximum allowable 25 per cent stake in the leading terrestrial network, Antena 3 TV. Since Antena 3 TV holds 15 per cent of CSD, this move gave Telefónica a stake in both the rival DTH platforms. The incursion was achieved with the assistance of the two banks which were already partners in Antena 3 TV, Banco de Santander and Banco Central Hispanoamérica, in effect acquiring Antonio Asensio's share on behalf of Telefónica. Importantly, the deal also included a controlling interest in Audiovisual Sport, the company which Antena 3 TV and Sogecable had set up to manage soccer rights (del Valle 1997*c*; Hopewell 1997*c*). As with the decoder issue, CSD has appealed to the EU. This recourse to supranational government by a corporation aggrieved by the actions of its national government or its agencies provides an interesting sidelight on the impact of globalization in the European setting, particularly since one of the Portuguese private channels also has sought to use the EU in a similar way (Sousa 1996*b*: 8).

Antena 3 TV has become broadly transnationalized in its ownership, and as such is important to Telefónica in its internationalization strategies, quite apart from the acquisition's shorter-term value in the immediate struggle over digital platforms. Whereas the major CSD partners Canal Plus and Prisa are each significant media powers in their own countries, and Canal Plus is a prime mover in the spread of post-broadcast television services throughout Western Europe, Antena 3 TV, like Telefónica, is more oriented to beyond Europe, and particularly to Latin America. Although Murdoch withdrew from his initial participation, Antena 3 TV now also includes Recoletos, with 10 per cent. This is a newspaper publishing company, 20 per cent owned by Telefónica, and 80 per cent by the British Pearson Group, in their first venture at 'the other end of the Tunnel' (del Valle 1997b; Godard 1997: 20).

Antena 3 TV had been one of the partners in Telenoticias, the original international Spanish-language satellite news launched in 1994, with Reuters and Artear of Argentina, as mentioned in Chapter 4. Although this was sold to CBS in 1996, Antena 3 TV still supplies news to Telenoticias, but, much more importantly, in that same year Antena 3 International was commenced. This is a satellite channel of Antena 3 TV's own programming, transmitted to all Latin American countries. In Mexico, it was the most successful satellite channel in its first year, gaining a higher audience share than the US-based ones such as CNN. The channel also was made available in the US during 1987, making Antena 3 International as extensive in its global reach to the Spanish-speaking world—Spain, the US, and Latin America—as only Televisa has been in the past, but coming from the opposite direction.

Telefónica itself has a strong international orientation, evidenced by its activities in Argentina, the most 'European' of Latin American nations, as noted in Chapter 3. Furthermore, while CSD is a client of the European satellite Astra, Telefónica is a 22.7 per cent owner of Hispasat, the Spanish domestic satellite first launched in 1992, which not only serves to carry the Vía Digital signal to its subscribers in Spain, but is the only European satellite system serving both sides of the Atlantic (Puente 1997). The first Hispasat, incidentally, was designed to transmit to Latin America, but not to receive from there, prompting comment about how little Spain's attitude had changed in 500 years. However, although the next-generation Hispasat launched in 1994 could carry television signals in both directions, the main use to date has been for Televisión América, a selection of TVE programming distributed to several cable systems in Latin America (Bulloch 1992).

In addition to Televisa and TVE, Telefónica's original partners in DSD/Vía Digital, it has since brought in the Japanese company Hichu with 5 per cent, and has undertaken extensive negotiations with the Hughes global DTH enterprise, DirecTV, for them to take up 20 per cent (Puente 1997). This is of interest, because when the Spanish venture was first announced, DSD was aligned with Murdoch's competing Sky consortium, as in Latin America, while it was CSD which was associated with Hughes (Martínez 1996: 50). The implication is that international strategic alliances are fluid and adaptable to different national and world-regional situations, although such adaptation might not necessarily suit all partners involved, especially the relatively minor ones. For example, Televisa will find itself in alliance with Hughes in Europe, but in competition with them in Latin America.

Portugal

From Authoritarianism to Liberalization

Portugal endured authoritarian rule for nearly half this century, the era of 'O Estado Novo', the Salazar–Caetano 'new state' of 1926 to 1974, during which time both radio and television were established. As in Spain, broadcasting was made an instrument of church and state, first with a duopoly in radio which lasted from the 1930s until the 1980s, and in television, with a quasi-private monopoly which began broadcasting in 1957 (Sousa 1994: 2–4). Although António de Oliveira Salazar, the architect of the 'Estado Novo', 'deeply mistrusted' television, as he did most other forms of modernization, with the introduction of television he was indulging the enthusiasm of Marcello Caetano, his 'dauphin' and subsequent successor, according to a former Chair of the state television organization, RTP (Rádiotelevisão Portuguesa) (quoted in Sousa 1996a: 135).

Caetano took a personal hand in setting up RTP as a state–private entity owned by the government in conjunction with commercial radio stations, banks, and other companies. As in Spain, the system was a hybrid, funded by a receiver's licence fee system (later abandoned), in conjunction with the sale of advertising time. At first reaching only 58 per cent of the population, it achieved national coverage by the time it launched a second, more 'cultural' network in 1968, once again matching the system in Spain (Optenhögel 1986: 240–1; Sousa 1996a: 135–6). Caetano used television as a medium of propaganda to maintain an increasingly untenable and isolated regime, and even after the overthrow of the old order by the Left in the 'Carnation Revolution' of April 1974, and the nationalization of RTP, it remained highly politicized. Succeeding democratic governments did not find cause to disagree with Caetano's 1972 observation, 'In the times that we live in the effective control of television is essential for the government' (quoted in Traquina 1995: 227).

RTP was confirmed as a state monopoly in the democratic constitutions of 1976 and 1982, but precisely because of its continued use as an 'ideological state apparatus', to use a metaphor conventional at the time but most appropriate in this context, public opinion was amenable to the urgings from commercial interests and social elites alike, that Portugal should join the broad movement towards privatization then prevalent elsewhere in Europe. A consensus in the parliament permitted the removal of the constitutional barriers to the privatization of television in

1989, and a new Television Law was passed in 1990 to set up the Alta Autoridade para a Comunicação Social (AACS), and open the way for the licensing of two private channels to commence. A number of generic social objectives were declared, such as the promotion of national identity and a critical conscience, but the law does not mandate any enforceable programming requirements (Traquina 1995: 225–6; Sousa 1996b: 10–12).

There were three bidders for the two licences. First, there was Sociedade Independente de Comunicação (SIC), headed by Pinto Balsemão. Although he had been Prime Minister in 1981–2, Balsemão had established credentials as a media owner in the Controjornal print group. Of more interest here is the fact that, right from the beginning, the maximum allowable to a foreign owner of 15 per cent (more stringent than in Spain) was held by Globo Participações, a company wholly owned by the Globo organization of Brazil. A second media-based bidder was Rede Independente (TV1), headed by a former RTP director. One other potential commercial media bidder did not proceed, which was presumed to be because it was associated with the opposition. The remaining bidder was Televisão Independente (TVI), a venture which included both the Catholic radio network and other organizations directly or indirectly linked to the church, as well as Antena 3 TV. The process was basically of the 'beauty contest' type, with the Prime Minister and cabinet deciding, though taking into consideration the very tentative advice given by the AACS. The licences went to the Balsemão/Globo SIC, and the church/Spanish television investors' company TVI (Sousa 1996a: 193–6).

The licence fee, the traditional source of revenue for RTP, was abolished around the same time, in revised statutes for RTP in 1992. The sale of advertising time had risen from 30 per cent of RTP's income in the 1970s to become the majority source in the 1980s, reaching 80 per cent in 1990, the last year before RTP funding was put on an almost wholly commercial basis. The statutes also restructured RTP as a private company, but one in which the government selected the board of directors. As well, RTP's public service obligations were put on to a contractual basis, whereby RTP would be paid for providing particular services to the government (Traquina 1995: 227–9).

Both the broad structural characteristics of the new system which has been adopted and even the time-scale in which the transition was effected show close parallels with those of Spain, perhaps something like an 'Iberian model' of private television institutionalization. However, there are some distinctive features of the Portuguese system which are worth further comment. First, there is the contractual arrangement just mentioned under which RTP undertakes to provide specific 'public service' functions for government. The first contract, in 1993, listed the transmission of television signals to all Portuguese, including those living abroad, and the production of programming for them; the concession of airtime to designated organizations, such as political parties; the maintenance of an audiovisual archive; the promotion of Portuguese cinema; and other such public interest activities, all cast in terms of the generic objectives set out in the 1990 Television Law (Contrato de Concessão do Serviço Público de Televisão 1993).

This at least amounted to a series of identifiable tasks, if not an affirmation of a public service ideal. Nevertheless, the private channels were then able to claim that the funds which RTP received under its contract were a subsidy to a commercial competitor for services which they too would willingly provide for the same payment (Sousa 1996a: 197–8). Interestingly, in the 1996 contract, the government has since affirmed its commitment to a special role for RTP as a national network of record, with particular obligations to provide programming diversity, an alternative to commercial programming, and other such classic objectives of national public service broadcasting (Contrato de Concessão do Serviço Público de Televisão 1996). Consequently, for example, RTP now provides local news services, and presents its second network cultural programming without advertising. These moves represent something of a retrieval of the concept of public service as a social ideal, a step back from the abyss, unlike Spain where, as has been suggested, TVE, RTP's counterpart, has been subjected to an economic rationalism which undermines the very grounds for the maintenance of public television as an institution.

Secondly, there has been the strong presence of the Catholic church within broadcasting. Just as radio had formerly been consolidated into one government and one church network under the Salazar–Caetano regime, the church found its way into a prominent position within the new privatized order of television. It was not given the preferential treatment it expected, but neither did it meet any obstruction. While deference to the church as an institution might be a cultural tradition, and consistent with the entrenched Catholicism of the 'Estado Novo', Spain (and the entire Latin world) has a similar religious tradition, as well as a heritage of authoritarian regime-sponsored Catholicism under Franco. However, from the start, Spain opted for a thoroughly secular and commercial system of television. In the next section, it will be seen that the church's apparently strong beginning in television was not in any case sustained in Portugal, though more for economic rather than ideological reasons.

The Empire Strikes Back

By 1997, TVI had been sidelined by the competition between RTP and SIC as the market leaders, but it had begun with different concerns, and had gone on to pursue a different direction again. In other words, the subsequent development of TVI has diminished the role of the church, but this has not just been a question of reconciling its expressed commitment to 'Christian humanism' with commercial realities in programming, but also of attracting capital into its more recent venture, the building of its own telecommunications infrastructure, which is aimed at providing market entry to that area of the communications business. By 1994, France Telecom was reported to have 45 per cent in that venture, Rede de Teledifusão Independente ('TVI promete o que não tem' 1994), while the church's participation in the television broadcaster still stood at 22 per cent, compared to a total of 44 per cent foreign, though mainly EU, capital. Most of this foreign capital was not media-related, but it did include 2.5 per cent from Antena 3 TV, which has assisted TVI with developing programme formats and training (Sousa 1996a: 210–11). There is now also some nominal participation from Lusomundo (Cintra Torres 1997b), so a much more commercial approach can be expected from TVI. As noted earlier regarding its connections with Sogecable, Lusomundo is a cinema distributor and exhibitor, the main one in Portugal, which also is involved in press and radio (Sousa 1994: 11). Like the other channels, TVI has international connections through which to source programming, notably in the UK and US, and it also buys Brazilian *telenovelas* from SBT and Bandeirantes in Brazil (Sousa 1996a: 211).

Prior to the advent of the private channels, Globo's links were with RTP. As noted in Chapter 3, Globo started selling *telenovelas* to RTP as early as 1977, and persuaded RTP to keep taking them over the next decade. Although Portuguese companies produced some of their own *telenovelas*, and there were some also imported from the other Brazilian networks, Globo *telenovelas* always were the most popular, so RTP felt it had a trump card in the programming battle which was to come with the privatized era. However, we have seen how Globo became a shareholder in one of the new channels, SIC. In spite of Globo's failure to gain a European foothold with Telemontecarlo, and the heavy loss it sustained there, Roberto Marinho was convinced by his son, the heir apparent Roberto Irineu Marinho, and also Pinto Balsemão, head of SIC, that this was an ideal strategic investment. For Balsemão, it was not just a question of getting access to Globo programming, but their entire repertoire of commercial and technical expertise, since his own experience was with newspapers.

Thus, in much the same way as Globo acquired its initial commercial television know-how from Time-Life in the 1960s, now Globo was in a perfect position to take on the tutelage of its Lusitanian protégé. At least for the first two years, while Globo was assisting SIC with every aspect of commercial television from engineering to marketing, it continued to sell its coveted *telenovelas* to both RTP and SIC, but SIC argued that this was devaluing the product with overexposure, and obtained an exclusive deal with Globo in September 1994. Within six months, SIC overtook the market leadership which RTP had been able to sustain until then (Sousa 1997: 7–12), and continued to increase market share at RTP's expense. As of April 1997, SIC had 51.5 per cent of the national audience; RTP's Canal 1 had 31.9; TVI had 11.3; and RTP's TV2 had 5.4 (Sousa 1997: annexe 1). Meanwhile, in much the same way as Spanish cultural elites had denounced the Latin American *telenovelas* as all-devouring serpents (*culebrones*) during the vogue for them in that country, Portuguese elites no longer joked about cultural imperialism in reverse, but worried about the incursion of Brazilian words into everyday language, and the adoption of Brazilian names, fashions, festivals, and social behaviour into popular culture (Sousa 1997: 8).

The eclipse of RTP by commercial competition has serious implications, although RTP continues to provide some quite distinct services. We have seen how it has been put on to a wholly competitive commercial basis, to the extent that it has no subsidy from licence fees, although it is exclusively charged with the responsibilities of the government's public service objectives. It operates five channels: Canal 1 is designed to serve the general population; TV2 is a more educational and cultural channel aimed at minority audiences; RTPi (International) is a satellite service sent out to the Portuguese-speaking countries of the world, as well as to the various diasporic settlements of Portuguese; while RTP-Madeira and RTP-Açores are for the 'autonomous regions' of those particular Portuguese islands in the Atlantic.

RTP has continued to commission productions in Portugal, but has not been successful in commercializing them in other markets. RTP productions are well received in the former colonies in Africa, but serving those nations is part of RTP's public service role, rather than the capturing of a market as such. Like its Spanish counterpart, RTP is much more an importer than an exporter of programming, first from the US, and secondly from Brazil. While *telenovelas* from Latin American countries other than Brazil have found some success in Portugal, RTP's experience is that Spanish, French, and German programmes do not attract audiences (Sousa 1996*a*: 198–200). Programming on Canal 1 is wholly commercial, but TV2 does carry out its role as an educational/ cultural channel—there are no *telenovelas* (nor advertising) on TV2. RTPi provides the Portuguese diaspora with a mixture of Canal 1 and TV2 programming, which is also the greater part of what goes out to the island communities, although they produce some of their own programming as well (Sousa 1996*a*: 201–4).

Post-Broadcast and Postcolonial Services

As elsewhere in Europe, individuals owning satellite dishes in Portugal were able to pick up services on an unregulated basis during the 1980s. Indeed, this form of demand for the circumvention of national television monopolies was one of the factors conducive to the liberalization of terrestrial television broadcasting, as surely as the extralegal services eventually attracted the attention of government regulation. The first licences to distribute satellite-to-cable signals in Portugal were issued in 1994, and although telecommunication companies were permitted to provide such services, start-up cable companies could not enter telecommunications. By early 1995, the licensees were TV Cabo Portugal, Bragatel, and Multicanal (Sousa 1996*a*: 212–14). TV Cabo Portugal is fully owned by Portugal Telecom, the national telecommunications monopoly which in 1995 commenced a process of up to 70 per cent privatization. Its initial thirty-channel service included Televisa's Galavisión and the Spelling TeleUno channels as well as the usual US-based ones such as CNN and Discovery, and the European global channels from the BBC and RAI. Bragatel, linked to Philips, operates only in the northern city of Braga, while Multicanal is owned by Lusomundo in conjunction with US capital (United International Holdings) (Sousa 1996*a*: 173–5 and 214).

Because the initial cable legislation only provided for operators to redistribute signals, no channels specifically for the Portuguese market had been developed, and subscriber take-up, possibly for that reason, had been slow—less than one-fifth of more than a million homes passed by TV Cabo cable were subscribers in early 1997 (Cintra Torres 1997*a*: 20–1). However, with the law being modified in April to permit licensees to package their own programming, it was reported before the end of the year that TV Cabo would join with a new company called Portusat to develop subscription television 'in Portugal and other markets'. Portusat is a joint venture of none other than SIC and Globo, with Globo as the main investor. The information was that Portusat was to have 42 per cent of the new company and TV Cabo the equivalent, with another 8 per cent being held by the film exhibition and distribution company Luso-mundo, and the remainder expected to go to a sports rights agency, Olivedesportos, which holds all the major soccer rights (Cintra Torres 1997*b*; 1997*c*; 'Lusomundo Joins TV Cabo' 1998). This new venture clearly can be expected to put Globo into as influential a position in the satellite-to-cable realm as it has achieved through its relationship with SIC in terrestrial free-to-air television in Portugal. Furthermore, given its alignment with Televisa, TCI, and News Corporation in the Sky DTH consortium, Globo is well placed to be instrumental in bringing a commercial digital television service to Portugal.

The first Portuguese broadcaster to use digital transmission, however, is RTP's international arm RTPi, which, amongst several other services, digitally transmits a channel new as of 1997, RTP África, for terrestrial redistribution in the five former Portuguese colonies in Africa (Angola, Cabo Verde, Guinea-Bissau, Mozambique, and São Tomé/Príncipe), and also incorporates programming from them ('Steps towards Digital' 1997). As noted, RTPi transmits to other world regions where there have been Portuguese colonies, or where there are diasporic or other communities of Portuguese-speakers. AsiaSat-2 carries RTPi as far as East Timor in Asia (Cane 1995; 'Portugal Broadcasts into East Timor' 1996), while Globo's rival TVA includes it in its digital bouquet in Brazil ('RTPi: The Five-Year Mission' 1997).

It was noted how TVE in Spain has a service which it sends via Hispasat to the Americas. The Italian public broadcaster RAI has a similar international satellite service, quite commonly available in Latin American countries, while the French Government has TVN-5 servicing its geolinguistic region. However, RTPi is perhaps the most serious effort by any national government in the Latin world to provide a service for its geolinguistic region as a matter of policy, albeit oriented more to Africa than to Latin America, where the great majority of Portuguese-speakers live. Commencing in June 1992, RTPi was motivated by the consideration that 'a third of Portuguese live abroad', according to the first director of RTPi, and that there are 25 million speakers of Portuguese outside of Portugal, without of course counting Brazil (Baptista Rato 1993).

At an estimated annual cost of over $US1,400,000, RTPi is intended to defend the Portuguese language from the incursions of French and English, especially in Africa where it competes against French channels with its popular music and soccer programming ('RTPi: The Five-Year Mission' 1997). This is a wholly political enterprise, more neocolonial than postcolonial—in Mozambique, for instance, which joined the British Commonwealth in 1995, English-speaking intellectuals question why they should continue as a lusophone nation, and be linked into the Portuguese invocation of a common *latinadade* ('Latinity'). Meanwhile, the most popular programme on television is the daily Brazilian *tele-novela* (Rønning 1997: 50–2). On the other hand, the possibility that there might be potential in commercializing at least some of the ex-patriate Portuguese is suggested by the fact that late in 1997 the Balse-mão/Globo SIC also commenced a digital service, not for Africa or Brazil, but for the 750,000 Portuguese who live in France ('Big Deals and Rating Roundup' 1997*b*). Tendencies such as these will be considered further in the next and final chapter.

References

Akyuz, Gün (1997), 'Heart of the Community', *TV World* (January), 49–52.

Alvarez, Maria (1997), 'Proof is in the Numbers', *Variety* (24 February–2 March), 198.

Anuario El País (1992), *El País*, Madrid.

Baptista Rato, Afonso (1993), 'An "I" Added to RTP', *Espace*, 18: 7.

'Big Deals and Rating Roundup' (1997*a*), *Broadcasting & Cable International* (June), 6.

—— (1997*b*), *Broadcasting & Cable International* (October), 6.

Bulloch, Chris (1992), 'Hispasat Up, Ready—and Waiting', *Via Satellite* (December), 62–4.

Bustamante, Enrique (1989), 'TV and Public Service in Spain: A Difficult Encounter', *Media, Culture and Society*, 11/1: 67–87.

—— (1990), 'Galavisión en España y la CEE', paper presented to international colloquium, 'La televisión en Español: una perspectiva global', University of California at Berkeley, June.

—— and Giu, Inmaculada (1988), 'Televisión: desequilibrios en cadena', in E. Bustamante and R. Zallo (eds.), *Las industrias culturales en España* (Ediciones Akal, Madrid), 109–62.

Cane, Alan (1995), 'Satellite Opens up New Era for Communications', *Australian* (1 December), 31.

Cintra Torres, Nuno (1997*a*), 'Portuguese Men of War', *Cable and Satellite Europe* (June), 20–4.

—— (1997*b*), 'SIC, Globo, TV Cabo Join Forces', *Cable and Satellite Europe* (October), 14.

—— (1997*c*), 'TV Cabo Reveals Premium Pay-TV Offer', *Cable and Satellite Europe* (November), 14.

Contrato de Concessão do Serviço Público de Televisão (1993), contract between the Portuguese Government and Radiotelevisão Portuguesa, Lisbon.

—— (1996), contract between the Portuguese Government and Radiotelevisão Portuguesa, Lisbon.

Contreras, José Miguel (1996), 'Ante un nueve punto cero: diez tendencias de evolución del mercado televisivo español', in *Informes Anuales de Fundesco, Comunicación social 1996/tendencias* (Fundesco, Madrid), 283–8.

'Country Profile: Spain' (1994), *TV International* (24 January), 5–8.

Davis, Andrew (1993*a*), 'ONCE Reportedly Sells 18% Stake in Tele 5', *Broadcasting & Cable International* (October), 42.

——— (1993*b*), 'Spain Waits Anxiously for New Cable Law', *Broadcasting & Cable International* (October), 41–2.

del Valle, David (1997*a*), 'EC Pushes for Spanish Change', *Cable and Satellite Europe* (September), 12.

——— (1997*b*), 'Telefónica Buys 20% Stake in Recoletos', *Cable and Satellite Europe* (November), 10.

——— (1997*c*), 'Telefónica Moves in on Antena 3', *Cable and Satellite Europe* (September), 18.

——— (1997*d*), 'Vía Digital CA "Out of Operation"', *Cable and Satellite Europe* (November), 12.

Franquet, Rosa (1988), 'Radio: un oligopolio en transformación', in E. Bustamante and R. Zallo (eds.), *Las industrias culturales en España* (Ediciones Akal, Madrid), 77–107.

García Jiménez, Jesús (1980), *Radiotelevisión y política cultural en el Franquismo* (Instituto Superior de Investigaciones Científicas, Instituto Balmes de Sociología, Madrid).

Godard, François (1997), 'The Urge to Merge', *Cable and Satellite Europe* (July), 20–4.

Hernández Lomeli, Francisco (1992–3), 'Televisa en España', *Comunicación y Sociedad*, 16–17: 74–105.

Holland, Jonathan (1997), 'El Pais Prexy Propels Prisa Growth', *Variety* (24 February–2 March), 206.

Hopewell, John (1997*a*), 'New Kid in Town', *Variety* (24 February–2 March), 197 and 205.

——— (1997*b*), 'Politicians Weigh in on Digital TV Rules', *Variety* (24 February–2 March), 204.

——— (1997*c*), 'Spain Telco Picks Up Antena 3 in Surprise', *Variety* (28 July–3 August), 32.

——— (1997*d*), 'Telefonica Sews up Lola Films Pact', *Variety* (11–17 August), 10.

——— (1998), 'WB Creates Spanish Axis', *Variety* (5–11 January), 28.

——— and Guider, Elizabeth (1997), 'Sogecable, WB in Pact', *Variety* (14–20 July), 33.

Kinnane, Jo (1991), 'Report on Visit to Eurovisa and Protele in London', unpublished research assistant's report, Victoria University.

Larraya, J., and Beaumont, J. (1992), 'Godó dimite como presidente de Antena 3 TV', *El País* (17 June).

'Lusomundo Joins TV Cabo' (1998), *Cable and Satellite Europe* (January), 10.

Madinaveitia, Eduardo (1991), 'Tendencias en medias audiovisuales', in *Informes Anuales de Fundesco, Comunicación social 1991/tendencias* (Fundesco, Madrid), 54–5.

Martínez, Sanjuana (1996), 'Televisa se asocia a Radio Televisión Española, con la bendición de Aznar', *Proceso* (8 September), 48–50.

Nosty, Bernardo Díaz (1996), 'Televisión: la aventura digital', in Informes Anuales de Fundesco, *Comunicación social 1996/tendencias* (Fundesco, Madrid), 159–94.

Optenhögel, Uwe (1986), 'Portugal', in H. Kleinsteuber, D. McQuail, and K. Siune (eds.), *Electronic Media and Politics in Western Europe* (Campus Verlag, Frankfurt), 239–50.

Peralta, Braulio (1997), 'España: autorizan a Televisa para participar en la televisión digital', *La Jornada* (9 March), 53.

'Portugal Broadcasts into East Timor' (1996), *Australian* (30 January).

Puente, David (1997), 'Spanish Bulls', *TV World* (October), 22.

Roncagliolo, Rafael (1995), 'Trade Integration and Communication Networks in Latin America', *Canadian Journal of Communication*, 20/3: 335–42.

Rønning, Helge (1997), 'Language, Cultural Myths, Media and *Realpolitik*: The Case of Mozambique', *Media Development*, 44/1: 50–4.

'RTPi: The Five Year Mission' (1997), *Cable and Satellite Europe* (June), 22.

Sampedro Blanco, Victor, and van den Bulck, Jan (1995), 'Regions vs States and Cultures in the EC Media Policy Debate: Regional Broadcasting in Belgium and Spain', *Media, Culture and Society*, 17/2: 239–51.

Schweid, Richard (1997), 'Spain's Digital Decoder Box Battle', *International Cable* (September), 34.

Seymour, Abigail (1997), 'Pic Maker Sogetel Pacts for Indie Prods', *Variety* (24 February–2 March), 202 and 205.

Sousa, Helena (1994), 'Portuguese Media: New Forms of Concentration', paper presented to the conference of the International Association for Mass Communication Research, Seoul, July.

—— (1996a), 'Communications Policy in Portugal and its Links with the European Union', unpublished Ph.D. thesis, City University, London.

—— (1996b), 'Portuguese Television Policy in the International Context: An Analysis of the Links with the EU, Brazil and the US', paper presented to the 20th Conference of the International Association for Mass Communication Research, Sydney, August.

—— (1997), 'Crossing the Atlantic: Globo's Wager in Portugal', paper presented to the conference of the International Association for Mass Communication Research, Oaxaca, July.

'Spanish TV the Latest to Go Private' (1989), *Broadcasting Abroad* (November), 8.

'Steps towards Digital' (1997), *Cable and Satellite Europe* (June), 24.

Traquina, Nelson (1995), 'Portuguese Television: The Politics of Savage Deregulation', *Media, Culture and Society*, 17/2: 223–38.

'TVI promete o que não tem' (1994), *Público* (8 June), 44.

Vilches, Lorenzo (1996), 'The Media in Spain', in T. Weymouth and B. Lamizet (eds.), *Markets and Myths: Forces for Change in the European Media* (Longman, London), 173–201.

Williams, Michael, and Hopewell, John (1997), 'Sogecable Timeline 1972–1997', *Variety* (24 February–2 March), 198.

6 | *Non plus ultra*: Latin Geolinguistic Markets at their Limits

Classical scholars tell us that the known limits of the ancient world were marked by the twin pillars of Hercules which were set at the mouth of the Mediterranean and carried the inscription, *non plus ultra*: no more beyond. Spain and Portugal dared to prove this wrong when their colonization of the Americas began in 1492. This book has examined the institutional development and international expansion of the major television industries of Latin America within the context of the linguistic and cultural similarities which colonization established, and with attention to how language and culture, in conjunction with new communication technologies, have been commercially exploited in extending markets for programmes and services beyond national borders, not only within the Americas but reaching back into Europe. However, it remains for this final chapter to analyse more closely the mechanisms that have favoured the rise of the particular corporations which have been under consideration, and to ask how much further their strategies for development can take them, or whether they have reached their limits in a more intensively globalized industry: that is, whether or not there really is 'no more beyond' for them now.

Cooperation towards a 'Latin Audiovisual Space'

While it would come as no surprise that the national broadcasters of Spain and Portugal are supported by their governments in providing satellite television services to their respective postcolonial worlds, as we have just seen, perhaps more striking are various intergovernmental initiatives, mostly aimed at consolidating the Spanish and Portuguese languages and cultures on an international basis, even including one committed to creating a 'Latin audiovisual space' as such. These efforts have been augmented by the activities of international broadcasters' associations and professional bodies. However, it should be understood that the international orientation of both Spain and Portugal is as modern nations of a united Europe, not one-time imperial centres brooding on their glorious pasts. Even though Portugal's former empire has only recently been given up and it evidently retains more *saudade* or nostalgia for it than does Spain for its long-lost colonies, in terms of trade and investment, the Iberian countries have become much more important to each other than their postcolonial worlds are to either of them (Drago 1991: 9; Birmingham 1993: 190–2). In this regard, their engagement as metropolitan nations in the promotion of their languages and cultures throughout the world is no more significant than that of the other former imperial nations of Europe, such as Britain, France, and Italy, and satellite television is a useful medium for that purpose. As the last chapter has shown, if anything Spain and Portugal have become more the objects of desire for the communication enterprises which have grown up in their erstwhile colonies. As early as the 1960s, Spain was seeking to establish international links between TVE and Latin American television programme producers, in which a major concern was its interest in the maintenance of the Spanish language under its hegemony, as well as the fostering of news and cultural programming exchanges (García Jiménez 1980: 401–9). The advent of satellite television has given a new kind of vision to these efforts, or, to quote the responsible executive of Hispasat:

Satellites have become a key element for the diffusion of a full range of television channels in markets which are homogeneous for linguistic, cultural or economic reasons. In this way, satellites today are the most appropriate telecommunications infrastructure for the development of digital television platforms directed to specific linguistic markets, leaping national barriers to form homogeneous markets composed of countries separated by thousands of kilometres.

And thanks to communication satellites and their capacity to transmit to millions of homes, we find before us the option of making real the old dream of creating an Iberoamerican Audiovisual Space, with its own accent. Ultimately, digital satellite platforms offer us an opportunity to develop an audiovisual market in 'Spanish', composed of more than a hundred million homes, led by the creators, producers, and media groups of our own Iberoamerican countries. (Díaz Argüelles 1997)

It is not as if Spain is the only nation wanting to bring the Spanish-speaking world together. For example, Latin American and Caribbean governments supported the development of a regional news agency, ASIN (La Acción de Sistemas Informativas Nacionales), which was joined only later by the Spanish national agency, EFE (Drago 1991: 11). Similarly, the creation of the CPLP (Comunidade dos Países de Língua Portuguesa—Community of Portuguese-Speaking Countries) in 1996 was not only the initiative of Portugal, whatever reservations about its motives might have been harboured in some of the member nations in Africa (Rønning 1997). Over the relatively short time in which both Portugal and Brazil have become more democratic nations, they have been willing to open up relations which had lapsed considerably since independence. Indeed, a former Brazilian Minister of Culture has been a prime mover not only in the CPLP, but also in founding the Instituto Internacional de Língua Portuguesa (International Institute of the Portuguese Language) (Marques de Melo 1995: 2–8).

No doubt the most ambitious extent of intergovernmental collaboration of this kind was reached in 1982 when the Ministers of Culture from Spain, Portugal, France, Italy, Mexico, and Brazil met to promote, in their words, 'cooperation between countries with a language of Latin origin'. It was left to the French (who, after all, had first invented the concept of Latin America, as was noted in the Introduction) to explore the possibility of building a 'Latin audiovisual space' (Mattelart, Delcourt, and Mattelart 1984: p. ix). This initiative was prompted by concerns over the internationalization of both the television and film industries (hence the concept of 'audiovisual'), and came in the wake of the 1970s debate over cultural imperialism, a phenomenon which was by then seen to have become a problem for Europe as well as the Third World. While the scheme produced some fine research (Mattelart and Mattelart 1990), and although France was later instrumental in ensuring that audiovisual production was not made subject to the free trade obligations under the GATT (General Agreement on Tariffs and Trade) signed by many leading countries in 1993, the initial impetus towards a Latin audiovisual space has not been sustained by the governments concerned.

However, if we set aside film, which requires a quite different line of analysis, it is clear that the activities of private entrepreneurial interests, at least in television, have gone much further than any intergovernmental collaboration in building up and coordinating international markets of Spanish- and Portuguese-speaking nations across the world. For example, perhaps the most durable and effective organization for international cooperation in television has been the OTI (Organización de Televisión Iberoamericana), which, as noted in Chapter 2, has had a close association with Televisa in Mexico, the country in which it was formed in 1971, as well as with some of the other major Latin American entrepreneurial channels such as Venevisión and the channels owned at the time of OTI's formation by Goar Mestre in Argentina and Chateaubriand in Brazil (García Jiménez 1980: 527). An organization of broadcasting companies, public as well as private, OTI exists to coordinate the transmission of such premier international events as the soccer World Cup. As noted in Chapter 1, Latin American entrepreneurs have maintained themselves as an international lobby group as well, in the form of AIR (Asociación Interamericana de Radiodifusión—Interamerican Broadcasting Association).

However, it is not so much the entrepreneurs' formalized international collective action as their individual corporate dynamics and strategic alliances which have been decisive in commercializing their respective geolinguistic regions. It is precisely that process which has been chronicled in this book, from the era when an international trade in actual programmes was opened up, to the present, which is characterized more by the provision of continuous services to subscribers over international satellites. The next sections will look more analytically at the mechanisms through which the Latin corporate entrepreneurs have exploited their strengths in the past, followed by an assessment of the challenges they face in maintaining their pre-eminence as they make the transition to the new era.

Latin Television: A Cultural Industries Analysis

[C]ultural production in television cannot be understood outside the framework of the institutional apparatuses which produce and the fundamental economic and production relations which organise these apparatuses, and which link and connect them, within and between nation-states. . . . But it must also be said that the level of economic determination is the necessary but not sufficient condition for an adequate analysis of cultural production. (Hall 1978: 239)

As well as the political and economic structures in terms of which television has developed, the modes in which it has commercialized language and culture have to be taken into account. British and North American political economists of communication have done this with a 'cultural industries' approach which links the nature of broadcasting commodities with language. However, where their analysis is aimed at explaining the dominance of US production in the English-speaking or 'anglophone' world, it will be argued here that a similar analysis can be used to explain the rise of the major Latin American corporations such as Televisa and Globo.

The cultural industries are not so much about the stock of domestic consumer hardware goods such as television sets, videorecorders, and compact disc players, as they are about the flow of software which they carry, such as television programmes and subscriber services. As commodities, such goods and services have some distinctive characteristics. While viewers might have some favourite programmes they like to see again and again, for the most part they want a continuous flow of new material. To maintain this comes at a high cost for producers, so there is an incentive for them to seek 'economies of scale' and to sell their cultural products and services into as many markets as possible. This they can do because cultural products are not used up in consumption, like food or clothes. Furthermore, the costs in reproducing copies for those additional markets are negligible: it is as if all the real costs are in making the original programme—in production rather than reproduction, so to speak. It follows also that it is more profitable for cultural producers if they can also control the distribution of their products.

On the basis of this economics of cultural production, there is a tendency for the cultural industries to favour concentration, as well as audience maximization. The high costs of developing and producing tradeable cultural products such as television programmes are a barrier to entry against smaller producers. Larger producers, as well as having economies of scale, achieved through factory- or at least studio-style continuous production, are also better placed to absorb the considerable risks in cultural production. Whatever the cultural imperialism theorists seemed to think, audiences do not just accept whatever programmes are churned out for them, even of quite generic material like situation comedies or *telenovelas*. Thus, while the producer of just one new series cannot afford for it to fail in the market, large producers are in a position to subsidize their failures with their more successful products over a continuous range of output. They are also better placed to adjust the prices of their output for different markets, or at different stages of the product's life-cycle (Collins, Garnham, and Locksley 1988: 6–19).

This analysis can be taken a stage further by incorporating what the classical economists called 'comparative advantage', now more often referred to as 'competitive advantage'. Hoskins and McFadyen use this concept to explain the traditional dominance of the US in cultural production. In addition to the 'first mover' advantages accruing from the exploitation of new technologies as they become available, US producers enjoy economies of scale and scope attributable to their 'unique access to the largest market' (1991: 209–12), that is, to the largest English-speaking nation in a world where English is 'the language of advantage': 'not only are anglophones the largest and richest world language community... but English is the dominant second language of the world' (Collins 1990: 211). The producers' access is 'unique' to the extent that they are able to exclude imported cultural products, as US producers very largely can do. Some other media economists use the concept of 'domestic opportunity advantage' to refer to the same phenomenon, but formulate it in such a way that it is a principle applicable to other geolinguistic regions as well, observing that

producers in larger countries, and producers in countries that belong to large natural-language markets, have a financial incentive to create larger budget films and programs that will generally have greater intrinsic audience appeal, a clear advantage in international competition. (Wildman and Siwek, 1988: 68)

Apart from their implicit recognition that having a large domestic market within a major geolinguistic region is only a potential and not a necessary competitive advantage, Wildman and Siwek identify two decisive factors which can determine whether or not that potential is realized. First, they make the point that it is not just the absolute numbers of speakers of a certain language in a particular nation which matter, but their relative income. Although they do not provide figures for 'non-market economies', and so exclude the People's Republic of China, the largest nation in the largest geolinguistic region of the world, they do include India, Hindi having the second largest number of speakers in the world after Chinese, and easily demonstrate the great discrepancy between India's population size and its gross national product. Significantly, however, Spanish is the third largest geolinguistic region, and, on the basis of the 1980s data Wildman and Siwek give, at a much more commensurate fifth rank in GDP, while Portuguese weighs in at sixth and eighth respectively (1988: 83–5). It is in this light that we can appreciate the significance of Televisa's strenuous efforts to obtain and hold distribution outlets for its products in the US and Spain, markets that are wealthier than its domestic market of Mexico; likewise Globo in Portugal; and furthermore, the increasing attention which the largely US-based global media corporations have been giving to both the Spanish and Portuguese geolinguistic markets in recent years.

Wildman and Siwek's second factor is broadcasting policy, claiming that less regulated countries, in particular the US, Mexico, and Brazil, tend to be the most successful exporters (1988: 95–6). The corollary of this is that more strictly regulated nations are less likely to be able to export their television programmes. Thus, to refer again to the case of China, Chinese does not fulfil its potential as a language of advantage not just because of the relative poverty of most of the people who speak it in its largest market, but also because of the restrictions on television production and export, within both the PRC and the geolinguistic region of 'Greater China' (Man Chan 1996).

More to the point in the context of this book, but none the less yielding an instructive contrast with the more state-controlled television regimes of most of Asia, the prevalence of the US commercial model of broadcasting in Latin America seems to have facilitated the growth of the programme export trade. Furthermore, the relationship which Televisa and Globo have borne to their respective states, as explored in Chapters 2 and 3, is pertinent here. Convivial relations with government certainly appear to have been an element in their successful rise to dominance within their nations. Yet it should be stressed that such relations, although enabling, are a secondary element in a corporation's internationalization. The basic factor is the size and wealth of the domestic market, or, in these cases, the fact that Televisa and Globo are the largest producers in the largest nations within their respective geolinguistic regions. On the other hand, the basic model upon which these markets have been structured, as distinct from government regulation and relations as such, is also decisive. After all, there are other Latin American countries with quite large populations, notably Argentina and Colombia, but these have not achieved a proportional television export leadership. Wildman and Siwek's argument suggests that if these had not experienced unusual government controls, or, more specifically, had been styled more conventionally on the US model during the development of television as an institution, then they might have become more significant producers and exporters of television than in fact they have done.

Thus, home market size in itself does not provide any necessary competitive advantage. Rather, membership of that nation in a large and relatively wealthy world language community or geolinguistic region is the more consequential factor in enabling it to project itself into international exchange. For the English-speaking world and the place of US producers and distributors within it, this might seem to be so much a truism as to require no further comment. However, what a cultural industries approach is able to demonstrate is that the prevalence of English-language, and especially US, material on the screens of the world is not imperialist domination as such, but the outcome of the intrinsic economic as well as cultural logic of production within the cultural industries. Importantly, in assessing the role of language in world exchange, the cultural industries theorists acknowledge that as a language in common between nations facilitates trade in cultural products (however unequal it might be), just so do linguistic and cultural differences throw up a 'cultural screen', a natural barrier against trade.

Although these differences are routinely overcome by dubbing and subtitling, and large sections of the world have become accustomed to a diet of material processed in those ways, there is still a 'cultural discount' factor present (Hoskins and Mirus 1988).

Indeed, even when the world language is the same, foreign material requires audiences to cross a cultural gap, to step outside the comfort, familiarity, and deep resonances of their own vernacular. This step might be minor and quite easily negotiated, like watching *Seinfeld* in Alice Springs, but when the cultural gap is large, especially when exacerbated by the dissonance of dubbing and the extra audience work required by subtitles, language and cultural difference can become a considerable disincentive. Nevertheless, argue the cultural industries theorists, producers in English are still at an advantage, because of the prevalence of English as the world's second language. English is not only the world's most widely taught foreign language, but it is pre-eminent in its cultural power as a global language. Two questions not raised by these predominantly anglophone theorists, however, are how robust and resistant might the Spanish-speaking geolinguistic market yet prove to be, given that Spanish is outstripping English in its number and distribution of mother-tongue speakers (Crystal 1997: 3–5)? but also conversely, what happens when US producers begin to make a large output of material tailored specifically for major geolinguistic markets other than English? That is, will the Latin American corporations which have built themselves up through exploiting their geolinguistic positions be able to sustain themselves against competition on their home turf from global services in Spanish and Portuguese?

Against the Flow

As noted first in Chapter 1, the demonstrable dominance of US material on world television screens in the 1970s provoked a debate about the flows of programming from one nation to another, manifested in the theoretical paradigm of cultural imperialism, and in demands for national and international communication policies designed to create more 'balanced' flows. Since that time, there have emerged the general worldwide tendencies for audiences to prefer programming produced in their own nation, to the extent that can be done, and for more regional exchange to take place, particularly where there are linguistic and cultural affinities rather than cultural discounts prevalent across borders, as in Latin America. Anxieties about foreign cultural influences being absorbed via television imports have nevertheless persisted, kept on the agenda by the formation of world trading blocs at one level, and the pressures towards global free trade under GATT at another, not to mention the ubiquitous spread of satellite television—all tendencies which we encompass with the all-embracing concept of globalization.

A study carried out at the beginning of this decade by a UNESCO research centre established in the 1970s for such purposes, CIESPAL (Centro Internacional de Estudios Superiores de Comunicación para América Latina: International Centre for Higher Studies of Communication for Latin America), confirmed the trend towards more regional exchanges in television programmes which had been remarked upon by Varis a decade before. Drawing upon a sample of seventy television stations in Latin America and the Caribbean, the study found an overall decrease in imported programming from 60 per cent of all programming in 1979 to 43 per cent in 1990. However, the greatest proportion of the local production was in news and informational material rather than entertainment programmes, of which 53 per cent were imported. Setting aside the special case of feature films, the largest category of imports and the one in which the US continues to dominate, a range of programming was being imported from Mexico, followed by *telenovelas* from Venezuela, Brazil, and Argentina. Not to overstate how much of a redress of the balance has been achieved, it should be noted that while over 62 per cent of the imported programming came from the US, not quite 30 per cent came from all Latin American and Caribbean sources combined— in other words, US material was more than double the rest, even though it was mainly in the distinct genre of films (M. Estrella, cited in Sánchez Ruiz 1996: 51–2 and 79–80).

In his discussion of this study, Enrique Sánchez Ruiz makes the point that while the evidence of a degree of regional counter-flow is apparent, it has been slow to develop, and involves only a limited number of participants. Furthermore, he notes that while language and cultural affinities are comparative advantages which have given the likes of Televisa, Globo, and Venevisión an assured niche to date in their geolinguistic regions, particularly with their *telenovelas*, there are other comparative advantages that the US enjoys in other audiovisual genres, notably feature films (1996: 52). These include those factors identified by the cultural industries theorists as discussed above, such as economies of scale and scope, which facilitate bigger budgets and hence production values, but also more specifically cultural advantages, such as the capacity of the US to exploit its own cultural diversity (Collins 1990: 214–15). It is important in this regard once again to draw attention to the fundamental distinction between the analysis of film and that of television, and not be deceived by the catch-all category of 'audiovisual'. As the CIESPAL study shows, the bulk of programming imported into Latin American countries, including those such as Mexico which are net programme exporters, is actually US feature films. Similarly, in the previous chapter, it was noted how, in Spain, films are a substantial proportion of the programming offered on television, and broadcasters vie for secure sources of supply from the US.

In fact, a recent study of the audiovisual trade flows of the Iberoamerican geolinguistic region, drawing on 1996 industry-supplied data from Mexico, Brazil, Venezuela, Argentina, and Chile, as well as Spain and Portugal, identifies Spain as one of the biggest importers of audiovisual products, second only to Brazil. Looking more widely, the vast majority (44 per cent) of all audiovisual imports in the national markets named was of films and programmes destined for broadcast television, followed by satellite and cable television services (especially important in Argentina) with 28 per cent, then 16 per cent for videos and 12 per cent for cinema. For all the regional trade in television programmes, the major traded product being the *telenovela*, only 6 per cent of total audiovisual imports came from within the region itself, the same amount as originating in Europe (and mostly imported by Spain and Portugal), with the overwhelming majority of 86 per cent coming from the US. Even the figures for television programming alone (though including the important category of films bought for television) showed a massive preponderance (79 per cent) of US material, with Spain being the biggest market, accounting for half of all such imports (Media Research and Consultancy Spain 1997: 12–15).

Because of the continued attraction of films within television schedules, and not just in Spain, there might be little in these figures to challenge the world-view of the cultural imperialism theorists, but a rather different perspective is gained from looking at the region's exports. Television programmes were found to be by far the largest sector of all audiovisual exports (76 per cent), with satellite and cable services a distant 17 per cent and cinema a sorry 7 per cent. With over half of these exports (54 per cent) going to other Iberoamerican countries, the study sees the region as 'a true economic space' of audiovisual exchange. The US is the second largest destination (20 per cent), a revealing measure of the importance of the Univisión network there to its principal Latin American suppliers, Televisa and Venevisión. European countries were taking 11 per cent of Iberoamerican exports, with 15 per cent going to the rest of the world (1997: 16).

Just as audiovisual production and distribution in the US has become dominated by a few major suppliers, pricing their products according to each national market, the same study found that in television programming exports from the region, five companies accounted for 94 per cent of programmes exported. In order of importance, these were Televisa, Globo, Venevisión, RCTV, and RTVE. However, without citing any figures, the study reports that export sales still represent only a small percentage of the income of these companies. Not surprisingly, the distribution pattern of destinations for television programmes in particular varies little from that for audiovisual goods and services in general: 50 per cent to the region, 23 per cent to the US, 9 per cent to Europe, and 18 per cent to the rest of the world. Note, however, that just as the US is the most important market outside the region for the main Spanish-language producers, Portugal has special importance for Globo: half of its regional sales go to SIC (1997: 16–17).

At this stage it should not be necessary to labour the point that the largest Latin American producers and distributors of television have capitalized on their dominance of the largest national markets in their respective geolinguistic regions in a pattern similar to the global market power achieved by the cultural industries based in the US as the world's largest English-speaking nation. Wilkinson quotes Marcel Vinay, the former head of Protele, Televisa's international distribution company, who formulates 'the classic "aftermarket" strategy of international program sales' available to corporations with such economies of scale:

When we produce a show we are not thinking about the international market. We're thinking mainly of Mexico, to be successful in Mexico, to recoup our costs in Mexico, to earn money. As an ancillary income is the sale of our programs around the world. (1995: 213)

Furthermore, differences in how Spanish is spoken throughout Latin America (though perhaps not in Spain) have been smoothed over, on television at least, thanks to decades in which Televisa and its predecessors have been the major agents for the dubbing into Spanish of most English-language and other foreign films and television programming shown throughout the Spanish-speaking countries of the entire region. Similarly, Globo has been able to put its stamp on much of the material in English and Spanish imported into Brazil. Thus, both the dominant television powers in the region have been able to minimize cultural discount on all the material they deal in, not just their own considerable output (Wilkinson 1995: 3).

While the logic of the cultural industries produces structural and strategic similarities between the major television corporations of the English-speaking and Latin worlds alike, it is also worth while taking stock of some differences exhibited in the Latin American model of media corporate development. As was outlined in Chapter 3, the trend to cross-media ownership and the integration of production and distribution can be identified as major features of this model. While not unique to the Latin American corporations, and steadily returning to become part of the US mediascape, these are two structural features which have enabled, even impelled, Televisa and Globo to trade on their linguistic and cultural position so as to spread beyond their domestic markets. However, some of the other characteristics of the model, such as these companies' oligarchical and autocratic mode of management, might have been useful in maintaining strong relations with national governments and so consolidating their domestic position over the years, but, as the recent crisis in Televisa and its former clashes with both US and Spanish governments would indicate, can be ill-adapted to operating effectively at an international level.

Sánchez Ruiz argues that Televisa in particular, though it could also be said of Globo to a lesser extent, has the comparative disadvantage of lacking experience in competition (1996: 67). Indeed, while Televisa does engage in some film production and distribution, and has been concerned over the last decade to expand its repertoire of exportable television programme genres, particularly in variety and current affairs, it has avoided full-on competition with the US in film and in the television genres in which the US has the greater comparative advantage, such as action series and situation comedies. As for Globo and the more emergent Latin American producers and distributors, the *telenovela* is a niche genre with which the US does not compete. Lopez observes that while film in Latin American countries has only ever flourished when subsidized and protected by the state, the *telenovela* has come to occupy a place in both cultural production and popular culture in Latin America, corresponding to that occupied by film in the US—it is commercially profitable and exportable; it has its star system, for writers and directors as well as actors; and it is expressive of national and pan-regional cultures, a means by which its audiences can 'recognise themselves in the world' (1995: 258–61).

The *Telenovela*

Because the international expansion of Latin American television production and distribution has been identified so much with the particular genre of the *telenovela*, it is worth some further consideration here as both a cultural and an economic phenomenon. There is a flourishing literature on *telenovelas*, in which the condemnatory discourse on the sexism, escapism, and consumerism of their contents in the 1970s has given way to a more audience-based perspective which 'has attempted to take the genre seriously without accepting it uncritically' (McAnany 1993: 135). The history of the genre's origins under the auspices of sponsors such as Colgate-Palmolive in pre-revolutionary Cuba, and its subsequent diffusion to continental Latin America, especially via Argentina and Mexico after 1959, has been well canvassed, as has its prehistory in the *radionovela*, print serials, and other traditional popular culture forms. There is as well a consensus on the distinctions between the *telenovela* and the US soap opera, which are both quantitative (*telenovelas* are shorter, and move towards a definite ending), and qualitative (for example, *telenovelas* often draw dramatic motivation from social conflicts). It is also conventional to draw attention to national differences in *telenovelas*—Brazilian ones have relatively good production values and more complex plots, while the Mexican tend to go for more obvious melodramatic and lachrymose effects (Straubhaar 1982; Klagsbrunn 1993; Mazziotti 1993; Lopez 1995).

As well as its pivotal role as a tradeable genre, the *telenovela* has attracted research attention because of its fusion of commercial exploitation and popular culture, an embodiment of 'the marketplace's long experience in condensing knowledge that both shapes human aspirations and social demands and makes them motives of profit' (Martín-Barbero 1995: 281). Stuart Hall's perception that the series as a genre 'constructs its own audience' (1978: 239–43) has been well borne out by studies of Brazilian *telenovela* production in particular, notably the practice of writers developing plots in conjunction with audience focus groups, and, furthermore, matching each *telenovela* to the expectations of the distinct commercial market segment at which it is aimed (Marques de Melo 1988: 50–2).

However, given that Globo and other *telenovela* producers in Brazil rely on initial domestic market success as the basis for subsequent export strategies, there is a tension between such 'Brazilianization' of the genre, and the broad acceptability of the products to international audiences (Lopez 1995: 261–70). This has meant that not all *telenovelas* can be exported—Globo distributes internationally only a third of those it produces—while those that are exported have to shed or at least play down precisely those more familiar characteristics which make them appealing to Brazilians (Katz 1997: 2). This dilemma is not so much a problem for Televisa so far as the US market is concerned, given the Mexican origins of the majority of US Hispanics, but, as has been noted, Televisa has not been able to sustain a market for its *telenovelas* in Spain, where their more Mexican qualities have become a liability.

Thus, the cultural reasons for the success of the *telenovela* as a genre need to be assessed in different terms for domestic and international audiences, a problem which the producers themselves have to manage carefully. Some elements are common, and are also to be found in other series genres. The appeal of melodrama for audiences, such as was found in Ien Ang's *Watching Dallas* (1985), seems to be universal, as is the series's very 'seriality' (Allen 1996), and the habitual everyday shared ritual quality of watching and discussing in specific social settings (González 1994). Yet without disparaging the very challenging task of achieving an anthropological understanding of the universal narrative structures and allegorical themes of the *telenovela* as a genre, there are some basic economic as well as cultural determinants of their international growth in particular which need to be taken into account in explaining the phenomenon.

It would be apparent from the chapters on Mexico and Brazil that there is a common pattern in which international expansion of the market for *telenovelas* has proceeded. Consistent with the geolinguistic regions hypothesis, the initial export successes were in countries which shared a similar language and culture with the exporting nations, and these similarities became the basis upon which strategies to expand the programme export trade were elaborated. Globo's rise in Portugal, and Televisa's hold, not on Spain but on the Spanish-speaking US and Latin American markets, are the most striking cases which have been examined. However, the second phase of *telenovela* export successes was in countries which had no linguistic and cultural similarities whatsoever with the exporting nations. By 1985, for example, Brazilian *telenovelas* were finding audiences in Poland, China, and the then Soviet Union (Marques de Melo 1988: 44).

While the universality of melodrama and allegory and the social rhythms of viewing provide some of the explanation for this leap beyond the geolinguistic region, there are some basic economic reasons as well. For one thing, even though a Brazilian *telenovela* can cost up to fourteen times more than a Mexican one (Marques de Melo 1988: 30), suggesting that the differences between nations in the 'look and feel' of their *telenovelas* are at least in part a function of budget size, even the more expensive *telenovelas* are cheaper than most other programming available on the international market, including that from the US. As of 1997, the range of costs in Venezuela, for instance, varied between $US20,000 and $US135,000 per episode, while Globo's average was towards the top end of that scale, at around $US100,000 (de la Fuente 1997: 47). To take an albeit extreme point of comparison, around that time new episodes of series like *Seinfeld* were costing NBC $US5 million (Alexander 1998).

Although the international rise of producers such as Televisa and Globo has overthrown the verities of the cultural imperialism paradigm of the 1970s, this does not mean that dependence has been relativized into oblivion. On the contrary, economic disadvantage within the global system has generated its own mode of television programme distribution and exchange amongst nations we would not long ago have been calling Second and Third World. One response to the debt and inflation crisis and scarcity of hard currency in Latin America in the 1980s was to introduce a system of barter. To take a notable instance, Televisa began providing its programmes to other Latin American countries in exchange for four minutes per hour of advertising time which it could sell to pan-regional advertisers. Globo made a similar arrangement when it exported its first *telenovelas* to China (Mattelart and Mattelart 1990: 12). Co-production is another means by which costs can be kept down, at the same time as the partners gain access to each other's markets. It has been noted already that in 1997, both Globo and Televisa were claiming to have sales in up to 130 countries (de la Fuente 1997: 47; Symmes 1997: S14). Yet it would be misleading to give the impression that Latin American television programmes circulate only in the less developed world. Certainly, the newer television markets without a production capacity of their own find them most attractive, but it is really only in the English-speaking countries that programmers ignore a genre which is not only relatively inexpensive to acquire, but is known to be able to draw and keep audiences for extended periods.

None the less, for all their reach and the strength of their attraction within their own region, there are grounds for believing that *telenovelas* might prove to be much more finite in their appeal as an export genre than it seemed in their glory days of the 1980s. First, there is the fact that they have not penetrated the cultural screens of anglophone markets, except of course in their considerable success with Spanish-speakers in the US. Secondly, evidence from Western European markets, including ones such as Spain and Italy where they could have been expected to gain a more durable audience, is that they have been a transitory fad. This seems certainly the case with the Mexican *telenovelas*; as the previous chapter showed, however, Brazilian *telenovelas* have secured a sustained following in Portugal. Thirdly, outside their geolinguistic region, *telenovelas* do best in some of the least developed national markets. What will happen as even these markets mature and are better able to substitute their own programming for imports? It may turn out that, unless Latin American producers are able to diversify their range of programming and enhance the quality, they will find that they have a created a secure niche within the flows of exchange, only to be left behind in it as their existing markets become more affluent and discerning.

Convergence and the Challenge to Geolinguistic Monopolies

Like 'globalization', one of the great buzzwords of the 1990s is 'convergence'. It most often refers to the digitization of information, which permits image, voice, and data to be reduced to a common code in which they can be interchanged; or, more concretely, to the obliteration of fundamental differences between what previously were quite distinct means of communication and information—the television, telephone, and computer. The communications satellite, in both symbolic and practical terms, is one of the most significant instances of this epoch-making fusion of broadcasting, telecommunications, and data transmission. Much of the discourse about convergence presents it as a technological phenomenon, but that needs to be kept in perspective:

The penetration of societies in Latin America, Asia, or Africa is not primarily due, as some seem to argue, to the expansion of the technological infrastructure of distribution (such as satellites, telecommunications, computers), but the mechanism of industrial production and market distribution that is more basic than the technological innovation as such. (McAnany 1984: 188–9)

Thus, as well as at the technological level, convergence is also occurring within the structure of the communication and information industries themselves, as telecommunication companies take up strategic holdings in more entertainment-based cultural industries such as subscription television, as we have seen in the case of Telefónica in Spain and Argentina, and as some of the very largest companies build vertically integrated structures for content production and distribution. Such integration was formerly one of the more distinct features of the Latin American model of corporate organization, but now is becoming globalized. As is apparent in the case of the Hughes Galaxy DTH venture in Latin America, these integrated structures can cross the former divide between hardware or 'carriage' (in this case, satellite design, manufacture, and management), and software or 'content' (television programme production and distribution). This kind of convergence has also transformed the international television business from an import–export trade in programmes as products, to a post-broadcast industry which provides not so much particular products but continuous transmission of services, whether delivered via cable or delivered direct to subscribers.

Such immense technological and structural transformation has consequences for how we understand communications theoretically, and this includes the implications for language and culture. Following the Spanish geographer Manuel Castells, Morley and Robins argue that what Harold Innis called the 'space-binding' properties of communications media now are redefining space in terms of flows, rather than of places as such, although with key economic and cultural 'nerve centres' in the network of flows (1995: 26–9). We can think of geolinguistic regions as prime examples of such virtual restructured spaces, in which new centres have emerged. As was noted in Chapter 3, these include not just Mexico City and Rio de Janeiro, the home bases of Televisa and Globo, but also Miami. More than a strategically located centre for television production and distribution to serve both Americas, Miami has assumed a mythical place in the Latin American 'collective imagination' (Monsiváis 1994: 124).

But while respatialization, understood in this way as a dimension of globalization facilitated by convergence, seems to be overflowing geographical barriers to create global markets, the barriers of language and culture seem more resistant. As Collins observes:

Although new communication technologies have reduced the costs of transmitting and distributing information over distance (space binding), distinct information markets remain; here the most important differentiating factors are those of language and culture. (1994: 386)

Thus, while paradigmatic of global respatialization, the transcontinental niches which the Spanish- and Portuguese-speaking television markets have carved out for themselves are also emblematic of the reassertion of linguistic and cultural difference which is taking place in the face of globalization. Even within those geolinguistic regions, there is further linguistic and cultural differentiation, as seen in the advent of the 'autonomous communities' channels in Spain. Another example is perhaps more prophetic. Just as in Asia, where Sony first elaborated its strategy of 'global localization', and Murdoch's Star TV tailored its offerings to the major linguistic groups rather than seek a pan-Asian audience, some US-based cable channels in Latin America have found it necessary to adapt and differentiate their services to the local market. This is a significant trend because it shows how the drive for global economies of scale, a force towards homogenization, is attenuated by the heterogenizing factors of language and culture, although, as Morley and

Robins note, 'the local' is usually not more specific than national, regional, or even pan-regional differences (1995: 117).

Clearly, for the Latin American market, the provision of audio tracks in both Spanish and Portuguese is elemental, usually as well as English, but there are now much more culturally sensitive bases for differentiation, such as musical taste cultures. Viacom's MTV not only has a separate service for Latin America, and, within that, one for Brazil, but has created special programming feeds for Mexico at one end of the Spanish-speaking zone, and Argentina at the other. Based in the mythical space of Miami, so as to be seen to be above national partisanship, the core international material is augmented with distinct Mexican and Argentinian segments for those respective feeds. As well as increasing its total subscribers in the region, this strategy has also attracted local advertisers, in addition to the global ones that one expects to find everywhere on MTV (Goldner 1997).

MTV Latin America represents the kind of challenge which Televisa, Globo, and the other major producers and distributors of the region now face on their home ground in the era of convergence. As noted in the chapters on these companies, the technical properties of the new digital compression on the current generation of satellites not only allow the satellites to transmit many more channels than ever before, whether from the US, Europe, or elsewhere, but facilitate the provision of multiple audio tracks. This means that one image, say a Hollywood film on HBO Olé, or a Discovery channel travelogue, can be made available to cable operators and DTH subscribers dubbed into Spanish or Portuguese, as well as in the original version.

Thus, the comparative advantage of language difference which the Latin American companies once enjoyed as a kind of natural monopoly is under threat. It is not only the new satellite technologies of digital compression and conditional access DTH reception which have brought this about: several of the global channels have gained their experience in the US with the potential audience of over 26 million Spanish-speakers there, and the move into Latin America represents immense opportunities for them to exploit. At the very least, it is well worth their while to dub programmes which have been produced in English. It could even be said that the prospect of 'more beyond', the 300 million or more Spanish-speakers of Latin America, gives US producers an incentive to develop programming for the Latino market in the first instance, with Latin America, and Spain, as aftermarkets. The development of the CBS Telenoticias news channel from a US domestic to an international service is a good case in point. A CBS executive observes that Latin America is more attractive than Europe for such ventures because the whole region only requires channels in two languages, as against the multiple languages needed for Europe (Francis and Fernandez 1997: 38–40). As Mexico City and Rio surrender their monopoly to Los Angeles and Miami as centres of dubbing from English to Spanish and Portuguese (Wilkinson 1995: 22), US capital flows into new channels: one US investment company has joined with the Cisneros Group 'to create a pan-Ibero-American media network' based in Miami (Sutter 1998).

Recalling that as well as CBS and MTV there is Turner's CNN, the Time-Warner/Sony venture HBO Olé, Murdoch's Fox Latin America, Spelling's TeleUno, ESPN, Discovery, and other US-based global channels providing satellite and cable services in Spanish and/or Portuguese to Latin America, it is not surprising that, as of 1996, 90 per cent of television services (that is, satellite and cable signals rather than programmes) imported into the Iberoamerican region were found to be from the US (Media Research and Consultancy Spain 1997: 14). The same study found that the export of such services from the region mainly (70 per cent) came from Televisa and Multivisión in Mexico, especially by virtue of their involvement with the Murdoch Sky and Hughes Galaxy DTH ventures respectively.

Even though 90 per cent of the services exported from Iberoamerican countries went to other regional nations of the same language (the rest mainly to the Spanish-speaking networks in the US), evidence of the geolinguistic cohesion of the region's trade, it also shows that the US services have been able to cross the language barrier without much movement back in the other direction. This trend is likely to consolidate if, as the study predicts, the trade in services rather than programmes soon becomes the major form of audiovisual exchange (1997: 17–18).

Given that the US-based and other global corporations such as Hughes not only have taken over the technological vanguard in the region once held by PanAmSat, but have also faced up to the content issue by extending into services in the regional languages, if post-broadcast services do come to eclipse programmes as the core of the television trade, then much of the comparative advantage once enjoyed by the major Latin American companies would be undermined. It has been argued in this book that the era of cultural imperialism in the 1960s and 1970s, when television programme imports from the US reached their high-tide mark, has proven to be just an initial phase of television development. It was overtaken by a phase in which audiences learned to have more appreciation for programmes which came to them out of their own language and culture. Beginning in the late 1970s, this has been the era in which Televisa and Globo have exploited their advantages to become the market leaders in their respective geolinguistic regions, but the indications are that this stage also will pass. As McAnany predicted, the fact that a nation can develop a strong cultural industry 'may be no guarantee that the threat of external influence will not surface at a later date' (1984: 196). By the same token, the reassertion of US corporate dominance should not be interpreted teleologically, that is, as the inevitable victory of American capitalism, but analytically, as the logic of a cultural industry in which the US has advantages able to overcome those of its competitors, even in their own national and regional markets.

The Return of the Repressed

While there can be no doubt that the advent of digital television via satellite marks a whole new phase in the technological development of the medium and in the nature of television as an international business, it does not follow that it is about to replace broadcast television as we have known it at the national and regional levels. As long as DTH and even cable services are subscription services and broadcast television remains free-to-air, we can expect there to be a significant socioeconomic division between those who can afford to upgrade to the new modes of delivery, and those who cannot, particularly in developing countries. Brazil, for example, is the sixth biggest world market for subscription television, but the number of subscribers represents little more than 6 per cent of the population, a 'well-informed elite' in the cities (Costa 1997).

Drawing on his own and other research in Latin America, Joseph Straubhaar maintains that there is a class factor in the now frequently observed mass preference for television programming which derives from one's own language and culture:

New research seems to point to a greater traditionalism and loyalty to national and local cultures by lower or popular classes, who show the strongest tendency to seek greater cultural proximity in television programs and other cultural products. They seem to prefer nationally or locally produced material that is closer to or more reinforcing of traditional identities, based in regional, ethnic, dialect/language, religious, and other elements. (1991: 51)

On the other hand, for the elite strata of the region, the dictum of global marketing guru Theodore Levitt appears to hold true: 'globalisation does not mean the end of segments. It means, instead, their expansion to worldwide proportions' (quoted in Morley and Robins 1995: 113). While the emergence of such social sectors as markets on a transnational basis was also identified long before by critical communications scholars such as Nordenstreng and Varis in their concept of 'the nonhomogeneity of the national state', the links between class preferences in television programming and dependency have not been followed through. However, Kenton Wilkinson's research on the Latin American television trade brings to light differences between the *telenovelas*, variety shows, sports, imported action series, and movies programmed for mass audiences on broadcast television, and the much more internationalized material on the cable and satellite services subscribed to by the social elites: 'the regional program market is itself segmented according to characteristics of the target audience' (1995: 238–90).

In other words, the mass audiences not only tolerate but rather enjoy seeing locally made programming (much of it not at all exportable), nationally produced and distributed material, and the characteristic generic programming of the region, such as *telenovelas* from the major exporters, though they do also watch films and series from the US. The elites that subscribe to satellite and cable services get their MTV, HBO, CNN, Discovery, Disney, Playboy, and other US-based services, but in their own language if they want it, along with some Latin American channels such as ECO, and European feeds from RAI and RTVE. This is a much more global, cosmopolitan mix, although with some local inflections, as in the case mentioned of MTV. Cultural stratification of this kind corresponds to the multiple levels of television flows identified by scholars such as Straubhaar and Wilkinson, and as discussed in this book: the local, national, regional (that is, world-regional, including geolinguistic regional), and global. While there might appear to be a complex mix of choice in the middle of the scale, the range of offerings between local live shows on free-to-air television at one extreme, and the global channels on DTH subscription services at the other, is analytically comprehensible and need not induce postmodernist vertigo in either viewers or theorists. Precisely because audiences are stratified, relatively few viewers have the full range of choice anyhow.

Furthermore, it is worth emphasizing at this stage that, partly for this reason, the different levels are not mutually exclusive—that is, the build-up of global channels in Latin America does not drive out local, national, and regional programming, any more than the rise of regional programming could ever have hoped to replace the global. Rather, consistent with world trends, 'the productive capacity of regional players has increased along with the total volume of programmes transmitted' (Wilkinson 1995: 236), and, as well, with the differentiation of audiences. If Televisa and Globo had ever aspired to join the global league, rather than just maximize their advantages within their geolinguistic regions, this would have involved competing head-on with the entrenched US corporations on their home ground: the US market and the anglophone geolinguistic region as a whole. This they have not done: Televisa's ECO might be modelled on CNN, but it did not set out to compete with it; Globo has concentrated on the fullest development of the *telenovela* genre, but does not have a film division.

However, while the Latin American corporations have cultivated their geolinguistic regional-level niches rather than challenge the US-based majors at the global level, those niches themselves are now being forced open to competition as the global corporations have recognized their potential value, and gained experience and economies of scale in production for them. Thus, a service such as ECO, for which Televisa has been prepared to sustain recurrent losses in order to develop on a regional basis, now finds itself being overtaken by CBS Telenoticias and CNN en Español. One reason given for this is that ECO's pan-regional perspective is actually less attractive to subscribers than the strategic 'global localization' combination of international and local news offered by the new services (Kepp 1997: 41). Again, while the inclusion of Televisa and Globo in the Murdoch DTH scheme, and Venevisión in that of Hughes, is a recognition of the Latin American companies' strengths in being able to supply traditional entertainment programming to their region, we have seen in Chapter 2 that this represents only a minor proportion of the whole bouquet in each case.

The pattern which emerges is that the US-based corporations have been quick to occupy the global level of distribution opened up by digital technologies, and they also have begun to penetrate the regional level, at least so far as the elite subscriber audiences are concerned. The Latin American corporations have been granted a limited but significant measure of participation in the new services at the global level, but have had to face the unwonted competition of global channels in Spanish and Portuguese at the regional level. However, we have seen that, by and large, they continue to dominate the regional trade in programmes for broadcast television as a relatively mass medium, and maintain predominance over domestic competition in broadcast television within the national markets where they have their roots and still earn by far the bulk of their income.

The coalition of interests arranged around the different levels of television flow and the markets for them makes manifest the links between the local and the global, but also points to the relative inequalities between the participants. Some observers, such as Straubhaar (1991) and Sánchez Ruiz (1996), invoke Johan Galtung's concept of 'asymmetrical interdependence' as a means of conceptualizing the structural inequalities of globalization within the context of a more complex theorization of dependence than prevailed during the heyday of 'cultural dependency' in the 1970s and 1980s. Thus, for example, it could be said that Hughes 'depends' on Venevisión for its regional programming and distribution contacts in developing the Galaxy service, but not so much as Venevisión depends on Hughes for the provision of the hardware and 60 per cent of the capital investment. Venevisión is perhaps more dependent than the other Latin American corporations, it might be added, because it is much more reliant on export income (de la Fuente 1997: 46).

Classically, however, dependence is about relationships between nations rather than corporations, and in this respect it is worth taking account of the considerable degree to which the Latin American television producers and distributors have their fortunes tied to those of the nation-states within which they have secured their market power. In spite of the fact that only a small proportion of their total sales revenues comes from their various international activities, the heads of Televisa and Globo in particular have declared that the limits for growth imposed on their respective national economies by debt and inflation in the 1980s served as a stimulus for them to further develop external markets (Sinclair 1996: 51–2). Conversely and more recently, as was seen in Chapter 2, Televisa's expansion plans were much curtailed by Mexico's devaluation crisis of 1994, illustrating how the shifting sands upon which a nation is located within the world economy can impact upon these 'multinationals of the Third World' (Mattelart, Delcourt, and Mattelart 1984: 54).

Such instances underscore the need to understand the particular historical and structural circumstances of individual countries, which this book has sought to do, rather than think of dependence as a uniform and immutable condition in which all developing countries find themselves. As Rafael Roncagliolo has it, 'all Latin American countries are dependent, but some are more dependent than others' (1995: 338). This does not mean that they, and the corporations which develop out of them, are perpetual victims of globalization to some greater or lesser extent. Rather, their possibilities are circumscribed by more stringent limitations and subject to circumstances beyond their control, relative to the richer and more powerful nations and 'their' corporations.

The capacity of the Latin American corporations to build the geolinguistic markets which they have over the last few decades is largely due to their discoveries that they had a comparative advantage in being the largest producers in their respective languages, and that language and culture were 'market forces'—that mass audiences, at least, were

169

attracted by linguistically and culturally proximate programming. If US producers and distributors are now in on the secret and threaten to cream off the more affluent subscription viewers with 'global localized' programming, such a turn of events probably means that the Latin Americans have no choice but to collaborate rather than to compete at the global level of televisual flows, while their hegemonies over mass broadcast audiences at the regional and national levels will remain more secure. *Vamos a ver*—we shall see.

References

Alexander, Garth (1998), 'The Entertainment Glut', *Australian* (24 February), 32.

Allen, Robert (1996), 'As the World Turns: Television Soap Operas and Global Media Cultures', in E. McAnany and K. Wilkinson (eds.), *Mass Media and Free Trade: NAFTA and the Cultural Industries* (University of Texas Press, Austin), 110–27.

Ang, Ien (1985), *Watching Dallas* (Methuen, London).

Birmingham, David (1993), *A Concise History of Portugal* (Cambridge University Press, Cambridge).

Collins, Richard (1990), *Television: Policy and Culture* (Unwin Hyman, London).

—— (1994), 'Trading in Culture: The Role of Language', *Canadian Journal of Communication*, 19: 377–99.

—— Garnham, Nicholas, and Locksley, Gareth (1988), *The Economics of Television: The UK Case* (Sage, London).

Costa, Luiz (1997), 'Brasil é sexto mercado mundial no sector', *O Estado de São Paulo* (6 February), D2.

Crystal, David (1997), *English as a Global Language* (Cambridge University Press, Cambridge).

de la Fuente, Anna Maria (1997), 'Endless Love', *TV World* (January), 45–7.

Díaz Argüelles, José (1997), 'Los satélites como vínculo económico y cultural entre Europa e Iberoamérica', *Fundesco Boletín* (March–April), 17.

Drago, Tito (1991), 'La Comunidad Iberoamericana de Naciones: un reto científico y tecnológico', *Telos*, 26: 9–11.

Francis, Greg, and Fernandez, Robustiano (1997), 'Satellites South of the Border', *Via Satellite* (February), 28–42.

García Jiménez, Jesús (1980), *Radiotelevisión y política cultural en el Franquismo* (Instituto Superior de Investigaciones Científicas, Instituto Balmes de Sociología, Madrid).

Goldner, Diane (1997), 'MTV Rocks to Latin Beat', *Variety* (19–25 May), 22.

González, Jorge (1994), *Más (+) cultura(s)* (Consejo Nacional para la Cultura y los Artes, Mexico DF).

Hall, Stuart (1978), 'The TV Feuilleton or the Domestication of the World: Some Preliminary Critical Notes', in *The Feuilleton in Television*, vol. i (ERI/Edizioni RAI Radiotelevisione Italiana, Turin), 235–49.

Hoskins, Colin, and McFadyen, Stuart (1991), 'The US Competitive Advantage in the Global Television Market: Is it Sustainable in the New Broadcasting Environment?', *Canadian Journal of Communication*, 16/2: 207–14.

—— and Mirus, Roger (1988), 'Reasons for the US Dominance of International Trade in Television Programmes', *Media, Culture and Society*, 10/4: 499–515.

Katz, Michael (1997), 'Latin American Telenovelas: Stories in the Language of Love', *Broadcasting & Cable International* (June), 10–14.

Kepp, Michael (1997), 'News Addicts', *Cable and Satellite Europe* (August), 39–43.

Klagsbrunn, Martha (1993), 'The Brazilian Telenovela: A Genre in Development', in Anamaria Fadul (ed.), *Serial Fiction in TV: The Latin American Telenovelas* (School of Communication and Arts, University of São Paulo, São Paulo), 15–24.

Lopez, Ana (1995), 'Our Welcomed Guests: Telenovelas in Latin America', in Robert Allen (ed.), *To Be Continued... Soap Operas around the World* (Routledge, London), 256–75.

McAnany, Emile (1984), 'The Logic of Cultural Industries in Latin America: The Television Industry in Brazil', in V. Mosco and J. Wasko (eds.), *The Critical Communications Review*, ii: *Changing Patterns of Communications Control* (Ablex, Norwood, NJ), 185–208.

—— (1993), 'The Telenovela and Social Change', in Anamaria Fadul (ed.), *Serial Fiction in TV: The Latin American Telenovelas* (School of Communication and Arts, University of São Paulo, São Paulo), 135–47.

Man Chan, Joseph (1996), 'Television in Greater China: Structure, Exports, and Market Formation', in J. Sinclair, E. Jacka, and S. Cunningham (eds.), *New Patterns in Global Television: Peripheral Vision* (Oxford University Press, Oxford), 126–60.

Marques de Melo, José (1988), *As telenovelas da Globo* (Summus Editorial, São Paulo).

—— (1995), 'A Cultural Community without Physical Borders: The Case of the Community of Portuguese-Speaking Countries', paper presented at the Borders and Cultures Conference, Montreal, February.

Martín-Barbero, Jesús (1995), 'Memory and Form in the Latin American Soap Opera', in Robert Allen (ed.), *To Be Continued... Soap Operas around the World* (Routledge, London), 276–84.

Mattelart, Armand, Delcourt, Xavier, and Mattelart, Michèle (1984), *International Image Markets: In Search of an Alternative Perspective* (Comedia Publishing Group, London).

Mattelart, Michèle, and Mattelart, Armand (1990), *The Carnival of Images: Brazilian Television Fiction* (Bergin & Garvey, New York).

Mazziotti, Nora (1993), 'Acercamientos a las telenovelas latinoamericanas', in Anamaria Fadul (ed.), *Serial Fiction in TV: The Latin American Telenovelas* (School of Communication and Arts, University of São Paulo, São Paulo), 25–32.

Media Research and Consultancy Spain (1997), 'La industria audiovisual iberoamericana: datos de sus principales mercados 1997', report prepared for the Federación de Asociaciones de Productores Audiovisuales Españoles and Agencia Española de Cooperación Internacional, Madrid, July.

Monsiváis, Carlos (1994), 'Globalisation Means Never Having to Say You're Sorry', *Journal of International Communication*, 1/2: 120–4.

Morley, David, and Robins, Kevin (1995), *Spaces of Identity: Global Media, Electronic Landscapes and Cultural Boundaries* (Routledge, London).

Nordenstreng, Kaarle, and Varis, Tapio (1973), 'The Nonhomogeneity of the National State and the International Flow of Communication', in G. Gerbner, L. Gross, and W. Melody (eds.), *Communication Technology and Social Policy* (Wiley, New York), 393–412.

Rønning, Helge (1997), 'Language, Cultural Myths, Media and *Realpolitik*: The Case of Mozambique', *Media Development*, 44/1: 50–4.

Sánchez Ruiz, Enrique (1996), 'Flujos globales, nacionales y regionales de programación televisiva: el caso de México', *Comunicación y Sociedad*, 27: 43–88.

Sinclair, John (1996), 'Mexico, Brazil, and the Latin World', in J. Sinclair, E. Jacka, and S. Cunningham (eds.), *New Patterns in Global Television: Peripheral Vision* (Oxford University Press, Oxford), 33–66.

Straubhaar, Joseph (1982), 'The Development of the Telenovela as the Pre-eminent Form of Popular Culture in Brazil', *Studies in Latin American Popular Culture*, 1: 138–50.

—— (1991), 'Beyond Media Imperialism: Asymmetrical Interdependence and Cultural Proximity', *Critical Studies in Mass Communication*, 8: 39–59.

Sutter, Mary (1998), 'Hicks Sets $500 mil Latin Fund', *Variety* (22 December 1997–4 January 1998), 34.

Symmes, Patrick (1997), 'The Hacker Tourist Maps Brazil', *Wired* (October), S11–15.

Wildman, Steven, and Siwek, Stephen (1988), *International Trade in Films and Television Programs* (American Enterprise Institute/Ballinger Publications, Cambridge, Mass.).

Wilkinson, Kenton (1995), 'When Culture, Language and Communication Converge: The Latin American Cultural-Linguistic Television Market', unpublished Ph.D. dissertation, University of Texas at Austin.

Index

Index

Index